NOT TO BE REMOVED
FROM THE LIBRARY.

A HISTORY OF ENGLISH LITERATURE

A HISTORY OF
ENGLISH LITERATURE

The Middle Ages and the Renascence
(650–1660)

By ÉMILE LEGOUIS

Translated from the French by
Helen Douglas Irvine

Modern Times
(1660–1970)

By LOUIS CAZAMIAN
and RAYMOND LAS VERGNAS (Book VIII)

REVISED EDITION

Bibliographies by
Donald Davie *and* Pierre Legouis

J. M. DENT AND SONS LTD

Made in Great Britain
at the
Aldine Press · Letchworth · Herts
for
J. M. DENT & SONS LTD
Aldine House · Bedford Street · London
First published in England by J. M. Dent & Sons Ltd
and in America by The Macmillan Co., New York

I. The Middle Ages and the Renascence . . .	1926
II. Modern Times	1927
Revised and reset two volumes in one . . .	1930
Further revised editions 1933, 1934, 1937, 1940, 1943, 1945,	
	1947, 1948, 1951
Revised with additional chapters . . .	1954
Reprinted and revised bibliographies . . .	1957
Further revisions	1960
Reprinted	1961
Reprinted with a new Book VIII by R. Las Vergnas .	1964
Reprinted	1965
Further revisions	1967
Further revisions	1971

© Revisions (1960) and Book VIII, J. M. Dent & Sons Ltd, 1964
© Further revisions J. M. Dent & Sons Ltd, 1967, 1971

ISBN: 0 460 03583 5

PREFACE

SOME little while ago a number of English professors in our various universities and university colleges discovered a common indebtedness to Émile Legouis (no honorifics can improve a name now so eminent) and a common impulse to thank him; an impulse, that is, of personal gratitude, warming and colouring the respect due to the achievement of a great scholar.

Viewed dispassionately, of course, that achievement were monumental enough; the purpose of a life time—he was born in 1861—carved out by long and delicate labour; a large purpose, yet simple, definite, practical—to attract young Frenchmen in the great university of Paris to the study of English literature, to widen their knowledge, quicken their understanding of it, and through the immense authority of the Sorbonne to disseminate that understanding through educated France. Now so massive is our literature that the mere task of grappling with it must, for a foreigner, have been enormous, let be the task of seeing and presenting it in right proportion of parts. With what devotion he and his younger confrère, M. Cazamian, have laboured, and with what skill attained, the following pages bear witness.

They would have done *beneficently*, too, had their success ended with their primary object. Since more than half—and more likely ninety per cent—of public wars or private quarrels spring out of misunderstanding, he does well indeed who interprets to a quick-witted nation the best of another nation's mind. Seeing then that the best of Great Britain's mind—the true secret of its working—resides in our literature; seeing too how much, and how often, from the days of the Breton saints and of Bede, in the story of our civilization France and Britain have borrowed from one another and Europe from both, with a mutual benefit that should dwarf all a we can scarcely overpraise MM. Legouis and C y their primary purpose here fulfilled.

But they have had a secondary succ eir book Legouis says of this, too modestly. d English it authors was exceeded when th d be attrac- received in Great Britain th deemed desirable; th they pursued was a certain n would not

tive and useful.' This modest way of putting things, however
becoming in the writer, must not be stretched to cover our
gratitude. I remind myself that among the least pretentious
herbs of the field is a little plant of the family *Euphrasia*
(or 'good cheer') of which country housewives brew a lotion
for tired or ageing vision. Their grandmothers gave it the
happy name Eyebright—and I have tested its virtue. Even
so medicinal have some of us English teachers found the surveys (to name no others) of M. Jusserand, M. Maurois, and
MM. Legouis and Cazamian, in their various fields. For an
instance, from the earliest pages of this book: Over more
than a generation teachers of our literature on its native
soil, enslaved by school-philology, exalted our Anglo-Saxon
'origins,' out of all proportion to our later literature. In revolt
from this, some of us, as special pleaders for a livelier sense of
the living word, went too far no doubt in challenging the
pre-Chaucerian caskets of which the mere antiquity of dust
deserved, of decency, a holier respect. M. Legouis's opening
chapter had, of course, to deal with the subject; and it seemed
to me, one of the disputants, that a natural fair-mindedness
here reinforced an onlooker's proverbial advantage in seeing
most of the game. The chapter proved of happy augury.
As the reader went on, the qualities of fair judgment and
disinterested enthusiasm persisted, with frequent flashes of
insight as it were from an unexpected angle. These stimulate
curiosity, and even when we find this or that writer thrown
into a focus which our second thought obliges us to correct,
still the stimulus has been valuable in compelling that second
thought. No teacher of English literature would belittle
such surveys as Chambers's *Cyclopaedia of English Literature*
(those engrossing volumes, wherever opened), Courthope's
History of English Poetry, Professor Elton's four volumes
tilling the century 1780–1880, or Saintsbury's smaller
ones—to name but these out of many useful ones; nor
the series *Periods of European Literature* published by
Blackwood; while, for reference always, and often for
more, there is the great *Cambridge History of English*
almost all. But the singular value of this present
English students of university age, lies
enlargement of the vision to see our
as it is, in European perspective—
comparison, but more winningly,
operation upon it of two

critical minds trained in another great literature which, more
than ours, conforms with logic and measure. (Perhaps, too,
I may be allowed to interpose a word on the enterprise of the
publishers, who have ventured to compress the original two
volumes of this work into one of over 1,400 pages, well printed
on opaque paper, yet easily handled and to be had for half
the original cost.)

To resume, however: If criticism may be offered by one
who admires this work the more through some acquaintance
with the mass of its difficulties overcome, I feel that here and
there in the second part (where, as we approach the present
day, the material accumulates enormously while he who
handles it is left with lessening authority to quote in support of
his own judgments) M. Cazamian has been forced back upon
his Gallic instinct for logical neatness, to overstrain it somewhat; that he is driven to classify our authors by 'movements'
and 'tendencies' rather than by individual merit, even as his
predecessor M. Taine generalized them by 'environment.'
Now movements and environments are facts, important facts;
but for vital study of a vital literature by the young, some of
whom (as the teacher hopes) are destined to perpetuate it,
neither movements nor environments can challenge the actual
and individual work of individual authors as the first main
object of concern. And if this be true of any literary study,
it is notably true of English, wherein genius has so often
mated itself with eccentricity. For instance, Mrs. Radcliffe
and 'Monk' Lewis exemplify a 'movement,' Landor and
Peacock simply genius; yet who would compare the first pair
with the second in any quality worth our concern? How
sensitively our two authors can appraise eccentric genius in
itself, let any reader judge who will turn to M. Legouis's twin
estimates of Robert Burton and Sir Thomas Browne, or to
M. Cazamian's condensed pages on Blake. To revert to
'tendencies,' one can only congratulate M. Cazamian on his
courage in essaying to extract some intention (let me not
say 'drift') from the welter of our post-War poetry, fiction,
biography. His is pioneer work, at any rate, and may be
a reproach to some of us older men, who withhold our
judgments (with our prejudices), simply trusting to youth,
energy, the evident virtue of being alive, to what end soever
tending.

ARTHUR QUILLER-COUCH.

1933.

CONTENTS

PART I

BOOK I

ORIGINS (650–1350)

BOOK II

THE FOURTEENTH AND FIFTEENTH CENTURIES (1350–1516) FROM CHAUCER TO THE RENASCENCE

BOOK III

THE PREPARATION FOR THE RENASCENCE (1516–78)

BOOK IV

THE FLOWERING OF THE RENASCENCE (1578–1625)

CONTENTS

BOOK IV
The pre-Romantic Period (1770–98)

BOOK V
The Romantic Period (1798–1832)

BOOK VI
The Search for Balance (1832–75)

BOOK VII
New Divergencies (1875–1914)

CONTENTS

BOOK VIII

GENERAL INTRODUCTION

THE literature of the English language, one of the literatures richest in original beauty, is the most extensive ever known to the world. Literary production in the past and the present, taken together, has attained to a greater mass in English than in any other tongue, ancient or modern. Long though this work is, it does not attempt to cover the whole field. It has confined itself to the English literature of the British Isles, leaving to others both the literature of the United States and the literature of the various British dominions, a vast subject which is growing with prodigious rapidity. Only by forgoing any picture of literary expression overseas has it been possible to trace the history of English literature not too superficially, and to show its development coherently and harmoniously, because with unity of place.

This history was first written for the students of English who, year by year, are becoming more numerous in the universities of France. Its appeal was also to all those Frenchmen who have a curiosity regarding England and things English, who desire to reduce the results of scattered reading to order, to grasp the dominating features of succeeding periods and follow the reflection in books of the development of a great people. The authors had not the ambition to reach the English public, which was, they already knew, richly provided with histories of literature, both erudite and brilliant, ample or condensed, the productions of one or of several minds.

The expectation of the authors was therefore exceeded when their work was so favourably received in Great Britain that its translation into English was deemed desirable. It may be that their enterprise was thus fortunate partly because of the character they intentionally gave it. Their experience as university professors had warned them that, if they were to prepare their own students for knowledge of a foreign literature, they must take into account certain demands proper to the mentality of their nation: they must satisfy that need for connected composition, for the presentment of a chain of facts and ideas, without which the French do not easily assimilate the matter they study. The unforeseen result of the method they

xiii

therefore pursued was that the English critics found in their book a certain novelty; they considered that even in English it would not overlap with any other work, but would be attractive and useful. Moreover, the authors' view of English literature is that of outsiders, who are indeed fervent admirers of its strength and splendour, but yet have an independence of mind due to their foreign training, to the fact that they have not inherited nor been nurtured on this literature, but have approached it consciously and of deliberate choice, as men rather than as children; and their judgments may in consequence have an added impartiality, their praise more weight. In these ways there is compensation for the inevitable inferiority of a foreign historian, his lack of the instinctive, almost innate, love, which immediately affects the subconscious mind and may inspire the critic of his own nation's work with some such moving, profound epithet as reveals the race. Duly conscious as they are of this original taint, the authors were the more pleased when they found their conception of English literature to be far from unacceptable to British minds. The agreement seems to them proof that the friendly effort they have made to penetrate the mysteries of an intellectual nationality, and to share it in so far as outsiders may, has not been entirely in vain.

It is true that the generous reception accorded to this book does not stand in isolation. French study of English literature has had no more valuable encouragement than the benevolent interest with which it has been followed in England during the last half-century and especially during the last thirty years. It is encouragement justly bestowed considering, merit apart, the lack of prejudice and the fervour, even enthusiasm, with which English is now studied in France.

Although the production of theses for the doctorate was naturally hindered for a time by the War of 1914–18, those existing already deal with all the various periods of English literature from the beginning to the present day. Among those of which the subjects are general, we find *The Feeling for Nature in Anglo-Saxon Poetry, The English Masques of the Renascence, The English Public and English Men of Letters in the Eighteenth Century, The Social and Literary History of the Town of Bath, English Poets and the French Revolution, The Sociological Novel in England in the Middle Nineteenth Century, The Influence of Science on the English Novel and on English Thought, Socialism and the Evolution of Contemporary England.*

More numerous are the monographs which have for subject Renascence writers, for instance, John Lyly, Ben Jonson, Milton, Marvell, or Herrick; or writers of the classical period, such as Locke, Defoe, Swift, James Thomson, Edward Young, Horace Walpole, Wesley, or Sterne; or pre-Romantics like Cowper, Crabbe, and Burns; or Romantics properly so called —Wordsworth, Shelley, Keats, Charles Lamb, or the so different Jane Austen and Sydney Smith, or again the moderns —Ruskin, Meredith, Swinburne, Thomas Hardy.

To these works, which go deep, cover their whole subject, derive from sources directly, and often reveal new evidence or a new interpretation, which are erudite and yet aspire to a public beyond the initiate, English criticism has not been niggardly of approval. It has immediately admitted several of them to rank in their own sphere as classics, if the term may so be used, and has demanded and insisted that they should be translated into English.

Our list has dealt only with the theses, the immediate fruits of academic labour. It might well have included the works which the same authors have written freely, and also those individual books of wider reputation to which the English-speaking public have finely rendered homage, Taine's work in a former day and now those of J. J. Jusserand and André Chevrillon.

The work now presented to the British and American public was thus born in a propitious atmosphere. It is no summary of the studies enumerated above, for it aspires to more than the mere noting of results obtained in France. It cannot, therefore be said merely to focus the conclusions of earlier monographs. In its defects and its qualities it claims entire independence. Undoubtedly, however, its birth was encouraged by the ardent curiosity and sympathy which its subject aroused in France, and also, to a high degree, by the feeling that England herself looked favourably on French efforts to understand her character and interpret her literature.

E. L. L. C.

LIST OF WORKS FOR GENERAL
REFERENCE

WITH SPECIAL REFERENCE TO PART I

THE history of English literature from the beginning to 1660 is traced in certain authoritative works, either entirely or almost entirely. To refer to them at the opening of each chapter would be wearisome. It has seemed better to give here a list of works which will not again be separately noticed unless they develop a particular point in a way not found elsewhere.

The Cambridge History of English Literature, 14 volumes (1907–16). The first seven volumes go down to 1660. Each volume contains very full bibliographies.

Henry Morley, *English Writers*, 11 volumes (1887–95). This work ends about 1616, at Shakespeare's death.

W. J. Courthope, *A History of English Poetry*, 6 volumes. The first four volumes, published from 1895 to 1903, go down to the end of the seventeenth century.

Chambers's Cyclopaedia of English Literature, 1903 edition in 3 volumes. This is less a consecutive history than a collection of extracts. The first volume goes down to 1700.

B. ten Brink, *Geschichte der englischen Literatur* (2nd edition revised by A. Brandl, 1st part 1899, 2nd part 1912). English translation of the first edition in Bohn's Standard Library in 3 volumes (1895–6). This incomplete work goes down to about 1550.

H. Taine, *Histoire de la littérature anglaise*, 4 volumes (1864). The first two volumes go down to the Restoration, 1660.

J. J. Jusserand, *Histoire littéraire du peuple anglais* (1st vol. 1896, 2nd vol. 1904). This work stops at the end of the reign of James I, 1625.

The development of the language and literature cannot be better followed than in the texts published by the Clarendon Press:

Sweet, *An Anglo-Saxon Reader in Prose and Verse.*

Morris and Skeat, *Specimens of Early English.* Vol. i, 1150–1300; vol. ii, 1298–1393.

W. W. Skeat, *Specimens of English Literature*, 1394–1578.

To these should be added:

The Cambridge Bibliography of English Literature. Ed. by F. W. Bateson, 4 volumes (Cambridge, 1940).

A Literary History of England. Ed. by A. C. Baugh (New York, 1948).

The Oxford History of English Literature. Ed. by F. P. Wilson and Bonamy Dobrée (Oxford, 1945).

Walter Allen, *Reading a Novel*, 1949.

The following works have taken the place of Morris and Skeat's *Specimens*, no longer reprinted:

J. Hall, *Selections from Early Middle English* (Oxford, 1920).

Bruce Dickins and R. M. Wilson, *Early Middle English Texts* (Cambridge, 1951).

K. Sisam and J. R. R. Tolkien, *Fourteenth Century Verse and Prose* (1921).

Biographies of authors will be found in the *Dictionary of National Biography*.

INTRODUCTION—PART I

THE MIDDLE AGES AND THE RENASCENCE
(650–1660)

THE division of the book into two parts, the first dealing with origins, the Middle Ages and the Renascence, the second with the modern and contemporary periods, entails obvious differences of presentment and even of method. It would be vain to deny that they are partly due to the different habits of thought of the two authors. Yet even had the whole book been written by one man, he would have been led, almost inevitably, to pursue a different method in treating of the past and of the present.

The past has been for many years the material of scholars. Its literary monuments follow each other less closely and are less overwhelming in their bulk, but they are weighed down by commentaries, surrounded by exegetic works, which sometimes, especially in the case of the giants—Chaucer, Shakespeare, Milton—attain to truly formidable proportions. There is here no question of breaking new ground. The historian's task is to hew a way through all the barriers of earlier criticism, which yet must not be neglected, and attain to contact with the original works. It behoves him to use the best conclusions of his predecessors without repeating their accomplishment, for the publication of a new book is justified only if it makes a new contribution to knowledge.

This, to particularize, is to say that every new French history of English literature must take into account two works, variously remarkable, among those which have in France been devoted to this subject. Taine's famous book, published in 1864, remains one of the most characteristic productions of this philosopher whose ideas left a profound imprint on the second half of the nineteenth century. The doctrine expressed in it, its brilliancy and vigour, and the author's reputation, will always find its readers, whatever progress time and the researches of scholars may bring to new histories of literature. It is desirable that Taine's luminous and enthralling book should continue to introduce the English to French criticism, and there is no danger that oblivion will overtake this, one of the master achievements of an exceptional mind.

More recently M. Jusserand returned to the same subject in his *Histoire littéraire du peuple anglais*, of which the first volume appeared in 1896 and the second in 1904. His work was conceived on quite other lines than Taine's. An historian first of all, whose scholarship was such that he had made numerous discoveries and closely discussed many special problems, he painted with the greatest accuracy and picturesqueness England as she is revealed by her writers. To attempt to do over again what he has accomplished to such perfection would be no less vain than presumptuous.

These two works have, the one of them mainly and the other exclusively, the same subject as the first part of the present book. Taine, writing over a hundred years ago, could not know the history which is contemporary for the men of our day. Moreover his picture, full enough for the earlier periods, leaves gaps with increasing boldness from the eighteenth century onwards. Thenceforward he supplies rather a series of brilliant articles than a complete, closely written, and continuous story. As for M. Jusserand, his history stops before Milton, about 1625.

The duty of him who travels the country crossed by these pioneers is surely not to follow in their footsteps, but to seek, as much as possible, the paths they have explored least willingly, the points of view which have most seldom been theirs. There is no occasion to attempt, after Taine, to rear an imposing determinist construction, to deduce, from categorical assertions on race, conditions, and clime, both the general characteristics of English literature and the special marks of the writers who made it. Against Taine's seductive and imperious theory strong objections have been raised, principally in the introduction to Auguste Angellier's *Robert Burns* (*Les Œuvres*, vol. ii). To restate it in its entirety is no longer possible, and to revise it would change what is and should be a calm and free exposition of known facts into a long controversy. On the other hand, all who seek mainly to conjure up for themselves the manners, the institutions, and the life of the past, may be referred to the learned and vivid pages of M. Jusserand's work, simply because it exists and admirably fulfils its author's purpose.

What seems not indeed to have been omitted, but to have

been given a secondary place in both these histories, is the aesthetic aspect of their subject, and by divergence from them in this respect an essential task may be accomplished. It can be neither idle nor ill-timed to endeavour before all else in a history of literature to show the earliest signs, the early gropings, the progress and retrogression and the triumphs of the artistic sense. To this end the study of form is quite as important as that of thought or even feeling. The evolution of language, now slow, now quickened by a catastrophe of history, the formation or deformation of metre, the hardly won advances of prose, passing from its original aim of mere intelligibility to that of measure and beauty: these are subjects worthy of the leading place in a work on literature. It will be seen that the first part of the present book does not disregard ideas, or, on occasion, historical considerations, but it does not make them its chief object. It does not seek them nor suffer itself to be detained by them for long, and it reserves the space, thus left free, for the direct presentment of significant works, describing their matter and their manner. Thus it is hoped that a useful complement to earlier histories of value has been supplied. These remarks apply to the first part. The second, which follows its own method, has a separate introduction.

The translator deserves all thanks for the accomplishment of her difficult task. No less than her wide knowledge of English literature and most patient industry was required to find out all the hints and allusions to the original writings scattered without any direct reference throughout the French text.

E. L.

INTRODUCTION—PART II

MODERN TIMES (1660–1970)

To pass on from the study of medieval and Renascence literature to that of modern times (1660–1970), is to meet with lighter difficulties in some respects, and heavier in others. So many conditions of the problem are new that the very nature of the task is no longer the same. The case here is not one of superabundant authorities, but of scattered and insufficient guidance. On many points, and more and more as one proceeds, the necessary spadework is still wanting. While the matter to be dealt with is really, within a shorter compass of time, much more plentiful, fewer attempts have been made to survey and clarify it. Even the division into periods is far from being agreed upon. It was therefore inevitable, if some sort of order was to be evolved, that much should be ventured, as much indeed remained to be done.

Under these circumstances, the author has been anxious to select the most efficient principle for a classification. Warned by the example of Taine—a critic of genius, steeped in the spirit of a dogmatic philosophy—he has not sought to deduce the course of English literature from any number of exterior influences. Such a scheme of rigorous determination is no longer conceivable. However, the day has come, it seems, when the broad facts of literary history can be more closely connected not merely with physical or social agents, but with a moral one—namely, the development of the national mind itself. That a relation of this kind obtains always more or less, is admitted on all hands; but no explanatory ordering of the data could be thought of, so long as no definite elements were shown to reappear, in at least analogous forms, at the various stages of the psychological process. It is now possible to reckon with such elements, and to speak of recurrences in literature. The more searching analysis which has been effected of the movements in intellectual history, has brought out certain correspondences between equivalent terms. Those words, classicism, romanticism, and so forth, are seen to

answer to distinct attitudes of the mind; and the transitions
from one period to another show themselves as governed by
a law of rhythmic change, the sway of which extends to most
moral happenings.

From this point of view, it has proved possible to regard
two centuries and a half of English literature as a succession
of moments in the history of the English mind, each stage of
which obeyed a craving for novelty and contrast, while consciously or unconsciously preserving the accumulated capital
of all previous experiences. Such, in fact, is the normal
development of that collective personality, a nation. That
the national mind of England should have reached full growth
at the time of the Renascence, made it easier to apply this
method throughout the centuries of maturity that followed
the age of Elizabeth.

The working out of this principle has allowed modern
English literature to be presented in some sort of genetic order,
and divided into periods, each of which really corresponds
with a broad phase in the moral history of England; and with
her social history as well, in so far as the facts of society and
those of intellectual life offer a natural harmony. In consequence, not only has the field of literature been extended so
as to include philosophy, theology, and the wider results of
the sciences, whenever the expressions given them had
awakened general interest; but the chapters within each
period have been arranged so as to answer in principle, not the
customary distinction between literary kinds, based on form,
but the diverse aspects in the creative activities of writers,
and thus the various psychological attitudes which these
activities imply. The traditional separation between prose
and poetry has therefore had very often to be ignored.

Although this method makes large demands upon the
attention of the reader, and involves the upsetting of not a few
cherished habits, the price to pay is perhaps not too high, when
balanced with the facilities which our desire not only to
remember, but to understand, may find in an orderly view of
a vast number of facts. It is the author's hope that the disadvantages inseparable from such an effort may not be deemed
so heavy as to condemn his attempt altogether.

Whatever its further aim may be, a history of literature
must before all deal properly with writers who, if interesting,
are more or less original; and with periods which, however
similar to others, are more or less unique. No attempt to

classify tendencies and works, and explain the common elements in them, would be in the present case tolerable, unless it allowed free scope to the direct, unhampered study of ages, men, and artists. Earnest care has been taken here not to overstress the general at the expense of the particular. While a regular recurrence, with gradually shortening beats of the rhythm, is emphasized all through, no pains have been spared to throw light on the proper features of each period, the infusion of the present with an ever richer past producing results which are really ever new. Again, the individual temperaments of the authors have received the utmost attention, and the qualities of their art and language have been given the fullest consideration which the narrow limits of this study would allow.

Indeed, excessive compression, due to lack of space, is the greatest difficulty under which this part of the work has laboured. For not only is the volume of literary output larger in the modern period; the interrelation of literature with an increasingly complex moral and social life is itself growing more complex. The result is that many and cruel sacrifices have had to be made. No quotation could be thought of. Even the greatest writers have been studied on a reduced scale. All that concerns the lives and careers of authors has had, almost without exception, to be transferred to the corresponding footnotes, each of which aims at being in brief a biographical and bibliographical summary.

It need hardly be added that the study of the most recent period has proved extremely arduous, for obvious reasons; and that this portion of the survey can only be regarded as especially tentative.

The obligations incurred to such comprehensive works as *The Cambridge History of English Literature*, Sir Leslie Stephen's *History of English Thought in the Eighteenth Century*, Professor Oliver Elton's *Survey of English Literature*, 1780–1830 and 1830–80, H. Walker's *Literature of the Victorian Era*, etc., have been acknowledged more than once; but that a debt of gratitude to these works and many others should not remain unrecognized, goes without saying. The author avails himself of this opportunity to make a general apology to the scholars and critics whose exertions and learning have rendered this modest attempt at a synthesis possible, without due appreciation of their help being expressed in every case.

L. C.

In this cheaper edition, the bibliographies have been again revised; the last chapter (Book VII, Chap. V) has been largely rewritten, so that a survey is now given of the period 1914–37.

L. C.

1937.

In this new edition, the bibliographies have been once more revised—those of Part I by Monsieur Pierre Legouis, Professor of English language and literature at the University of Lyons. Some changes, mostly additions, have been made in the text of the last chapter.

L. C.

1940.

A new book (VIII) has been added, dealing with the period 1914–50. Minor changes have been made in the preceding chapters.

L. C.

1954.

For this reprint the text has been revised by the author, and the bibliographies have been brought up to date by Dr. Donald Davie of Trinity College, Dublin—for Part I in collaboration with Professor Pierre Legouis of the University of Lyons—with a care and competence that deserve all praise.

L. C.

1957.

On this occasion Chapters III, IV and V of Book VIII have been revised and brought up to date by Raymond Las Vergnas, Professor of English at the Sorbonne, and the bibliographies have been further revised by Dr. Donald Davie of Trinity College, Dublin.

L. C.

1959.

Publisher's Note

For this edition Book VIII has been entirely rewritten by R. Las Vergnas, and the Index has been adjusted accordingly.

1964.

For these editions Book VIII has been further revised and brought up to date.

1967, 1971.

PART I

THE MIDDLE AGES AND THE RENASCENCE (650–1660)

BOOK I—ORIGINS (650–1350)

CHAPTER I

ANGLO-SAXON LITERATURE (650–1066)

1. *That Anglo-Saxon Literature is Distinct from English Literature.*—Until recently the English looked upon Chaucer as the father of their poetry. They discovered the earliest source of their literature in that fourteenth century in which, on British soil, the fusion of the Anglo-Saxons and the Franco-Normans was consummated. To-day they trace their literary origins back to the seventh century. They give out that Cædmon and the unknown author of *Beowulf* were their first poets, and would go beyond these were it not that they lack older monuments. The stages and the motives of this recession in conquest of the past are curious.

From the time of the battle of Hastings in 1066 until the religious reformation of the sixteenth century, works prior to the Norman Conquest lay forgotten in cloisters where they were deciphered only by a few monks among whom knowledge of the former language was traditional. The dissolution of religious houses resulted in the loss of a large number of these documents, but, in compensation, it brought to light others to which a few scholars turned their attention. At first, especially for polemical reasons, they were concerned only with the religious and historical origins of the nation, or else with the characters of the language in which the documents were written, but gradually, after the charters and the books of devotion, old works of literature were explored, and some sort of collection of poets was made. The idea arose that a real national literature had flourished before the Norman invasion. There was, in the beginning, no thought of identifying it with English literature, properly so called, and it was known as Saxon or Anglo-Saxon, words which marked it as separate and distinct. But during the last sixty years or so, the correctness of these very words has been disputed; they have been criticized as cutting what was an indivisible whole into two

3

parts, and many scholars of the present day speak instead of old or primitive English literature. To the question: 'When does English literature begin?' they answer unhesitatingly that it begins with the first verse sung, the first line written in a Germanic tongue in the country now called England.

It may be that, unknown to themselves, this answer has been dictated as much by sentiment as by history. Until Germany had given evidence of her power in the world of intellect, England seems to have been at little pains to discover the expression of her national genius in the works which the Anglo-Saxons have left behind them. It was Germany, in her desire to prove her near kinship with the people who had produced Shakespeare and Milton, who made all the advances. Afterwards, the glory won by the Germans at the end of the eighteenth century in the fields of letters and philosophy, together with hostility to the France of Voltaire and Napoleon, inclined the English to strengthen those distant ties of intellectual kinship which bound them to the Germans, a new tendency first noticeable in the works of Coleridge, De Quincey, and Carlyle. The political prosperity and growing military power of Germany ensued in the second half of the nineteenth century, and they had an influence which was decisive. It was at the very moment at which defeated France was submitting to the Treaty of Frankfort that German and English philologists began to suspect the legitimacy of the word Anglo-Saxon, and extended the word English to cover all the language spoken and all the literature written in Great Britain from the time of the Germanic invasion, thus implying that linguistic and literary progress had suffered no interruption important enough to make the use of distinct terms necessary.

This tendency met with an unconscious ally in democratic sentiment, then in vigorous and umbrageous growth, which made in England a rough distinction between two castes, the caste of the Franco-Normans which was the aristocracy, and that of the Saxons with which the whole remainder of the people were identified. Every loss of prestige to the former class, every doctrine which tended to give it an adventitious and foreign character, could not fail to please the majority.

At the same time the love, even infatuation, for the 'Gothic,' with which Romanticism slowly infused all Europe, had exalted the most mutilated products of the Middle Ages at the expense of the so-called classical literatures, and had even gone

so far as to surround the works of the barbarous ages with
prestige. Works hitherto unknown or despised had been
revealed as real treasures, glorious to appropriate. What
Addison rather contemptuously called the ' Gothic manner in
writing' (*Spectator*, No. 70), had come to be admired by artists.
It was a new enticement to the English to annex the most
copious medieval vernacular literature which had been
preserved before those of Scandinavia or France.

Philology countenanced the annexation with its high
authority. It placed beyond dispute the essentially German
character of the English language. It proved, with the help
of rediscovered texts, that the absorption into the old Germanic framework of foreign words, whether French or Latin,
was progressive although considerable, that here and there
the frames were perhaps strained or broken, but that they
nevertheless subsisted. Philology, with its attentive lens,
caught the slight successive modifications of speech, found
nowhere a break in continuity, and concluded that there was
a hidden unity behind the slow changes.

The transition from philology to literature seemed easy, and
for many critics of the present day the distinction, formerly
admitted, between Anglo-Saxon and English literature has
ceased to exist. If terminology alone were in question, to
waste time on assent or contradiction would be puerile. But
the new doctrine obscures fundamental truths. For it is the
property of the scientific study of languages to show that every
seeming revolution in speech derives from an unnoticed gradual
process. Philology succeeds unfailingly, where there is not
a lack of texts, in proving that no sudden break exists
anywhere in language. If supplied with texts, it will trace
language back to Adam. But reflection shows that it would
be as wrong, on this account, to give different names to Latin
and the Romance languages, and to the literature of ancient
Rome and the literatures of the nations now called Latin, as
to Anglo-Saxon and English. Whither might not such a
conception lead? To broaden meaning until all necessary
distinctions are lost, is, in this instance, to forget that varia-
tions of language, however gradual, have finally such a
cumulative effect that they render one age incomprehensible
to another, although the two be undeniably connected by a
progressive linguistic evolution. However it may be with the
English language, there is no other literature which has lived
and developed in as much ignorance of its indigenous past as

English literature. Italian and French were never quite weaned of their maternal Latin, but Anglo-Saxon literature, when the first great literary works of the fourteenth century appeared, was not only dead, but also unknown; its documents had been buried deep; they were written in a language which had become unintelligible, and could therefore exert no possible influence. The true unity of a literature is constituted by the persistence of a language which remains fairly intelligible from one age to another, and by the succeeding and more or less active influences, sometimes manifest and sometimes hidden, but none the less continuous, of the works which are literary landmarks. If this be so, Anglo-Saxon literature cannot be an integral part of English literature. It has rightly no other relation to English literature than the life of his father or mother has to the life of the hero of a biography.

It is the prologue rather than the first chapter of the book. Yet this prologue happens here to be indispensable. For if the Latin antecedents of Romance literatures are deposited in Latin literature, Anglo-Saxon literature is too slender and too special to have, at least for Frenchmen, its special place. Its most natural place is at the approach to English literature, its mere descendant, yet a descendant having certain derived characteristics and certain deep feelings which cannot be well understood until their germ has been descried in Anglo-Saxon works. Thus the right of Anglo-Saxon literature to open a history of English literature is again established, together with the justice of the term Anglo-Saxon.

2. *Anglo-Saxon Literature is not a Direct Expression of the Pagan Age.*—The Anglo-Saxon literature which has reached us is, on the whole, the work of clerks who lived from the seventh to the eleventh century. If they did not create all of it, they preserved it all. It is therefore an essentially Christian literature. The editors allowed nothing to survive which seemed to them to conflict formally with their religion. Hence came a vast elimination of which we cannot even conjecture the importance. Hence also arose modifications and amplifications of such of the old legends as were not sacrificed, changes which gave them an edifying turn certainly not theirs originally.

It is among these clerks that we must first place ourselves to understand not only the pages which emanated from them directly, but also the character and tone of the older fragments which they spared.

Let us go back to the end of the seventh century. The

conquest had reached its term.   Driven forward by the Huns, the Germanic tribes dwelling between the Elbe and the Oder and along the Danish coast, had invaded the eastern territory of Great Britain and held it for two hundred years.   The Angles were masters of the land north of the Humber, the Jutes of the land of Kent, and the Saxons of all the remaining country south of the Thames.   Pagans at their arrival, these peoples had undergone mass conversion at the end of the sixth century, and the first dated writings appeared at the end of the seventh.

The oldest collections of laws show a civilization which was already considerable and was permeated by the spirit of Christianity.   The Anglo-Saxons were already a settled people, tillers of the soil, enjoying protection against theft and plunder, and an organized justice which deprived the individual of the right to vengeance and, as much as possible, substituted fines for corporal punishment.   In each state a hierarchical society, in which centralization and democratic institutions were happily balanced, had been established.

Nothing is therefore more illusory than to take the extant Anglo-Saxon literature for a primitive product, and to seek in it the reflection of Germanic barbarism.   To blend the romantic picture Tacitus gives us of the first-century Germans with the picture of England in the eighth century is equivalent to placing on one plane the *Hymn of the Fratres Arvales* and the *Aeneid*.   In the pages of the Latin historian the remote germs of English political institutions or family customs may be discerned, but we must relegate to a dead past his descriptions of savages who went half naked or clothed in the skins of wild animals, whose sole occupations were war and hunting, those nomads incapable of prolonged labour who lived in sordid huts and caves, whose indolence kept them cowering by their hearths for days together, who knew nothing of agriculture and despised it.   There is no relevance in what Tacitus tells of the religion of these tribes, their gods who corresponded to Mercury, Mars, and Hercules, their cult of Ertha, the Earth Mother, the forests of their superstition in which their atrocious human sacrifices were consummated. These particulars are such as characterize any people not yet civilized.   They are doubtless interesting to know, but they belong to conditions of an earlier society which linger only vaguely in the memory of the age of civilization.   Between the time of which Tacitus speaks and the period of the Venerable

Bede, the Angles and Saxons underwent transformations compared to which all the revolutions of their later history, even the Norman Conquest, were trifling. They experienced migration and contact with a population of another race, the partially Romanized Celts, they relinquished a half-nomadic life for a life concentrated in fixed places, they exchanged war, misery, and famine for a state of relative peace and prosperity, and finally they underwent a deep and fervent mass conversion to Christianity, which disorganized the system of morals while it reformed it, which brought the clerks into communion with Latinity, and which severed most bonds with the still pagan Teutonic world.

During these convulsions, nearly every possible survival of primitive poetry was uprooted, together with the mythology on which it rested. The mythology of which Tacitus speaks, the gods Tuisco and Mannus, can and even should be forgotten by whoever wishes to understand *Beowulf*. The names of the deities had ceased, when *Beowulf* was written, to have interest for any one but a philologist, who might note the traces they had left in language, particularly in the names of the days of the week. The ancient rites had been totally submerged, save for some local practices or magic formulas or charms, which often had an alloy of Christian words, such survivals as folklore discovers to this day in the remote countrysides of Europe. Only traces of savage customs were to be observed, or such sporadic revivals of barbarism as the reigning code condemned. Everything derived from the barbaric past had been purified and ennobled, and also enervated, in an atmosphere of Christianity which already was almost one of chivalry.

It is no less dangerous to merge in a single whole Anglo-Saxon poetry and the poetry of the Scandinavians, or continental Germanic poetry where it was still pagan. The *Nibelungenlieder*, although compiled at a later date, give, at least in the Hagen epic, a powerful picture of the warlike furies and the atrocious vengeances of the earliest ages. Nothing like or approximating to them is to be found in the whole body of Anglo-Saxon verse. Scandinavia and Iceland preserved in the *Edda* and in their prose sagas abundant characteristics belonging to primitive beliefs and customs. In spite of manifest likenesses of form and versification, sometimes amounting to identity, the content of their legends is in extreme contrast with Anglo-Saxon literature. In the

Edda there is perfect harmony between the fabulous, immense, strange subject-matter and the vehement style. In Anglo-Saxon poems the excessiveness for the themes of the traditional form, the disparity of dulcified subjects and verbal violence, is immediately striking. The *Edda* is full of allusions to a mythology of extravagant proportions, to legends which may not be preserved in their original integrity, but of which the spirit at least is kept, and seems, indeed, to be strengthened rather than softened. The *Edda* presents, in abbreviated form, powerful dramatic pictures of fights between barbarous men, and of struggles between gods yet more barbarous and unbridled than the men. No wish to edify seems to have dominated or restrained the poet. At one time he gives full rein to his imagination, at another his realism is intense. He shows barbarism by turns in its acts and in its visions. But Anglo-Saxon poetry, taken as a whole, is a continuous piece of edification, elegiac in its dominant tone. It is a long Christian lamentation breathed by ingenuous and fervent men.

3. *The Anglo-Saxon Latinist Clerks: Aldhelm, Bede, and Alcuin.*[1]—Before dealing with the Anglo-Saxon poetical texts which seem most ancient, it is necessary to recall the Christian Latinists, about whom alone we have precise data. To them and to those like them we owe the preservation of the traces of primitive poetry. They spoke the native language and often themselves wrote verses in the vernacular, and in their Latin writings customs are indicated and scenes are sketched which reveal the life of their times more clearly than does Anglo-Saxon poetry. Sometimes, moreover, through their Latin, the imaginative background of their race makes itself felt with singular force, so that the characteristics of the national literature can thus be better understood.

The migration of the Germanic peoples into Great Britain was still in process when Christianity was first introduced among them. As early as 597, the monk Augustine came from Rome to convert them and founded in Kent, where the Jutes had established themselves, the church of Canterbury.

At much the same time, Christian Ireland was sending missionaries to the Angles, and was building the monasteries which were the earliest civilizing influences in Northumbria. From these two centres Christianity spread among the Saxons who were occupying the south and west of the island, that is from centres diverse as the mother-churches whence they

[1] The works of Aldhelm, Bede, and Alcuin are included in Migne's *Patrology*.

sprang. Their differences led to a struggle for supremacy which lasted until, in 664, the Synod of Whitby gave Rome the victory over Ireland. The distinction between the two disciplines subsisted, however, for a much longer time, and two distinct spirits are revealed in Christian writings, according to whether they emanate from the north or from the south, and are apparent through the Latin which was the invariable medium of the clerks.

Aldhelm (650?–709) was a product of the school of Canterbury. He was the pupil there of Abbot Hadrian, an African monk, and of Theodore, the Greek monk of Tarsus. A Saxon of noble birth, Aldhelm is said to have been a successful poet in the vernacular, but only his Latin works are extant. As abbot of Malmesbury, and afterwards as bishop of Sherborne, he was at once a saintly prelate and a humanist. He was as conversant with the Latin poets of the classical and of later periods as with the Scriptures and the writings of the Fathers. He was a seventh-century stylist, an artist who was at once a barbarian and a refined scholar. It is strange to find the expedients of Anglo-Saxon rhetoric intruding themselves into his Latin works, which abound, to an amusing degree, with alliterations and in which he indulges all his Anglo-Saxon taste for imagery and periphrasis. As a rule, he addresses himself to ladies, that is to nuns, and there is a curious coquetry in his discourses to them. It is the praises of virginity which he indites in prose, the praises of virgins in hexameters. His Latin is grammatically correct to a point which is rare at the end of the seventh century, but his origin is revealed by his too heavily decorated style, by his violent and numerous metaphors, and by his habit of materializing the abstract. He alludes, for instance, to the golden necklace of the virtues, the white jewels of merit, the purple flowers of modesty, the swanlike whiteness of old age, and he speaks of 'the opening of the gates of dumb silence,' 'the shining lamps of chastity in which the oil of modesty burns,' 'the unclean sink of impurity in which the vessels of the soul are miserably engulfed,' 'the bastion of the Catholic faith shaken by the war-machines of secular arguments and overthrown by the battering-rams of atrocious ingenuity.' These images are the very warp and woof of his prose. The same characteristics reappear, with less startling effect, in his verse. His riddles, which have a place between the riddles of Symposius and the Anglo-Saxon riddles of which we shall speak later, are ingenious and sometimes graceful. In his taste for riddles, as in his passion for metaphors, the Latinist Aldhelm betrays his origin.

The great Latinist of Northumbria, the Venerable Bede, affords a striking contrast to Aldhelm. Whatever may be thought of his taste, Aldhelm was first of all an artist with whom manner has precedence over matter. But of Bede (672–735) the reverse is true. This Angle, who was brought up in Wearmouth Abbey, and spent his whole adult life in the monastery of Jarrow, was the most learned theologian and the best historian of Christianity of his time. He absorbed and he summed up in himself the culture of an age which had lost its inheritance on the Continent. The variety of his knowledge and his interests appears in the subjects of his principal works—a treatise on metre, a natural history, a universal chronology of the Christian era, based on serious astronomical studies, a martyrology, lives of the abbots of Wearmouth and Jarrow, a life of Saint Cuthbert, above all, the *Ecclesiastical History of the Angles*.

The historical and biographical works are the most interesting for us. They are distinguished by an honest love of truth and by diligent documentary research. Bede's conceptions and style are impersonal, clear, simple, much above the level of his time. His pre-eminence is one of intelligence. He informs on points of fact and he interprets manners and customs. His *Ecclesiastical History* is still the chief authority for the early period of which it traces the history from a religious point of view, the years between Julius Caesar's conquest and 731, that is, four years before the author's death. The conversion and the struggle between the Roman and the Irish Church and final triumph of the former, are its principal themes. Yet Bede, the historian and learned man, has been too exclusively praised. His extreme simplicity, which is in so great contrast to the artificiality of Aldhelm, and the weakness of his surviving Latin verses, have done harm to his literary reputation. In Bede, more than in any other Anglo-Saxon Latinist or any vernacular poet, the poetry, the charm, and the meaning of this age of early Christian fervour are to be found. The spirit of his lives of saints and abbots and his *Ecclesiastical History* is more intimate and penetrating than any which breathes in other works. His direct narration of facts, and the marvels of an artless faith in which he clothes them, are far more eloquent than all the

effusions and the paraphrases of the poets. Moreover, Bede,
like Aldhelm, was a student of vernacular verse, of which his
lucid reason enabled him to interpret the genius. The whole
of the so-called Cædmonian epic could better be spared than
those few bald pages in which Bede tells us how the poor
peasant Cædmon received his inspiration. All the verses of
Cynewulf taken together would be poor compensation for the
ensuing scene, which has been quoted over and over again
and can never be quoted too often. It occurs in the account
of the conversion of Northumbria in 633. When Ædwin and
his nobles had been asked to embrace Christianity, one noble
spoke as follows:

> So, O king, does the present life of man on earth seem to me, in com-
> parison with the time which is unknown to us, as though a sparrow flew
> swiftly through the hall, coming in by one door and going out by the
> other, and you, the while, sat at meat with your captains and liegemen,
> in wintry weather, with a fire burning in your midst and heating the
> room, the storm raging out of doors and driving snow and rain before it.
> For the time for which he is within, the bird is sheltered from the storm,
> but after this short while of calm he flies out again into the cold and is
> seen no more. Thus the life of man is visible for a moment, but we
> know not what comes before it or follows after it. If, then, this new
> doctrine brings something more of certainty, it deserves to be followed.

Nowhere else is there anything at once so exact and so
ample. The image is as great as it is intimate, precise although
mysterious. Shakespeare never produced one which was more
striking or which better conveyed the feeling of life's strangeness. Nothing equal to it is to be found in the whole of
Anglo-Saxon poetry.

It is true and characteristic, if a fact of undetermined
importance, that Bede was the disciple of the Irish monks
settled in Wearmouth and Jarrow. The pious simplicity of
the way of life in these monasteries, a simplicity they created,
remained dear to him. Although he rallied to allegiance to
the Church of Rome, he never stifled regret for the pleasant
days of his youth, and the Celts or Gaels who were his masters
can hardly be denied an important share in the training of his
fine mind. To acknowledge this is to touch the insoluble
problem of what influence the Celtic spirit secretly exercised
on extant Anglo-Saxon poetry.

The illustrious Alcuin (730?–804), Charlemagne's collabora-
tor from 790 onwards, also came out of Northumbria. He was
brought up in York. Northumbria gave this great clerk to a
France which had relapsed into barbarism. Alcuin left his

country when the earliest civilization of the Angles was about
to be extinguished, for the terrible Danish invasions, which
ruined monasteries and centres of learning, were beginning.
Although as much of Alcuin's life as is historical was spent
among the Franks, he stayed in his own country until he
was sixty years old, and is therefore a representative, and a
brilliant one, of the culture and the character of the Angles.
His Latin poetry is less correct but more personal than Aldhelm's and sometimes has a fine ring. He finds moving
distichs in which to bid farewell to his monastic cell before he
leaves it for the court, and that cell, giving on to a blossoming
orchard and green lawns, beside a stream, seems indeed to
have been a place to regret. He sighs as he reflects that
another will occupy it, that he will no longer be able to
meditate verses in it, yet he recollects that all in this world is
fleeting, that such is the common lot.

Many lines of his work are addressed to Charlemagne, whom
he celebrates under the name of David, or compares to Homer,
himself assuming the name of Flaccus (Horace). It is, however, his prose which is of special interest to us. Alcuin,
writing prose, is an educationist who resumes all branches
of knowledge in manuals. He treats grammar, rhetoric, dialectics, and the rest in the form of dialogues or catechisms,
having questions and answers. Sometimes the conversation
is between a young Saxon and the young Frank whom he
teaches, sometimes between Alcuin and Charlemagne himself,
sometimes between Alcuin and his pupil Pepin, the emperor's
son. Often the questions are very like riddles, a proof of the
strong Anglo-Saxon taste for those ingenious exercises. The
answers are nearly always periphrases or metaphors. There
is no better introduction to an intelligent reading of Anglo-
Saxon poetry than any extract from these dialogues, in which
the pupil is the questioner:

What is the body? The spirit's lodging.
What is hair? The clothing of the head.
What is the beard? The distinction between the sexes, the mark of
age.
What are the eyes? The guides of the body, the vessels of light,
the index to thought.

Sometimes fancy becomes rich and beautiful as well as
curious:

What is the sun? The splendour of the world, the beauty of the sky,
the grace of nature, the honour of the day, the distributor of the hours.

What is the sea? The path of boldness, the earth's bourne, the divider of regions, the receiver of streams, the spring of showers. . . .

If the vulgar tongue be substituted for Latin, there is no difference in style between these didactic definitions and Anglo-Saxon poetry. Like Aldhelm, Alcuin carried into his Latin the turns of thought and the imaginative and slightly childish mentality of his fellow-countrymen. If the great clerks whom we have enumerated have left us no verses in the vernacular—such as they wrote have been almost all lost—they are yet hardly less representative of the Anglo-Saxon spirit than are the writers in the vulgar tongue. It was among these men, perhaps by them, surely by anonymous clerks like them, that the poems which have reached us were compiled or were, at least, edited and expurgated.

The characters of Roman writing seem to have been imported with Christianity, and to have taken the place of the runes, which the Germanic peoples engraved on monuments and used for brief correspondence, but in which they do not appear to have recorded the verses of their poets, the gleemen or scops. It follows that memories of the pagan epoch have invariably been transmitted to us through the medium of the clerks, and that what we call Anglo-Saxon literature has therefore been inevitably subject to the influence of Latin, and to no other foreign influence. It is a literature in which the direct and realistic expression of the national genius, unmodified by Christianity, is rarely found and dangerous to seek.

It is a literature compiled by clerks, but by clerks whose fathers were warriors and vikings, and who were very near the surviving memories of the warlike age. The word battle, the thought of prowess, awoke irrepressible ardours in them. It cost them little effort to call up the manners and the scenes of so recent a past. The terms of an unaltered language, the accents of unchanged prosody, the recurring combinations of words and images inevitable to alliteration: all these often took them back to the days of adventure by land and sea and led them to preserve such fragments as oral tradition had handed down to them. Thus their poetry, even when it is entirely Christian, is full of reminiscences and echoes of paganism. Less dominated by Latin than their prose, it deforms and reforms Holy Writ, in accordance with its own traditions, even while it reproduces it. It thinks Scripture anew and interprets it in national terms. It crowns biblical warriors with the helmet and shields them with the limewood buckler, and sends the saints of the Mediterranean to voyage over grey and ice-cold seas, while the low, rainy sky of the north broods over Palestine, wolves roam the Holy Land, and crows and wild swans fly above it. Thus this poetry presents a continual contradiction, yet constantly, by changes of scenery and of actors, creates anew while it claims to translate, so that its very inaccuracies are alive and partly original.

Such is the general character of this literature, which, although fundamentally Christian, is here and there still pagan in feeling and everywhere national in form.

4. *Anglo-Saxon Poetry: its Manuscript Sources, its General Character*.[1]—The way in which the texts of Anglo-Saxon literature have reached us is significant. Leaving on one side documentary and practical works, whether historical or religious, and also the chronicles, texts of laws and homilies, and the various translations, we find almost the whole exclusively poetical literature in four manuscripts attributed to the eleventh century. The first of these, the so-called Junius manuscript, named after the scholar, Milton's friend, who bequeathed it to the Bodleian Library, contains the paraphrases from the Bible known as the Cædmonian Poems. The second is the *Codex Exoniensis*, which was given to Exeter Cathedral by Bishop Leofric in the eleventh century and was almost forgotten until 1826. Its contents are a curious medley of pious poems, of half-pagan lyrical and elegiac compositions, and of riddles and sententious verses. Thirdly, *Beowulf* and the biblical fragment *Judith*, unknown until the end of the eighteenth century, are strangely associated in the British Museum manuscript. And lastly, in the manuscript which was discovered in 1832 in the capitular library of Vercelli in North Italy, there are entirely religious poems and, especially, metrical lives of the saints. To these must be added two

---

[1] C. W. M. Grein, *Bibliothek der angelsächsichen Poesie*, 4 vols., 1857–64, revised by R. P. Wülker, 1883–98 (Leipzig). G. P. Krapp and E. v. K. Dobbie, *The Anglo-Saxon Poetic Records*, 6 vols., 1931–53. Translations into alliterative verse in J. D. Spaeth's *Old English Poetry* (Princeton, 1922), into prose in R. K. Gordon's *Anglo-Saxon Poetry*, 1927.

Studies: Stopford Brooke, *History of Early English Literature to the Accession of King Alfred*, 1892, and *English Literature from the Beginning to the Norman Conquest*, 1898, two works which contain excellent verse translations; W. P. Ker, *The Dark Ages*, 1904, and *Epic and Romance*, 1897; E. Pons, *Le thème et le sentiment de la nature dans la poésie anglo-saxonne*, 1925; G. K. Anderson, *The Literature of the Anglo-Saxons* (Princeton, 1949); and, for the language, René Huchon, *Histoire de la langue anglaise*, vol. i, 1923.

short fragments of verse from some still more recently recovered pages of parchment, the one on the battle of Finnes-
burh and the other on an episode of the life of Waldhere,
otherwise Walter of Aquitaine, and also the important fragment, *The Death of Byrhtnoth* or *Battle of Maldon*, published
in 1726 from a manuscript which is lost. Such is almost the
whole of the known poetry of the Anglo-Saxons, and it is on
these texts that the attempt must be based to establish the
dominant features of this poetry, which is at once strongly
characterized and very uniform.

At the time when the extant texts were compiled, its form
was already fixed. This primitive metrical literature had been
subject, before it assumed its present guise, to a process of
ossification. The most ancient works are posterior to the
date at which versification and rhetoric assumed definite
shape, and every subject, whether Christian or pagan, epic
or personal, great or small, whether the story of the Creation
or a riddle on a rake, is clothed in the same dress. Literary
decoration and the turn that is given to a theme are always
identical. The singer's voice has unchanging volume. The
effect on the senses and the imagination hardly varies.

1. The most profound and also the most general element in
all poetry is to be sought in language. The qualities and
deficiencies of a language predetermine the field of poetry
and its successes and failures, almost independently of the
personal genius of the poets who use it. The chief task of a
poet is to take skilful advantage of the resources a language
offers to him. Words have a particular expressive value
which is outside or beyond their meaning, and although the
force of association of ideas may supply a grace or an energy,
a lucidity or a mystery other than that which belongs to a
word at its simplest, the fact remains true that the maximum
of suggestion is reached when sound and meaning are in
harmony. Thus it might be said, of the essence of the
English language, that in its Teutonic elements it surpasses
French by its vigorous strokes, but that it speaks with a less
melodious voice. What the French weakly call *force*, has an
English name, *strength*, from the Anglo-Saxon *strengthu*, in
which seven muscular consonants strangle a single vowel,
but in the French word *oiseau*, a solitary consonant murmurs
among soft vowels and diphthongs, with such effect that it
makes the English *bird* (A.-S. *bridd*) seem to have little power
of suggestion.

The primary character of the Anglo-Saxon language derives from the predominance of its consonants. Not only are syllables introduced by a consonant or group of consonants (*h, sc, sp, st, str, hr, thr*, etc.), but these consonants form the vital part of syllables. They are explosive, not quiescent, and their noise drowns the neighbouring vowels, a characteristic of which the persistence is proved whenever any French word passes through an English throat, as when *donne* becomes *ddonne* or *plaine pplaine*. The value given to the initial consonant, together with the tonic accent, which throws the root syllable into relief, and with the emphasis on the essential word of a sentence, make up the law of Anglo-Saxon versification. The comparative insignificance of vowels is shown in the rule that vowel sounds, which may be substituted for alliterations or repetitions of initial consonants, need not be identical. For here it is not the sound of the vowel but the absence of the consonant which is important. The effect is produced by the momentary softening of the line.

The normal line is made up of an undetermined number of syllables divided into two sections, in each of which there should be two rhythmic accents. The recurrence of the same consonant or group of consonants, to introduce the two accentuated syllables of the first section, and that of the first accentuated syllable of the second section, give the alliteration, as follows:

> *st*eap *st*anlitho—*st*ige nearwe (*Beowulf*, ii, line 159).
> Steep stone slopes, paths narrow.

There is often only one alliterating letter in the first section.

2. While the line is thus based on accent combined with alliteration, and while both of these depend on the predominating value of consonants, the style and the construction of the poetic phrase derive from another characteristic of the language.

Unlike modern English, which is one of the most analytical and least inflected of languages, Anglo-Saxon expresses changes of tense, number, and person either by modifications of the root vowels or by differences of termination. It is a language nearly as synthetic as Latin, endowed with four cases for either number, several declensions of the noun, two declensions of the adjective, and numerous conjugations of the verb. Its syntax, that of an inflected language, shows a very complex use of cases and great freedom in the arrange-

ment of words. This freedom of construction is to-day one
of the points in the old language which astonish an Englishman. Its effect in poetry is to cause the place of words to be
strictly governed by the needs of the alliterative line or the
exigencies of emphasis. There is an abundance of separate,
disconnected words in apposition, with something of the effect
of superimposed interjections.

It is impossible, even in the most literal translation into an
analytical language like English or French, to reproduce the
staccato of these phrases without either introducing connecting
links or becoming unintelligible. There is in the original a
greater abruptness, a more interrupted sequence than that of
which modern syntax allows.

3. Probably, however, no potentiality of the language had
more influence on the rhetoric of the Anglo-Saxon poets than
the ease with which it allowed them to make composites.
This primitive tongue is poor in the grammatical suffixes and
prefixes which transfer a word from one class to another, which
make an adjective of a noun or a noun of a verb, or make two
nouns into a new one, their separate meanings being lost in
the process. The constituent elements of derivatives and
composite words often remain clearly discernible and keep
their distinct sense. Thus to crucify is to fasten to the cross,
rod-fæstnen; a butcher is a slaughterer of cattle, *hrith-heawere*;
the third finger is the ring finger, *hring-finger*; a literate man
is one learned in letters, *stæfcræftig*. The passage from words
in current use and employed in prose to the words which
poets invent for a particular effect is unmarked, so that it is
often difficult to determine which terms are strictly poetic.
Alfred's prose gives us *æfter-genga*, or aftercomer, for successor;
ærend-gewrit, or written message, for letter; *cynestol*, or king's
seat, for throne; all words much like those composites which
are found only among the poets—for instance, *eardstapa*,
or earth-walker, for traveller; *breost-nett*, or breast-net, for
corslet; *death-reced*, or death-chamber, for grave; *ban-hring*,
or bone ring, for vertebra.

From language this process passed to thinking. Even when
they were writing Latin, the Anglo-Saxons developed their
ideas by means of accumulated periphrases. Their poets make
an extensive use of this possibility of the language, and the
peculiarity of their composite words is that they are used not
of necessity, for lack of a simple equivalent, but as ornaments,
to show a quality of the subject-matter and throw it into

relief, or, more frequently, for pure love of periphrasis, or again, for the sake of alliteration. The body becomes the bone-chamber; the heart, the treasure-chamber; thought, the treasure of the breast; the breast, the close of the heart; the warrior is the man with the corslet, the lance-bearer or the swordsman; the sailor is the traveller on the waters; armour, the warrior's garb or the shirt of battle; and man, the earth's inhabitant or the word-carrier.

Many primitive customs and beliefs are revealed by these poetic synonyms. The chief or king is the *beag*-giver—*beags* being rings which served at once as ornaments and as money —or he is the gold- or treasure-giver; the banqueting hall is the mead or wine hall, or else the roofed hall; and warriors are lime-bearers, that is, bearers of limewood shields.

Numerous composite words bear witness to the Anglo-Saxon enthusiasm for war; battle is the game of blades, the conflict of lances or the cracking of banners, and the sword is battle lightning, while blood is the sweat of war or the flow of carnage.

The elements and natural phenomena supply as many composite terms as war. The sea is the path of sails, the whale's road or the swan's pathway; the flood is the waves' journey; fog, the helmet of the air; and darkness, the helmet of night.

These composites are sometimes heaped upon a simple word, like heavy, barbaric jewellery. Cædmon has quite thirty synonyms to denote Noah's Ark. The more of them a poet collects, the more pleased he seems to be, and the poems often so closely recall the Litany to the Virgin—'Mystical Rose, Tower of David, Tower of Ivory, House of Gold, Ark of the Covenant, Gate of Heaven, Morning Star'—as almost to suggest an attribution of this prayer to an Anglo-Saxon clerk.

A poet will not say 'when night came,' but 'when the noble gleam its setting sought, darkened the northern firmament, dusk amid clouds, o'erveil'd the world with mist, with darkness cover'd, when night clos'd over the cultured land's adornments.' [1]

Often an object is designated only by composite words or periphrases, and its identity must therefore be guessed. Thus the eyes must be understood by 'jewels of the head,' the body by 'fleshy clothing,' armour by 'the eorl's raiment.' It was a sport of the poets to cause an object to be divined by one

[1] B. Thorpe's translation of the *Legend of St. Guthlac*, line 1212.

of its attributes, an amusement known as 'kenning' which led to the riddle, so that collections of riddles are naturally among the most interesting of these poetical productions.

Almost the whole rhetoric of the Anglo-Saxons is made up of such perpetual periphrases. These poets abound in abrupt metaphors, condensed in single composite words, but they hardly ever make the consecutive and extensive comparisons which are born both of imagination and of reason. Only the artist who is master of himself and at peace can note the resemblances of different objects and study them side by side. He rarely does it if he feels passion, never if he is without culture. It would be hard to find in Anglo-Saxon poetry a metaphor which is not swift and violent, or of which the lines are amplified or merged in a harmonious picture.

The character of the language, of the metres, and of the style is so marked that there is among all the poems a likeness which does not escape monotony. These poets modulate their voices very slightly and lack the alternatives of solemnity and lightness. Their joy weighs as heavy as their sorrow, their irony is brutal as a blow from a sledge-hammer. The traditional form and the single line give an air of grandeur to particular poems, but imprison and restrict individual initiative. Throughout the three centuries for which Anglo-Saxon literature is known, hardly an approach can be perceived to that differentiation of *genres* which is the sign of vitality and progress. The epic unity of form and tone is at first impressive, but its continued tension grows wearisome, and the periphrastic accompaniment enriches but overweights and obscures the style. None the less, this is a strong and an impressive poetic form. It remains to examine the value of the themes which it clothes.

5. *The Poems which refer to the pre-Christian Age: 'Widsith,' 'Deor,' 'Beowulf.'*—The Anglo-Saxon poems in which the traditions of the pagan age have been preserved are both the most beautiful in themselves and the most interesting to us. It has been seen that we cannot expect ever to find in them a direct picture of pre-Christian times, since they were compiled or edited some time between the eighth and tenth centuries by clerks who knew Latin, whose minds were coloured by Christian morality, and who had access to some models from Graeco-Roman literature. Yet the authors of these poems had kept the old passion for adventure, together with the memory of the wild life of their

ancestors and the ancestral legends and verses. There is a certain analogy between their state of mind and that which the nineteenth century called Romanticism. From a distance, through the medium of their purified feelings, they caressed with their melancholy their dream of the past. They were civilized men who returned to barbarism in spirit and impregnated it with their moral sense. They were a little like Virgil nobly retracing the history of Rome's infancy, or Tennyson expurgating the perverse Arthurian legend. They often re-cast the poems which a tradition, doubtless oral, had handed down to them, suppressing whatever shocked their consciences, and intercalating new passages or adding edifying conclusions.

The short poems *Widsith* [1] and *Deor* lift a corner of the veil which hides the past. They purport to be the songs of two scops or poets living on the Continent in an age already fabulous. Widsith or 'Great Traveller' has wandered much from tribe to tribe, and he gives a list of the princes who have made him presents. Among these are Eormenric, king of the Goths, Attila, king of the Huns, and Alboin, king of the Lombards, whose date is more than two centuries later than Attila's, the second third of the sixth century instead of the middle of the fourth, so that Widsith is plainly no historical figure but a typical scop who is an excuse for bringing together names famous in history and legend. The enumeration of Germanic tribes is valuable to historical geography, and the literary attraction consists almost entirely in the lustre of the proper names and their suggestions. Both Hrothgar, who recurs in *Beowulf*, and Hagen, celebrated in the *Nibelungenlieder*, figure in *Widsith*. The poem gives an idea of the wandering minstrels who went from court to court, singing the praises of the princes from whom they received or expected largesse. It concludes as follows:

> Thus the gleemen
> Say in song their need, speak aloud their thankword!
> Always South or Northward someone they encounter,
> Who,—for he is learned in lays, lavish in his giving—
> Would before his men of might magnify his sway,
> Manifest his earlship.
>   Till all flits away—
> Life and light together—land who getteth so
> Hath beneath the heaven high established power. [2]

---

[1] R. W. Chambers, *Widsith, a Study in Old English Medieval Legend* (Cambridge, 1912); Kemp Malone, *Widsith*, 1936.
[2] Stopford Brooke's translation.

The Lament of Deor is the effusion of a more sedentary and less happy scop than Widsith, one disgraced by his lord who has preferred his rival, but consoled for his ill luck by recollection of the normal inconstancy of fortune. He recalls heroes and gods who were not spared tribulations, and concludes every strophe—this is the only Anglo-Saxon poem which has this strophic form—with a sort of refrain:

> *That* he overwent; *this* also may I.[1]

But the only poem which attempts a picture of the primitive age on a large scale is *The Lay of Beowulf*.[2] The date of the compilation of this work makes it the most ancient epic of the Teutonic world, and historically its subject takes us back to the first half of the sixth century. It speaks of the victory of the Franks over the Goths led by Hygelac (the Cochilaicus of Gregory of Tours), which occurred about 512–520, a fight in which the young warrior Beowulf, one of the defeated army, is said to have distinguished himself by strength and valour.

Neither the subject nor the characters are in any way peculiarly Anglo-Saxon. Not only is there no question of the island of Great Britain, where the Anglo-Saxons were established as early as the fifth century, but there is also no mention of the lands near the Elbe which they inhabited previously. The scene is, by turns, the Danish island Seeland and the country of the Geats or Goths in the south of present Sweden, and Beowulf, the hero, is a Geat. This is thus no national epic; even if the common origin of the tribes be taken into account, it is remarkable that almost at the moment at which an unknown Anglo-Saxon poet was commemorating his forbears of Scandinavia, the still pagan people of that country were beginning their redoubtable descents upon the shores of Great Britain, visiting upon the Anglo-Saxons the very ills which these had once inflicted on the Britons. The question arises, therefore, whether *Beowulf* be not an adaptation into Anglo-Saxon of a Scandinavian legend, a hypothesis supported by the fact that the chief incidents of the story of Beowulf, the slayer of monsters, recur in the Icelandic saga

---

[1] Stopford Brooke's translation.
[2] Ed. by W. J. Sedgefield (3rd ed., Manchester, 1935); A. J. Wyatt (3rd ed., revised by R. W. Chambers, Cambridge, 1925); C. L. Wrenn, 1953. Translations by J. R. Clark Hall (prose, revised ed. 1950) and F. B. Gummere (verse, New York, 1909). See R. W. Chambers, *Beowulf* (2nd ed., Cambridge, 1932); J. Hoops, *Kommentar zum Beowulf* (Heidelberg, 1932); W. W. Lawrence, *Beowulf and the Epic tradition* (Cambridge, Mass., 1938).

of universal melancholy. It makes life seem sad, effort vain. The reason for this must be sought in its atmosphere. It takes one into a dark place whither the sun's clear light does not penetrate, where fogs and unwholesome vapours are never quite dissipated by the sun's rays. A certain joy in life is needed to make a work of imagination healthy, but Beowulf, or rather the poet who narrates his adventures, has introduced the Christian idea of earthly life among his gloomy scenery, has plumbed the emptiness of mortality, and found it of little worth at the very moment at which he celebrates mortal glory. This is indeed a poem which has come out of a cold cell in a Northumbrian cloister. It breathes the air of the tomb.

6. *Lyrical and Elegiac Poems:* [1] *'The Ruined Burg,' 'The Lover's Message,' 'The Maiden's Complaint,' 'The Wanderer,' 'The Seafarer.'*—The melancholy which weighs upon *Beowulf*, especially on its latter part, often recurs in several undated short poems, which are distinguished from those already mentioned by a complete severance of ties with the Continent and a break with pagan tradition. All the same, these poems are not distinctively Christian; rather they are Christian only in some of their details and in their conclusion. They are laments, usually desolate. Their voice is something like that heard in the so-called 'Songs of Ossian,' with which Macpherson conquered Europe at a moment in the eighteenth century when men were avid of the vague and the melancholy. These Anglo-Saxon verses strike, perhaps more truly than the authentic fragments of Celtic poetry, that note of lamentation, at once personal and human, to which the name of Ossianic has since been given.

There is, for instance, a complaint written on the ruins of an old town which might be Bath, the watering-place which was so magnificent in Roman times, before the Saxon invaders destroyed it. A poet comes to visit the remains of this splendid town, long after the days of its splendour, and is grieved by the sight of the 'ruined burg.'

> Many were the mead-halls, full of mirth of men,
> Till the strong-willed Wyrd whirled that all to change. [2]

The poem is a series of monotonous laments in which the word recurs incessantly like an inevitable refrain.

---

[1] N. Kershaw, *Anglo-Saxon and Norse Poems* (Cambridge, 1922).
[2] Stopford Brooke's translation.

There is also a series of lyrical poems, or rather elegies, which are more intimate and have reached us in the guise of personal effusions, but which are so obscure that the question has arisen whether they are not detached parts of longer romantic compositions. The habitual melancholy is missing only in one of them, *The Lover's Message*, in which an exile sends a message to his love by means of runes carved on a wooden tablet. By a fiction in harmony with the enigmatic style affected by this poetry, the wood itself is made to speak, to relate its origin in a forest and its voyage on a ship, and to marvel that man has been able to give it a tongue. This wood is employed by the lover to ask the maiden to join him in his place of exile where he has become powerful and prosperous and will surely make her happy.

> Soon as ever thou shalt listen on the edges of the cliff
> To the cuckoo in the copse-wood chanting of his sorrow,
> Then begin to seek the sea, where the sea-mew is at home.[1]

More obscure, but richer in feeling, is the elegy which might be called *The Wife's* or *Maiden's Complaint*, were it certainly the utterance of a slandered woman who laments that she is banished from the neighbourhood of her love. Equally well, however, it may be the complaint of a young thegn kept from joining his dear and exiled lord. The singer's suffering is caused by her faithfulness. She has been condemned to dwell in a cave 'in a grove amid this wood,' and thence, 'in the early dawning' she comes alone to spend a whole summer day mourning her griefs beneath the shelter of an oak. She dreams of her beloved, who also is consumed by sorrow and who is often compelled to assume an air of gladness. She imagines him sitting 'under the o'erhanging cliff, overfrosted by the storm,' where he endures

> Anguish mickle of the mind, far too oft remembers him
> Of a happier home![1]

The elegy *The Wanderer*, of fuller scope, is certainly a song of friendship. A young thegn has been obliged, after the death of his beloved lord, to seek another protector beyond the seas. His dreams on the path which leads to exile are sad.

> And it seemeth to him in spirit, that he seeth his man-lord,
> Clippeth him and kisseth him, on his knee he layeth
> Hands and head alike, as when he from hour to hour,
> Erewhile, in the older days, did enjoy the gift-stool.

---

[1] Stopford Brooke's translation.

> Then the friendless man forthwith doth awaken,
> And he sees before him only fallow waves,
> And sea-birds a-bathing, broadening out their plumes;
> Falling sleet and snow sifted through with hail—
> Then the wounds of heart all the heavier are.[1]

As, however, he considers that vicissitudes of fortune over-take even chiefs and that misery is common to all men, he understands that his grief is but a part of the universal order of change:

> Doom of weirds is changing all the world below the skies.[1]

He is like the old warrior who fights over again the battles of his younger days and cries out with Ossian:

> Whither went the horse, whither went the man?   Whither went the
>   Treasure-giver?
> What befel the seats of feasting?   Whither fled the joys in hall?[1]

The Seafarer, the most original of the Anglo-Saxon lyrical poems, may be taken as representative of this poetry, with its defects and qualities.   Its capital defect is its obscurity, which reaches an extreme point, and is such that the subject of the poem has been interpreted in many ways.   Is it a composition of a regulation type, in which the irresistible attraction of the sea for a seafaring man, well though he knows its evils and dangers, leads to the thought that as the sailor despises well-being on dry land, so man ought to reject earthly pleasures for the happiness which awaits him beyond death?   Or is it a poem which has been inspired from two distinct sources, a description of a seaman's rough life to which a pious Christian conclusion has been added?

Is it the monologue of a sailor who, with little order and more than one repetition, descants on his conflicting feelings for the sea, his love and hate, fear and desire?   Or is it, as some ingenious critics maintain, a dialogue between an old seaman, who recounts the misery of his life, and a youth who answers every warning with the voice of his irrepressible vocation?

Such ambiguity is enough to prove that this short poem is imperfect in form.   It is striking, none the less, by the sombre and violent picture it gives of northern seas in which suffering from cold mingles with the pains of water and wind.   The extreme redundancy at least has as nucleus a powerful and realistic impression.   Even though the ending is blurred

---

[1] Stopford Brooke's translation.

and lost among pious effusions, the opening lines are full of
energy:

> With a bitter breast-care I have been abiding:
> Many seats of sorrow in my ship have known!
> Frightful was the whirl of waves when it was my part
> Narrow watch at night to keep on my vessel's prow
> When it rushed the rocks along. By the rigid cold
> Fast my feet were pinched, fettered by the frost,
> By the chains of cold. Care was sighing then
> Hot my heart around; hunger rent to shreds within
> Courage in me, me sea-wearied! This the man knows not,
> He to whom it happens happiest on earth,
> How I, carked with care, in the ice-cold sea,
> Overwent the winter on my wander-ways,
> All forlorn of happiness, all bereft of loving kinsmen,
> Hung about with icicles; flew the hail in showers.
> Nothing heard I there save the howling of the sea,
> And the ice-chilled billow, 'whiles the crying of the swan!
> All the glee I got me was the gannet's scream,
> And the swoughing of the seal, 'stead of mirth of men;
> 'Stead of the mead-drinking, moaning of the sea-mew.[1]

Swiftly these memories are obliterated. The sailor soon
wearies of the facile pleasures of towns. Spring brings back
to his heart the passion for adventure:

> Trees rebloom with blossoms, burghs are fair again,
> Winsome are the wide plains, and the world is gay—
> All doth only challenge the impassioned heart
> Of his courage to the voyage, whosoever thus bethinks him
> O'er the ocean billows, far away to go.

And here the poet finds a strange and beautiful image to
express this lure:

> For behold, my thought hovers now above my heart;
> O'er the surging flood of sea now my spirit flies,
> O'er the homeland of the whale—hovers then afar
> O'er the folding of the earth! Now again it flies to me,
> Full of yearning, greedy! Yells that lonely flier;
> Whets upon the whale-way irresistibly my heart;
> O'er the storming of the seas.[1]

If it be impossible to follow all the truncated argument of
The Seafarer, at least, through its mists, a powerful vision of
polar seas and the fascination of their perils can be discerned.
And this is something which persists in literature. This very
passion for the sea and for adventure recurs in some great
modern English poets—Byron, Swinburne, and Kipling—

[1] Stopford Brooke's translation.

whether or not they have known the old Anglo-Saxon song.[1]

7. *The Songs of War: 'Brunanburh,' 'The Battle of Maldon.'*[2] —As might be expected, it was in their war songs that the Anglo-Saxons best retained the vestiges of their wild, primitive mood, especially in those which celebrated their own battles. This fact is independent of chronology. Nothing perhaps reflects their past better than the sort of ode which is inserted in the prose chronicles, compiled by some monk, to glorify the great victory which Athelstan, King of Wessex and Mercia, and his brother, Edward, won at Brunanburh in 937 over the Scots under Constantine and the Northmen whom Anlaf led out of Ireland. The fierce enthusiasm of victory breaks out in savage irony addressed to the slain or fleeing invaders. The swiftness, even lucidity, of the ode allows the hypothesis that it was one of those popular *cantilenas* which are known to have flourished among the Anglo-Saxons. While the narrative and elegiac poetry is often so obscure that we can hardly believe it to have been meant for the people and understood by them, we have here a song which it is easy to imagine intoned, and caught up by all the soldiers of the victorious army. The fact that it contains no original detail, that all its circumstances are general, and that it ends with the oldest of Anglo-Saxon commonplaces on slaughter, strengthens the impression that this is a work which connects with a long tradition of songs of war. The story, which in the epic fragments is continuous, is here cut up into a series of short, irregular stanzas. We can imagine it sung to the accompaniment of the harp.

The history of the battle is resumed in a sequence of short, enthusiastic stanzas, in which, in turn, the West Saxons and the Mercians are extolled, the Scots and the Northmen held up to ignominy. The poet's massive irony expends itself on Constantine who came to attack Athelstan after he had sworn fealty to him:

> To his home in the North, Constantinus.
> The hoar war-hero was unable to boast
> Of attendance of men; he was robbed of his kinsmen,
> Bereaved of his friends on the battle-field,
> Conquered in fight, and he left his son

---

[1] Douady, *La Mer et les poètes anglais*, 1912.
[2] A. Campbell (ed.), *The Battle of Brunanburh*, 1938; W. J. Sedgefield (ed.), *The Battle of Maldon, etc.*, 1904; E. V. Gordon, *The Battle of Maldon*, 1937.

> On the place of slaughter, wasted with wounds,
> The boy in the battle.   He durst not boast,
> The grey-haired warrior, of the clash of swords,
> The aged enemy . . .[1]

And the poem ends with the customary description of the
field covered with the dead:

> Behind them they let the corpses share
> The dark-feathered fowl, the raven black,
> The crooked-beaked, and the ashy-feathered,
> White-tailed eagle enjoy the prey,
> The greedy war-hawk, and the grey-clad beast,
> The wolf in the wood.[1]

Some sixty years after the ode on the victory of Brunanburh,
an unknown poet told the story of a national defeat, that of
Maldon, in which, in 993, Byrhtnoth, the old chief of the East
Saxons, met his death, as he strove to drive back a band of
Northmen whose ships were coming up the Blackwater, a little
to the north of the Thames.   We have only a fragment of 325
lines of this poem, which seems, since it does not name a single
one of the enemy, to have been written soon after the fight.
It is not a lyrical song, but a detailed epic narrative which,
by its rhythm and its general shape, recalls the battles of the
Iliad more than does any other Anglo-Saxon poem.   In spite
of the extreme simplicity and the wholly national character
of the poem, it provokes the question whether it be modelled
on the classical epics.   That poetry native to the country
should, by mere chance, have attained to such a likeness to
the classics seems incredible, and the surmise of imitation is
tenable, since all Anglo-Saxon literature had been impregnated
with Latin by the time this poem was written.   But it must
also be admitted that the copy, if such it be, is a very general
one, and is drawn from a distance.   The *Battle of Maldon* is
no paraphrase of an ancient model.   Its historical subject
is local and quite recent.   It is, in fact, the only extant fragment of a national epic of Anglo-Saxon.

The Saxons are Christians, repelling pagans, but all the noble
sentiments in the poem refer to martial valour, love of battle,
a leader's sacrifice of himself for his men, the loyalty of soldiers
to their leader.   Already the chivalrous point of honour is much
to the fore.   Out of his eagerness for battle, Byrhtnoth allows
the Northmen to pass over the Blackwater in order that the
fight may engage.   When the Saxon chief is wounded to death,

---

[1] Translation by J. M. Garnett.

he rejoices and breaks into laughter, and he dies thanking God that he has been suffered to strike great blows before his end, and that many joys have been vouchsafed to him on earth. His death is the signal for the flight of the cowards, led by the traitor Godrich, but it redoubles the ardour of the brave to avenge their fallen chief, and they die about his body. Their heroism is summed up in words spoken by the old chief, Byrhtwold, as he brandishes his ashwood lance:

> The braver shall thought be, the bolder the heart,
> The more the mood, as lessens our might.
> Here lieth our lord, all hewn to pieces,
> The good on the ground: ever may grieve
> Who now from this war-play thinketh to wend.
> I am old in years: hence will I not,
> But here beside mine own dear lord,
> So loved a man, I purpose to lie.[1]

This *Battle of Maldon* is like some embryonic *Roland*, a Song of Roland earlier than the legend. As in the French epic, there is a glorious defeat and an heroic death. It was long thought probable that about the beginning of the eleventh century, near the date of *The Battle of Maldon*, a first sketch, in the form of a lay, existed for the *Song of Roland*, and the question arises whether there was not, at this period, a close resemblance between the two poems. Probably not, for *Maldon* is a strictly historical poem, which does not magnify its subject and which neither introduces the marvellous nor leaves room for its introduction by an editor. It is not the germ of something greater than itself but the fragment of a completed whole. The sentiment of the two works is indeed almost identical. Byrhtnoth makes it a point of honour to allow the Northmen to ford the river unhindered, exactly as Roland refuses to sound his horn in order to summon Charlemagne. Both heroes, out of chivalrous pride, prepare disaster. Byrhtnoth's attachment to his king, Æthelred, and that of his brothers-in-arms to himself, their leader, are matched by the tie of duty and love which binds Roland to Charlemagne and all the Frankish warriors to Roland. The coward Godric is a pendant to the traitor Ganelon. And Byrhtnoth, like Roland, is a Christian slain by the pagans, whose last words are for God, the supreme leader of warriors, and who, because he is valiant and dies in battle, is sure of God's love.

[1] Translation by J. M. Garnett.

In spite, however, of all these points of resemblance, *Byrht-noth* is markedly distinct from *Roland*. It has the bare severity of history, while *Roland* has the prestige of legend. Heroic as they are, the exploits of *The Battle of Maldon* are not super-human. They are more solid and less poetical than those of *Roland*, not deeds of impossible prowess but the actions of men who do no more than fight to the death. Disaster in *Byrhtnoth* is not transformed by imagination, and, in spite of the proud words of the dying chief, the noble harangues of his friends, the blows they finely deal, and all the delirium of danger and death, this poem is sad, as *Roland* cannot be sad, with its hope and triumph enduring even in defeat, its un-failing confidence in the divine mission of the Franks, and its radiance of light and colour beneath so much blue sky.

Byrhtnoth has a unique place in pre-Conquest poetical literature. Its apparently strict adherence to the actual course of events was unmatched until the advent of the Anglo-Norman trouvères, in particular Wace who sang the battle of Hastings. But while this poem does not use legend to trans-figure facts, it yet dignifies them by the truly epical march of its story and the nobility of its alliterative verse, elements of greatness which are lacking in Wace's octosyllabic lines. It has a rough simplicity which is disconcerting at a time when Anglo-Saxon poetry was exaggerating its rhetorical character. This poem is like a sign of vigour, a promise of renewal, at a moment when the literature to which it belongs is overweighted with periphrases to the point of exhaustion. *Byrhtnoth* stands in such isolation that no theory can be founded on it, yet it poses the question whether native poetry was not capable, without foreign help, of a new development, an unexpected renascence.

8. *The Riddles*.[1]—It may seem strange to include among the most interesting of the poetical works of the Anglo-Saxons an extant collection of riddles, attributed by several critics to Cynewulf, although on unconvincing evidence. But that riddles are thus dignified ceases to surprise when the enigmatic turn always affected by Anglo-Saxon poetry is remembered, its way of denoting an object by qualities rather than an exact name, its cult of periphrasis, and its search for verbal subtleties, all tendencies which give a special tone to maxims

[1] A. J. Wyatt, *Old English Riddles* (Boston, 1912)—a good edition. Transla-tions into modern English by Stopford Brooke, *Early English Literature* (1892), and B. Thorpe, *Codex Exoniensis* (1842). F. Tupper, *The Riddles of the Exeter Book* (with introd.), Boston, 1910.

and which whet curiosity. That the scops used to put riddles, to test the sagacity of the guests at banquets before whom they displayed their talents, may be admitted. But the riddles which have come down to us are not original and are all Christian. Most of them are founded on the Latin riddles of the clerk Aldhelm, who had himself taken the riddles of Symposius as models, and others derive from the Latin of Tatwine, Archbishop of Canterbury. The Anglo-Saxon riddle is, however, a very free copy. It became poetical when, so to speak, it ceased to be utilitarian. From a mere ingenious definition, intended only to arouse attention and sharpen the wits, it grew into a description, often copious, and not only personified its subject, but also animated it and gave it life. The narrow frame of the Latin riddle had been broken. Thus did Phaedrus and, above all, La Fontaine, deal with the dry Aesopic fable. The Anglo-Saxon riddles are usually true poems, of varying and sometimes considerable length. They violate all the laws of the riddle at once, lack its curt precision and are too often diffuse and vague. As riddles, they must be allowed to be failures, but they make up for technical defects when the poet, led away by his subject, forgets to appeal to the intellect and speaks to the imagination. Anglo-Saxon prolixity, which wearies when it confuses and deforms the severe lines of the Bible, is easily excused when the translation of a riddle is in question.

The Anglo-Saxon riddles constitute a sort of encyclopaedia, in which figure the animals, especially the domestic animals, the celestial bodies and phenomena, contemporary products of art and useful objects, arms, tools, musical instruments, and articles of clothing. Several of them add to our picture of the customary life and implements of the Anglo-Saxons. If some are so obscure that they cannot be certainly solved, and some so marvellously gross that their presence in a pious compilation like the *Codex Exoniensis* is astonishing, others belong of right to literature, for instance the riddle on a shield:

> I am a recluse, with iron wounded,
> With falchion scarr'd, sated with works of war,
> Of edges weary; oft I battle see,
> Perilous fight; for comfort hope not,
> Or that safety to me shall come from martial strife,
> Ere I with generations shall all have perished;
> But they me shall strike with sword:
> The hard of edge, intensely sharp, hand-work of smiths,
> Shall bite among people: I must await

The hostile meeting: never the healing tribe,
In the battle-place, might I find,
Who with plants my wounds would heal,
But to me the edges' sores become increas'd,
Through deadly stroke, by day and night.[1]

The riddle on a bull's horn, which can be both a trumpet and a cup, is rich and brilliant. There is first an armed warrior who is the bull, then a maiden 'with rings adorned' who 'fills my bosom,' says the horn, and then warriors

On horseback bear me; then with wind I must,
Resplendent, swell from someone's bosom.

When the riddle describes the elemental forces of nature it becomes really lyrical. The riddle on the Wind or the Storm (Riddle IV) is one of the most original and most modern of short Anglo-Saxon poems. It has been compared, without hyperbole, to Shelley's *Ode to the West Wind*, or rather to his *Cloud*, for in it the storm in exaltation chants its deeds and the changes it works. The storm is first represented as held, by the will of the Creator, chained and captive beneath the earth, powerless within its dungeon. Set free, it stirs up the waters of the sea:

Foamy strives wave against wall,
Dusk rises mountain o'er deep;
Dark on its track, in ocean,
Another goes so that they meet,
The land's limit near, the high shores.
There the wood [2] is loud, the ocean-guests' noise;
Still remain the rocky cliffs
From the watery strife, the crew's outcry.
When the towering mass on the cliffs presses,
There shall be hope for the vessel, in the fierce contest,
If it the sea shall bear, at that terrific time,
Of guests full, so that it shall forthwith
Be borne away, though vitally assail'd,
Yet foamy ride on the waves' backs.
There shall be some terror to men display'd.[3]

The clatter of the tempest on land, as it pursues its destructive path over cities and the dwellings of men, is painted on as grand a scale, although the drawing is more confused and obscure.

Here the subject—the terror of the hurricane—and the necessary repetition of identical violent effects, combine to veil the habitual weaknesses of Anglo-Saxon poetry. Its

[1] B. Thorpe's translation of Riddle VI.
[2] i.e. the ship.   [3] B. Thorpe's translation.

qualities are thrown into relief, its defects momentarily hidden. The poem is powerful and arresting.

9. *Christian Poetry : the Cædmonian Poems and ' Judith.'* [1] —In all the poems hitherto examined there is some revelation of Christianity, or at least a certain attenuation of pagan characteristics, but they are not decidedly religious poems either in subject or in immediate intention. We have still to deal with the Christian poetry, properly so called, which is by far the larger, if the less original and, with few exceptions, the less formally beautiful part of this poetry. Whether because a greater volume of it was written, or because it was naturally more carefully preserved by the clerks, it fills almost all the extant collections of Anglo-Saxon verse.

This poetry is proof of the fervour with which, immediately upon their conversion, these Germanic pirates embraced the religion of Christ. At the end of the seventh and throughout the eighth century they made the great island they had conquered in an age of darkness into the most ardent and most radiant home of Christianity. Alliterative verse came to the aid of clerkly Latin to express their faith, spread it among the laity and made it really popular.

The origin of this Christian poetry in the vulgar tongue must be sought in the pages of Bede. He relates that in the monastery of Streoneshalh, now Whitby, in Northumbria, there was a brother whom God had honoured with His gifts and who excelled in glorifying piety and virtue in song. 'Everything the clerks taught him out of Holy Writ, he soon afterwards reproduced in the English language, in poetic words and most melodiously.' This man had reached old age without taking orders or learning any skill in poetry. 'Wherefore being sometimes at feasts, when all agreed for glee's sake to sing in turn, he no sooner saw the harp come towards him than he rose from the board and turned homewards. Once, when he had done thus, and gone from the feast to the stable where he had that night charge of the cattle, there appeared to him in his sleep One who said, greeting him by name, "Sing, Cædmon, some songs to Me." "I cannot sing," he answered, 'for this cause left I the feast and came hither." He who talked to him answered, "However that be, you shall

[1] G. P. Krapp, *The Junius Manuscript*, 1931; I. Gollancz, *The Cædmon MS. of Anglo-Saxon Biblical Poetry* (Oxford, 1927); F. A. Blackburn, *Exodus and Daniel* (Boston, 1907); C. W. Kennedy, *The Cædmon Poems* (translation, 1915), *Early English Christian Poetry*, translated into alliterative verse, 1952.

sing to Me." "What shall I sing?" rejoined Cædmon. "The beginning of created things,' replied He." [1] Then Cædmon sang verses he had never heard to the glory of the Creator:

> Now must we praise the Guardian of heaven's kingdom,
> The Creator's might, and his mind's thought;
> Glorious Father of men! as of every wonder He,
> Lord eternal, formed the beginning.
> He first framed for the children of earth
> The heaven as a roof; holy Creator!
> Then mid-earth, the Guardian of mankind,
> The eternal Lord, afterwards produced;
> The earth for men, Lord Almighty. [2]

Cædmon awoke, remembered the words of the song he had composed in sleep, and added to it many others, all to the glory of God. Then he went to the reeve of his village and told him of the gift he had received from Heaven, and the reeve took him before the abbess, who assembled all the clerks and bade Cædmon sing to them. All were agreed 'that a heavenly grace had been conferred on him by the Lord. They translated for Cædmon a passage in Holy Writ, bidding him, if he could, put the same into verse. The next morning he gave it them, composed in excellent verse, whereon the abbess, understanding the divine grace in the man, bade him quit the secular habit and take on him the monastic life. . . . He kept in mind everything that was taught to him, and as beasts of the field ruminate, so he turned it into melodious song, so sweet to the ear that his teachers became his hearers. He sang of the creation of the world, of the origin of man, and of all the history of Israel, of their departure from Egypt and entering into the Promised Land, and other passages of Holy Scripture, the Incarnation, Passion and Resurrection of Christ, and His ascension to Heaven, the coming of the Holy Ghost, and the teaching of the Apostles. He sang also of the terror of future judgment, the horrors of hell-pangs and the joys of heaven.'

There is nothing in the Christian poems to approach the charm of Bede's artless story, as appears if his short, very representative quotation of verse be compared to his Latin prose, with its wealth of precise circumstance which gives everything a character. In the verse there are no facts. Their place is taken by ejaculations, repetitions, and periphrases. Scholarship no longer admits the extant poems, written on the subjects Bede enumerates, to be the direct work of Cædmon,

---

[1] J. R. Green's translation.   [2] B. Thorpe's translation.

the old singer. They are paraphrases from other sources, at most later and altered versions of Cædmon's original. But their character has been little changed. The poems of the so-called Junius manuscript, which are not by Cædmon but are called Cædmonian in memory of him, are essentially biblical paraphrases. Some are on passages in the books of Genesis, Exodus, and Daniel, and other fragments, not biblical in the strict sense, have for subject the fall of the rebel angels, Christ's descent into hell, and His temptation by Satan. To these it is natural to add the fragment of a poem on Judith, although it is of later date and, strangely enough, not included in the Junius manuscript, but in the same manuscript as *Beowulf*.

What has been said of the origins of this biblical poetry makes the intention of the Anglo-Saxon poets sufficiently clear. They would not and could not invent. Their aim was to popularize Holy Writ. If sometimes they added to the Bible, their additions were based on pious commentaries or earlier Christian poems which they regarded as equally authentic, for instance on the poem in which Avitus of Vienne relates the fall of the angels.

What, then, is the original element which can be proved to exist in their poems? It is first and especially an originality of form. They recast the Bible in the mould of their national poetry, transposing it into alliterative verse, and giving it that half-epical, half-lyrical turn which characterizes all their poetry, and which made their rendering of several passages of the Hebrew poem a happy one.

Secondly, they transcribed not only with all the fervour of recent converts, but also with all the artlessness of an ignorant people, who imagined the Jews like themselves, who saw God in heaven with His angels like their own king surrounded by his thegns, who could not escape from themselves, their own customs and their own climate, and who instinctively put their own feelings into Jewish history, and pictured a Judaea washed by the sullen and icy waters of the North Sea.

This transposition is especially noticeable in the sea pictures, which testify to the nautical experience of the vikings, and in the battle stories, which rekindled the ardour of the scops, so that they drew on their pagan tradition for conventional details —the clash of spears, the helmeted warriors, the war-cries, the black crows cawing over carrion.

The misunderstanding has curious and picturesque effects,

and the too complete assimilation of the Bible makes for life and vehemence, but there is monotony in these poets' imagination, which unfailingly reduces the whole of the world's contents to two or three sentiments and two or three unvarying descriptions.

If, for a moment, these Anglo-Saxon poems are not read indulgently, if we cease to make allowances for them, almost as we do for the sketches of children and savage peoples, but, like some critics, overpraise them, the heavy pompousness of the paraphrases at once becomes evident, in contrast to the sober and sublime vigour of the Bible; and Ten Brink is seen to be guilty of flattery when he says that 'the originality of the Anglo-Saxon poet of *Genesis* is revealed only in detail and execution. The simple, terse expression of the Scriptural narrative is exchanged for a broad, often impassioned, epic style.' Very often, the Anglo-Saxon has overlaid beauties not apparent to him with the weight of his words:

The Bible	*The Paraphrase*
And the earth was without form and void; and darkness was upon the face of the deep. And the Spirit of God moved upon the face of the waters. And God said, Let there be light: and there was light.	The earth as yet was not green with grass; Ocean cover'd, swart in eternal night, Far and wide, the dusky ways.
	Then was the glory-bright Spirit of heaven's guardian
	Borne over the deep, with utmost speed:
	The Creator of angels bade, the Lord of life,
	Light to come forth over the spacious deep.
	Forthwith was fulfilled the High King's command;
	For him was holy light spread over the waste,
	As the Worker had ordered.[1]

Indisputably, the Anglo-Saxon diverges from his model; he is himself. But the sum of his originality is his promiscuous piling-up of words, which hides, rather than reveals, the great outline of the primitive chaos. Above all, it drags out the act of creation, which showed the might of God by its very swiftness. The God of the Anglo-Saxon fumbles awkwardly before He lights up the world. There could be no better lesson on the difference between grandiose verbosity and the true sublime.

[1] B. Thorpe's translation.

The effect is not accidental. It recurs in almost every passage of this paraphrase, which partial critics quote with approval. *Exodus* has the same defect, that of detailed description which aims at grandeur and misses sublimity. The Bible says:

'And Moses stretched out his hand over the sea; and the Lord caused the sea to go back by a strong east wind all that night, and made the sea dry land, and the waters were divided.'

Mr. Stopford Brooke praises what he calls the 'vivid realistic way' of the Anglo-Saxon poet in the paraphrase, but it is a very childish realism, which consists in making Moses describe the phenomenon to his people as he accomplishes it.

> Lo! ye now with your eyes behold,
> Most beloved of people, a stupendous wonder;
> How I myself have struck, and this right hand,
> With a green sign, the ocean's deep:
> The wave ascends; rapidly worketh
> The water a wall-fastness, the ways are dry,
> Rugged army-roads; the sea hath left
> Its old stations; where I before have never heard,
> Over mid-earth, men to journey,
> Are variegated fields, which until this time,
> Through eternity, the waves have covered.[1]

Thus the great wizard, whose silent gesture had worked the miracle, is changed into an artless gossip whom the miracle seems to amaze as much as it does his people.

Although the later poet who paraphrased *Judith*,[2] and who deserves gratitude for his choice of this admirable book of the Apocrypha, is more vigorous, a comparison of his Anglo-Saxon text with the original shows that he also has not recognized true sublimity, and stumbles beneath the enormous weight of his poetic ornament and conventions. It should perhaps also be said that to the confused intelligence of the Anglo-Saxon poet, that quality of keen, steely decision which constitutes the character of the heroine was inconceivable. The biblical Judith never says a word which does not lead straight to action; the Saxon Judith wraps her thought in periphrases, so that the feeling of action is lost. She repeats herself interminably. Her gestures, like her thoughts, reach us through a fog of words. Compare her words in the two texts—for instance, when she beseeches the Lord for help before she strikes Holofernes, or when, returning to Bethulia

[1] B. Thorpe's translation. [2] A. S. Cook, *Judith* (with English translation, Boston, 1904), ed. by B. S. Timmer, 1952.

with the Assyrian general's head, she summons the Jews to battle: always a showy, awkward verbosity is substituted for the cutting precision of lucid words. The woman of action has been changed into a sort of prophetess, drunk with excitement, exalted, vague, and frenzied.

There remains that part of the Anglo-Saxon biblical epic which treats of the fall of the angels,[1] and the machinations of the prince of the fallen angels to avenge himself on God, who has cast him into hell, by causing Adam and Eve to commit the first sin. It is the very subject of Milton's *Paradise Lost*, and this identity of theme, together with certain likenesses of emphasis and language, have given rise to a surmise that Milton, who was Junius's friend, was inspired by the old poem. The presumed imitation has even shed a sort of reflected glory on the Anglo-Saxon work. The paraphrase is here not of the Bible, but of a Latin poem by Avitus, and there is a freedom of imagination not found in the other Cædmonian poems, and an attempt at a psychological explanation of the first sin. The versification, the style, and even the vocabulary also, have special characteristics which make it resemble the continental Saxon poem, *Heliand*, or *The Saviour*, and critics incline to think that it is a translation or imitation of a lost poem of similar origin.

However this may be, *The Fall of the Angels* is interesting by its study of motives—those of Satan, jealous and ambitious but courageous and great; of Eve, seduced but not perverse; of Adam who yields to Eve because he knows her for lost and would share her fall. The lines spoken by Satan have outstanding energy. The conception of some of his monologues is worthy of Milton, as when he dreams of emancipating himself from the divine supremacy, or when, in the depths of hell, he plots his vengeance. Unfortunately, it was in the form of the poem that the author, since he had not invented the subject, had most scope, and his style is extraordinarily redundant and wordy. Without many cuts the poem can hardly bear translation. If Milton knew it, he may have owed to it some vigorous strokes of his brush, but he cleared away its terrible prolixities and repetitions, and reclothed their sentiment in the majesty of his close, strong language. Milton might be a Cædmon whom the lessons of classical antiquity and a better understanding of the Bible had taught to compose, to select, and to direct.

---

[1] F. Holthausen, *Die ältere Genesis*; F. Klaeber, *The Later Genesis* (Heidelberg, 1913–14); B. J. Timmer (ed.), *The Later Genesis* (Oxford, 1948).

10. *Cynewulf : 'Christ' and the Lives of the Saints*.[1]—While the critics, robbing Cædmon like another Homer, have bereft him of the biblical poems, they have brought out of the void a poet whose very name was previously unknown. It was noticed that two poems in the *Codex Exoniensis*, the *Christ* and the *Life of Saint Juliana*, and two in the Vercelli manuscript, *Saint Helen* and *The Fates of the Apostles*, included runic characters which, when deciphered, gave the same name, Cynewulf. The conclusion was that this must be the name of the author, especially as the passages containing the runes had a personal and almost autobiographical character which distinguished them from others. Starting from this discovery, the critics were for a time so daring as to claim for this poet the authorship of most of the other verses included in the same two manuscripts. On the basis of a dubious solution of the first riddle, all the riddles were attributed to Cynewulf. Doubtful resemblances of form and subject were a pretext for assigning to him other lives of the saints, those of Saint Andreas and Saint Guthlac, and other pious poems, *The Phoenix* and *The Dream of the Rood*. Almost, he was erected into the single author of all the Christian Anglo-Saxon poetry extant. Finally, a search was made in history for this Cynewulf, and after much conjecture he was identified, not certainly but probably, with a Cynewulf who was Bishop of Lindisfarne and lived in the middle of the eighth century. Every trace of a personal confession contained in these poems was then collected, and a portrait and biography of Cynewulf was constructed. He was a wandering singer or poet who lived a gay and secular life. The accuracy of some of his battle-scenes and seascapes showed that he had fought on land and sailed the seas. Finally, after a dream in which he had a vision of the Holy Rood, he changed his life, became a religious poet, sang of Christ, the apostles, and the saints.

The structure is ingenious but it is frail, and it was no sooner conceived than gaps were made in it, so that to take up a stand on it is to risk perpetual falls into the unknown. The fact is that nothing is known to show either which works are properly ascribed to Cynewulf, or the century in which he

[1] A. S. Cook, *The Christ of Cynewulf* (Boston, 1900), *The Old English Elene,* . . . (New Haven, 1919); I. Gollancz, *Cynewulf's Christ* (with translation, 1892); Krapp and Dobbie, *The Exeter Book*, 1936; G. H. Krapp, *The Vercelli Book,* 1932; B. Dickins and A. Ross, *The Dream of the Rood*, 1934. Translations by C. W. Kennedy, *The Poems of Cynewulf*, 1910, L. H. Holt, *Elene* (Yale Studies in English, 1904), and R. K. Root, *Andreas* (ibid., 1899).

lived or his place of birth.   While he seems to have been born
in Northumbria, his verses, like all those of his fellow-countrymen, have reached us in the dialect of the West Saxons.

It can hardly be disputed that Cynewulf's reputation with
critics has gained by the pleasure of discovery.   It is not
uncommon in these days to hear him compared to William
Cowper or even Dante.   His *Christ*, which seemed to its first
editor a tissue of obscurely tangled threads, is to-day translated, annotated, and published like a classic.   The severity
with which Cynewulf's work must be estimated is made
indispensable by the extravagance of the praise given to it.

Of the probable writings of Cynewulf—that is, of those
which contain his runic signature—the *Christ* alone is original,
at least in part.   Its seventeen hundred lines have been
disentangled by scholarship to show a composition in three
parts, a sort of triptych which celebrates the Advent of
Christ, that is, his birth, his going-away or Ascension, and his
second coming at the Last Judgment.   Even after patient
study has marked this distribution of the poem into parts,
it is difficult to read it without losing the thread on every
page, so profound is the obscurity of the thought and so
hesitating the march of the narrative.   The obscurity is a little
due to the loss of the beginning of the poem, but much more to
the radical weakness of a befogged intelligence, led away by
words rather than guided by ideas.   Cynewulf's verses are
vague effusions, based on anthems, homilies, and hymns, and
they suffer by a comparison with their frequently sublime
originals, even more than do the Cædmonian paraphrases
when these are put side by side with the words of the Bible.

This is proved if the third *passus* of the *Christ*, the fullest
and most imposing of the three, be examined.   Its basis is
the admirable hymn, *De Die Judicii*, formerly ascribed to
Saint Gregory, which is itself no more than a metrical version
of one of the most beautiful chapters of the Gospels, the
twenty-fifth of Saint Matthew.   Out of its twenty-three
distichs Cynewulf makes eight hundred lines, and the sole
effect of his vast additions is to draw a thick veil over the
sober grandeur of the images, to obliterate the sublime unity
of thought and sentiment, and to surround with darkness the
central idea so brilliantly clear in Christ's dialogue with the
righteous and wicked: 'Inasmuch as ye have done it unto one
of the least of these my brethren, ye have done it unto me.'

It is hardly credible that although Cynewulf has kept this

thought, he does not seem to have perceived its grandeur, to such a point has he smothered it with trite and commonplace developments. It is possible to read the third *passus* without noticing it.

Even those of Cynewulf's images which have been most praised by his commentators are often no more than weak embroideries on the severe and strong outline of his original. It takes him ten lines to render the first distich, 'Suddenly the great day of the Lord will come, Like a thief in the dark night falling upon unwitting sleepers,' and he adds to it only words, not a single exact circumstance. Or else, with thick, prosaic commentary, he drags out a phrase which impresses by its brevity. 'The glorious King will sit upon His heavenly throne, Surrounded by the trembling (*tremebunda*) ranks of His angels,' is rendered by Cynewulf as follows:

> Heaven's angels' King holy shall shine,
> Glorious o'er the hosts, the powerful God;
> And around him chiefs most excellent,
> Holy martial bands shall brightly shine,
> A train of blessed angels: they inwardly
> Tremble with fear, for terror of the Father.
> Therefore 'tis not any wonder, how of worldly men
> The impure race, sadly sorrowing,
> Shall sorely dread, when the holy race,
> White and heaven-bright, the archangel-host,
> Before that countenance is with dread affrighted.[1]

Even where he depicts the catastrophe of the Last Day, winning high praise from the critics for poetic power, and giving himself free rein, it is hard to discern anything in his work but unending, wearisome repetition of the words which express the idea of ruin and conflagration.

It is not suggested that Cynewulf is insincere, but it is maintained that all the many sighs and incoherent complaints of his gloomy spirit are not worthy to be compared with the high exaltation of a clear-eyed Christian. Exuberance of language and prolix facility of versification: these are the sum of Cynewulf's qualities. He has written some of the most fluent and melodious verses in Anglo-Saxon poetry, but he has done it by the sacrifice of all precision, and the accomplishment is not worth its price.

The runic signature of the same Cynewulf occurs in a *Saint Juliana* and a *Saint Helen*, poems which are pleasantly differen-

[1] B. Thorpe's translation.

tiated from the *Christ* by their continuous story and the respite they afford from vague effusiveness.   Two other lives of saints, Saint Andreas and Saint Guthlac, once also attributed to Cyne-wulf by some critics, are now denied to him.   The absolute decision of this question of authorship, when the author con-cerned is so hypothetical a person, has little importance.   It is more interesting to establish the distinguishing character-istics of hagiography in Anglo-Saxon verse.

Saint Juliana, Saint Helen, and Saint Andreas are exotic saints, whose legends, doubtless transcribed from Greek into Latin, have been, on the whole, faithfully followed by the Anglo-Saxon poets.   All of them have an oriental element of the marvellous, evidently seductive to the Anglo-Saxon imagination, a taste which was to affect profane literature also, and to make the English the first translators of the com-plicated romance of *Apollonius of Tyre*, whence Shakespeare drew the incidents of his *Pericles*.   Since invention had hardly any part in the writing of these lives of saints, their principal value, beyond the few modifications of the stories, is to show what were the themes which appealed to the imagination of their authors.

The life of Saint Juliana, a Christian maiden of Nicomedia, victorious over the demon Belial, who tries vainly to tempt her, and a martyr to her faith, is distinguished by the clearness and swiftness of the story.   But the pace involves dryness and an absence of poetry and emotion.

The life of Saint Elene or Saint Helen is told more expan-sively.   The story is that of the Invention of the True Cross by the mother of the Emperor Constantine after his victory over the Huns [*sic*].   Constantine's warlike expedition, the battle, and Helen's voyage over the sea to Judaea give scope for the traditional descriptive effects, so that the native verse is in its element and easily falls into the epic mood.

Saint Andreas is the most crowded and the most Byzantine of these legends.   Long analysis would be necessary to exhaust the list of the saint's miracles on his way to deliver the apostle, Saint Matthew, held captive by the cannibal Myrmidons.   He crosses a raging sea, Christ being, without his knowledge, the pilot of his boat; an invisible form, he enters the dungeon in which Saint Matthew lies; the cannibals are infuriated when their prisoner is set free; Saint Andreas is tortured but remains invulnerable; he avenges himself by the flood which he lets loose upon the town by an order to one of the columns of his prison to scatter torrents of water; his wrath is appeased by the prayers of the terrified people; he commands the mountain to be riven, and the waters, into which the people had been plunged up to their arm-pits, are cast into its breach; the astounded Myrmidons undergo mass conversion.

These are only some of the incidents which swarm in the seventeen hundred lines of the poem. The exuberant wealth of happenings saves *Saint Andreas* from the diffuse wordiness of most Anglo-Saxon Christian poems. It is less diluted than most of them. The unknown author is nevertheless to be suspected of a rhetoric not so innocent as that of his predecessors. As Stopford Brooke has well said, he is a 'sensationalist.' So, truth to tell, is Cynewulf, when in *Saint Helen* he piles up in cold blood the periphrases he loves too well. 'I was stained with crimes,' he says when he is confessing his sins, 'till the Lord my . . . bone-house unbound, breastlock unwound, song-craft unlocked.'

They are strange, these poems. The web of the Byzantine romances is studded with heavy Anglo-Saxon jewellery.

Besides the lives of these exotic saints, there is one of a native saint, Saint Guthlac. It is, unfortunately, the most imperfect of the four, made of two badly joined parts of which the first is confused and mediocre. Yet this poem deserves a brief attention, for it confirms and completes certain observations suggested by the Christian paraphrases.

It is founded on a story told in Latin prose by Felix, a monk of Crowland in Mercia. Saint Guthlac's life, as related by Felix, is worthy of a place beside the life of another saint which is told by Bede, that of Saint Cuthbert. It is rich in legends which are of the soil of Great Britain, redolent of artless popular beliefs. To read it is to feel oneself at the very source of the religious feeling of the past. Guthlac, the son of a Mercian noble and born near the end of the seventh century, has become a hermit, and has built himself a hut in a lonely island in the midst of wide marshlands north of the Granta. There he is tormented by hideous demons, 'who speak the British tongue'—perhaps none others than the first owners of the land the Mercians had engrossed. He makes every kind of humble divination, showing his simple shrewdness, and accomplishes numerous unambitious cures which pass for miracles. But what especially endears him is a fondness for animals worthy of Saint Francis of Assisi. The birds tamed by his kindness are all about him. He loves the beasts, knows their ways, talks to them, is really saddened if they are guilty of an unjust or malicious action.

His life in prose is full of true charm and fragrance. Together with the stories by Bede which have been mentioned, it gives an idea of the rich material which the ingenuous faith of this country and these ages offered to religious poetry. But the metrical life of Saint Guthlac makes a painful impression of emptiness. All that was concrete and picturesque in the Latin prose has given place, in these verses, to an exalted treatment of the subject which makes it unintelligible to a reader without other knowledge of it. The story has no thread; there are no outlines; everything is confused. The struggle with the demons has become an abstract argument. Even the second part of the poem, which deals with the death of the saint and has moments of beauty, cannot still the regret for the exactness of the prose original. Here again is evidence of the sins of this oppressive rhetoric, which so rarely allows the Anglo-Saxon poets to express themselves simply.

II. *Other Christian Poems: 'The Dream of the Rood,' the 'Bestiary,' 'The Phoenix.' Didactic Poems.*—The Christian poetry of the Anglo-Saxons is not all comprised in the biblical paraphrases and the lives of the saints. It also includes some noteworthy poems of a different kind.

It has been seen that Cynewulf was led by his devotion to the Cross to choose the legend of Saint Helen as a subject, and it is tempting to see in him the author of *The Dream of the Rood*, since such a dream is said to have determined his conversion. To personify the Holy Cross was a natural tendency of faith, more than once manifest in the Latin verses of the clerks. Thus in Saint Fortunatus's admirable and impassioned hymn, *Vexilla Regis prodeunt*, the poet's love is moved by the wood of the Cross which the cruel lance has stricken and which flows with blood and water. 'Beautiful and shining tree . . . chosen the holy limbs to touch, blessed Cross from whose arms hung the Ransom of the World. . . . Hail, Cross, sole hope! . . .'

The same sentiment and the same image have inspired the Anglo-Saxon poet. Incapable of the concentrated and poignant forcefulness of Saint Fortunatus, he has at least an ingenious dream of his own, not so diffuse as to be without outline. In it he sees the miraculous tree, by turns shining with jewels and bathed in blood. It speaks to him and relates to him its life from the day when it was struck down on the verge of the forest, to that on which 'the young Hero, brave and strong,' was lifted on to it, and it trembled as it received the kiss of God in Man. It is now honoured by men, their beacon-light and the cure for all their ills.

At an early date Christian literature gave symbolic meaning to natural phenomena, and particularly to animals which were especially fabulous. It followed, in so doing, both the parables of the Bible and Greek fables. Hence the *Bestiaries* of the Middle Ages, called *Physiologi* in Latin. Anglo-Saxon is the first vernacular language in which a *Bestiary* occurs, a mere fragment embracing the Panther, the Whale, and part of a passage on the Partridge. Anglo-Saxon verse lends itself to this poetic form much as it does to the riddle. The same stretch of imagination is needed. The description of the Whale—Fastitocalon, who is as large as an island, so that confiding ships anchor on his sides and sailors land on his back, to kindle a fire and feast—is on a scale which Milton repeats. Naturally, the enormous beast chooses the very instant at which pleasure reaches its height to plunge into the sea, taking ship and sailors with him. Even so the devil plays with the souls of men, duping them with his false lures that he may the better carry them off to hell.

The Phoenix is an independent poem, but it is very like these others in character. The fourth-century poet Lactantius, taking his subject from Ovid and Claudian, had transformed the mythological phoenix, which burnt itself to be reborn of its own ashes, into a symbol of Christ and the Christian soul. His short Latin poem, *Phoenix*, is a work of eighty-five distichs, conventional in style, a mosaic of the classical poets which is spoilt by its dryness and its too enigmatic turn.

This time the Anglo-Saxon poet, who has expended the theme to seven hundred lines, has the advantage over his model. Anglo-Saxon plenty here relieves happily the effects of a Latin drought. The poet brings new moving warmth into his treatment of a subject which mythological memories and terms had frozen to lifelessness. Instead of getting further away from nature, as he diverges from his model, he sometimes seems to put the fresh life of his own impressions into an entirely artificial composition. He thus more than compensates for his inevitable inferiority in lucidity and terseness. His endearing if diffuse description of the paradise in which the Phoenix dwells is preferable to the cold brevity

of the Latin. It is true that either northern impotence or
Anglo-Saxon rhetoric has made the poet unequal to painting
a flowery and sunny place of delights, and that he is most at
ease when he is paraphrasing the list of the scourges which this
Eden is spared. But even in this too negative description
there is more charm than the poets of his country were wont
to put into their pictures. His smooth and ample verses
succeed better than those of Lactantius in suggesting the
marvellous harmony of the songs of the Phoenix. The ardent
homily with which the poem ends is a commentary on Lactantius's last line: 'Aeternam vitam mortis adepta bono'—
which has a strong precision beyond the later poet. But
the homily has an unction and a melody which finally make
this poem probably the most attractive of all those written
in alliterative verse.

This survey of the Christian poetry must include several
short didactic pieces, the *Gifts of Men*, the *Weirds of Men*, and
Ten Instructions of a Father to his Son. In these, Anglo-
Saxon poetry is sententious. The *Dialogues between Solomon
and Saturn*, in which the fantastic varies the didactic, are more
curious. They are imitations of a lost Latin original, itself
taken from a vanished Greek source, and are the prototypes
of the dialogues between Solomon and Marcolf which were
so popular in the Middle Ages. Saturn, who has nothing in
common with the god of mythology, is a Chaldean prince
sprung from a family of demons. He is acquainted with all
books but not with the magic of the *Pater Noster*, which he
makes Solomon explain to him.

It is not always in such amusing fictions that Christian
morality finds expression. It loves to bring before men
lugubrious images of death and decomposition, to humiliate
the body which constantly leads the soul to stray from the
path of salvation. Hence the struggles between body and
soul which held so large a place in the imagination of this age
of faith. Anglo-Saxon poetry soon took possession of this
theme, of which the cruelty was aggravated by the habitual
heaviness of alliterative verse. Thus it is with the *Discourse
of the Soul to its Body*. The soul inveighs against the body,
already corrupt and the prey of the voracious worm with jaws
sharper than the needle, which once tempted it to the sins for
which it now suffers the pains of hell. The soul, in revenge,
describes with savage joy the decomposition of the fatal body.

The grave is similarly evoked at the end of a volume of

homilies, but this time it is Death who speaks and with sombre realism calls up the picture of man's last abode.

It is true that these images cannot be taken as peculiar to the Anglo-Saxon imagination. They are essentially Christian and also, it may be said, representative of the gloomiest of the Christian centuries. It is, however, impossible not to notice how aptly the rude verse and violent rhetoric of the Anglo-Saxons render their dismay and emphasize their horror.

12. *Anglo-Saxon Prose. Alfred, Ælfric, Wulfstan.*[1]—The breach between Anglo-Saxon and English poetry is everywhere apparent, and to pass from Cynewulf to Chaucer is to bridge a deep gulf. The poetry of the Anglo-Saxons is deliberately archaic. In order to produce a desired emotional state in its hearers, it reverts to traditional turns of expression, to words almost consecrated, as religion works its effects by the constantly recurring use of an ancient liturgy. This poetry is modelled on an earlier age of which the remoteness cannot now be determined. It retains many periphrases and locutions already obsolete, imitates and systematizes the disorder of primitive lyrical construction. The poetic form tends towards the past.

On the other hand, the tendency of the prose is towards observance of the rules of ordinary speech, unless it copies the Latin prose of the clerks. Its object is to instruct and inform, not to move, and since it thus educates the understanding, it necessarily turns to the future. There is therefore nothing surprising in the fact that the prose writings of the Anglo-Saxons, which are much less curious than their poetry, are also much nearer ourselves. No revolution seems to separate Alfred's pages from those of Caxton, Ælfric's from Wyclif's. There is a change but no break. National and linguistic continuity is felt to exist; there almost seems to be a continuity in the thought as it is framed in much the same mould as now. While an Englishman has to make a quite considerable effort in order to read the verse of the Anglo-Saxons, he finds it comparatively easy to understand their prose.

If such facility be not marked in the oldest prose literature, this is because it is either of earlier compilation than any of the poetry extant—like the laws of Ina, king of the West Saxons, which were promulgated at the end of the seventh century, although our transcription dates only from the time of

---

[1] *Bibliothek der angelsächsichen Prosa*, ed. Grein, Wülker, and Hecht (Cassel, 1872–1933). See R. W. Chambers, *On the Continuity of English Prose from Alfred to More*, 1932; G. P. Krapp, *The Rise of English Literary Prose* (Oxford, 1916); J. W. Tupper, *Tropes and Figures in Anglo-Saxon Prose* (Baltimore, 1897).

Alfred—or because some of this prose is more than half poetry and seems to be fragments of old epic tales. This character belongs to many passages of the chronicle usually attributed to the influence of King Alfred, of which we have distinct versions written by the religious of different monasteries, those of Winchester, Canterbury, Abingdon, Worcester, and Peter-borough, the last-named having continued its narrative to the middle of the twelfth century. In this chronicle several references to early times, brief but impressively vehement, are pagan in feeling and emphasis and seem to date from the pre-Christian period. Even in the references to the eighth century there are a suddenness and a roughness in the narrative which betray that mental and grammatical habits were still empirical. It is continually necessary to complete the ellipses and to relate the pronouns to their proper subjects, as with a story told by a small child. For instance, the chronicler relates, as follows, the beginning of the struggle between Cynewulf and Sebright in 755:

This year Cynewulf took from Sebright his kingdom, and the coun-cillors of the West Saxons [did as much], for unrighteous deeds, except Hamptonshire, and he [that is, Sebright] reigned there [that is, in Hamp-shire] until he slew the alderman who stayed longest with him. Then Cynewulf drove him to the forest of Andred, where he remained until a swain stabbed him at Privett, and he [that is, the swain] revenged the alderman Cumbra.

The alderman is not named until he is mentioned for the second time.

This formless prose was succeeded at the end of the ninth century by a regular prose, possessed of nearly all its essential parts. Since it is modelled on Latin texts, which are almost literally translated, it is very near English prose, as that was fixed, and also near French prose which was formed under the same masters.

Alfred, the glorious king of Wessex, was the pioneer of the prose-writers.[1] The exclusively poetic or Latin literature which had hitherto flourished had emanated principally from the north-east, the country of the Angles, or from central Mercia. About 800, the supremacy was passing to the south-west, and the king of Wessex was tending toward the sovereignty of all the Germanic groups settled in the island. But the Danish invasions supervened, and with them the

[1] The E.E.T.S. has published Alfred's translations of the *Cura Pastoralis*, ed. Sweet 1871-2, Orosius, ed. Sweet 1883, and Bede, ed. Miller 1890-8. Translation of Boethius, ed. Sedgefield (Oxford, 1899); retranslation by Sedge-field into modern English (ibid., 1900).

destruction of the centres of religion and letters. In the year 878 it seemed as though nothing would escape the invaders. It was then that the young King Alfred withdrew to Athelney in Somerset, formed there a nucleus of resistance, defeated the Danes, and won from them a treaty which left him the south of England while they remained masters of the old country of the Angles and northern Mercia.

After his victory, Alfred set himself to retrieve his country from the barbarism to which it had relapsed. A decadent and demoralized clergy had sunk into depths of ignorance. Alfred did for Wessex what Charlemagne, a hundred years earlier, had done for the country of the Franks: he endeavoured to teach the people, and to re-establish Christian discipline and culture, and to this end he brought foreign monks into his kingdom and reformed education. It was under his influence that the earlier poetic works, which had almost all been written in the Northumbrian dialect, were transcribed into the language of the West Saxons.

The part which the king himself took in this literary move-ment was considerable. His early education had been much neglected, and he had to learn before he could teach. He sur-rounded himself with scholars and learned men, learnt Latin after he was grown up, for Saxon had been the only language of his childhood, and had no sooner learnt it than he began to translate the works which seemed to him most apt to civilize his people. It was thus that he became the father of English prose-writers.

Whether in the works he inspired or in those he himself produced, an effort is apparent to regularize the old elliptical, abrupt style, with its obscurity and lack of continuity. Thus the Annals or Chronicles of Winchester, Alfred's capital town, were amplified and given smoothness until they are almost a continuous story, in which, for instance, the history of the king's war against the Danes can be read without any irritating difficulty in following the text.

Alfred himself is credited with a translation of the *Universal History* of Orosius, the compilation which made antiquity known to the Middle Ages. The task was difficult, for Orosius, a Spanish historian and theologian of the fifth century, writes an obscure, tortured Latin. Sometimes Alfred, as he himself says, translates 'word by word, sometimes meaning by mean-ing.' Although the literal translation had the most formative influence on prose, it is naturally the free version which most attracts us. Its very weaknesses are characteristic. Alfred, who does not know Latin very well and who has acquired no historical sense, aims at producing a work of pedagogy. The result is that he is often very inexact, and that, as he diverges from his author, he attains to a certain originality. While he deletes what seems to him of little use to his subjects, he also makes additions, especially in the geographical section. One of the stories he adds, that of Ohthere's sail along the shores of Scandinavia, is so simple and elementary in style that its vocabulary differs only slightly from modern English. The conclusion is that the spoken language was almost fixed.

Of Alfred's other translations, either made or ordered by him—Bede's *Ecclesiastical History of the Angles*, the *Pastoral Rule* of Gregory the Great, and the *Consolation* of Boethius [1] —it is the Boethius which is the most interesting. His choice of this book, which was again translated by Chaucer, is characteristic. Boethius has reproduced the Platonic and Stoic doctrines, coloured by Christianity and at their highest moral level—the distinction between true and false happiness, the lofty discussions on the existence of evil, on human liberty, and on divine prescience. He gives these abstractions a dramatic frame. Philosophy herself appears to him in his prison, and drives away the Muses, those prostitutes who were vainly seeking to console him. Thus he makes use of allegory, and although his style is not always pure and is often mannered, it is full of life and movement. His book could not but suffer gravely when it was translated by Alfred, who mistakes the meaning fairly frequently and is incapable of conveying the fine shades. When he renders the metrical passages, which have a classic elegance, his limitations obtrude themselves. But in nobility of sentiment he is the equal of the Latin author. He explains his reasons for undertaking this arduous task:

I have desired material for the exercise of my faculties that my talents and my power might not be forgotten and hidden away, for every good gift and every power soon groweth old and is no more heard of, if wisdom be not in them. Without wisdom no faculty can be fully brought out, for whatsoever is done unwisely can never be accounted as skill. To be brief, I may say that it has ever been my desire to live honourably while I was alive, and after my death to leave to them that should come after me my memory in good works.

This king's literary work was, like his political work, interrupted for almost a century after his death in 901. The sketchy civilization of Wessex was once more scattered to the winds, and the clerks relapsed into ignorance and inertia. They were gradually redeemed thence, during the tenth century, by a reform of the monasteries which was inspired by the similar movement accomplished in France under the influence of the Benedictines.   Religious houses were founded and organized in England, on the model of the abbeys of Cluny and Fleury, in which a strict rule enjoined intellectual work. This innovation was led by Dunstan, Archbishop of Canterbury, and his friend Æthelwold, 'the father of the monks.' Secular priests, not bound to celibacy, then abounded in the monasteries.   They retained something of the patriarchal constitution which the Church of Ireland had originally given to their communities, and therewith very disorderly morals, much laziness, and gross superstition.   The fact is proved by the so-called *Blickling Homilies*, a medley of canonical and uncanonical legends which swarm with strange arguments and allusions.[1]   It is to works of this kind that Ælfric alludes when he says: 'I have seen and heard many heresies in many an English book which unlearned men, in their simplicity, took for great wisdom.'   Stories of the saints, replete with the marvellous, and the obsession that the end of the world was at hand, take up most space in this collection.

It was at this time that the strict rule of Saint Benedict was introduced.   Morals once more became austere.   The lives of the saints did indeed remain the principal subject of study and the marvellous continued to fill a large place in them, but the stories, as compared with their predecessors, were pure and even reasonable.   Two men who with Alfred are the best writers of Anglo-Saxon prose are connected with this reform, Ælfric and Wulfstan.[2]

Ælfric was a pupil of the monastic school which Æthelwold founded at Abingdon, and he wrote in the first years of the eleventh century.   We owe to him a *Colloquium* for teaching Latin by conversation, and a vocabulary which was the first Latin-English dictionary.   But he made his name by his *Homilies*, that is, his compilations and translations from the Fathers of the Church which form two series of forty sermons each, and commemorate the various saints venerated by the Anglo-Saxon Church.

Ælfric's prose, unlike that of Alfred, is written not to be read but to be spoken to the people, in the conventional tone of a priest delivering a sermon.   It has therefore a rhythm which brings it near to verse: its sentences are divided into

[1] Ed. by R. Morris, with translation (E.E.T.S., 1874-80).
[2] Ælfric, *Selected Homilies*, ed. H. Sweet (Oxford, 1895).   Wulfstan, *Homilies*, ed. A. S. Napier (1883); *Sermo Lupi ad Anglos*, ed. D. Whitelock (1938). See C. L. White, *Ælfric: a New Study of his Life and Writings* (Boston, 1898).

sections, more or less equivalent to the metrical line, and it is frequently alliterative. For this reason scholars were long uncertain whether to classify it as verse or prose. It celebrates the saints, as the scops once sang the deeds of warriors. This poetic prose marks a great advance on that of Alfred. It aims at beauty, measure, and harmony. It is remarkably clear and finished. There is much less awkwardness and effort in the connection of phrases than in Alfred's writings. In fact, the author is consciously literate, even when he is using the vulgar tongue, and he excuses himself, with some shame, for the popular character of his translation of the Latin homilies, pleading the ignorance of his fellow-countrymen.

Wulfstan, who was Archbishop of York from 1002 to 1023, was first of all a preacher. The most remarkable of his homilies dates from 1012, the time when the English were suffering the ills of the Danish invasions. With deep feeling, the homilist deplores the irreligion and immorality of his people, to which he attributes their misfortunes, and he proclaims the near advent of the great chastiser, the Antichrist. Wulfstan is less of a finished artist than Ælfric, but the popular emphasis of his language gives its rich colour and lively tones.

After Wulfstan all was over: the Antichrist came indeed. The Danes became masters of the country, and then, after a short interval of independence, the Anglo-Saxons were brought under the Norman yoke. Such prose writings as we have prove, however, that, even without the Norman Conquest, Anglo-Saxon prose would have taken shape, modelling itself on Latin, and, with the exception of part of its vocabulary, would have become much what it was when in the fourteenth century it regained a place in literature.

It was poetry which was principally affected by the Conquest. The poetic form had outlived its time and had little life left in it. It was conventional and was getting further and further away from the real language of the people. It was fated to be abolished and superseded. The aesthetic ideal was to undergo a change, or rather a revolution. England was to learn to love verse of another kind, other cadences and new subjects. All the rich ornament which profusely decorated verse with a pomp still half barbaric was to go out of fashion. Poets were to shed their periphrases and ejaculations, and gradually to learn sobriety of style and an art almost unknown to them, that of stating facts clearly, grouping them, and inventing stories.

CHAPTER II

1. *General Character of Old French Literature.*—The literary ideal changed at the Norman Conquest of 1066. The conquerors were, it is true, of the race of the pagan Danes whose incursions had for so long afflicted Great Britain, but from the time they had become masters of the French province which has been called Normandy, they had been gallicized with a rapidity which was prodigious, and had forgotten their paganism with the country of their origin and its language and traditions. At the time of their conquest of the great island they were real Frenchmen, in language and civilization, nor had they failed to draw into their expedition many an adventurer from neighbouring French provinces.

It was therefore the French literary ideal which they imported into Great Britain, together with their laws and administration. Before their supremacy, the native language receded, was degraded so that it was kept alive only by the lower strata of the population. Anglo-Saxon literature seemed to disappear entirely, not only was silent for a century, but severed nearly all its ties with its past. The only literature other than Latin which was known to whosoever had any knowledge of letters was the literature of France. It was in its infancy at the time of the battle of Hastings, but a rapid growth made it the first of European literatures in the twelfth and thirteenth centuries, and spread its glory and influence far beyond the confines of France. One of its chief developments took place in Great Britain. Slowly, little by little, it permeated the conquered people, so that, when the English were ready once more to put their own language to literary uses, they took both matter and manner from French works, basing and forming their own productions upon them. Complete ignorance of Anglo-Saxon poetry is no barrier to understanding Chaucer, but to be ignorant of French medieval poetry is to be entirely unacquainted with Chaucer's literary origins.

There are thus two necessary prefaces to English literature, and the French is more indispensable than the Anglo-Saxon to comprehension of its final form. It is therefore important to discover which of the most general characteristics of established French literature were such as by their novelty to impress English writers, and by their beauty to persuade them to imitation.[1]

(1) The one of these characteristics which is most widely found, and which is most thrown into relief by a study of Anglo-Saxon, is undoubtedly clarity. To turn from *Beowulf*, or even *The Battle of Maldon*, to the *Chanson de Roland* is to come out of darkness into light. The impression is received from all sides at once. It is an outcome of the subject, the way of telling the story, its spirit and the mind behind it, but above all and always it results from the difference between the two languages. That the old French authors wrote clearly is generally recognized, but it has been too much the fashion to see this gift as merely consequent on the analytical tendencies and logical aptitudes of their thought, and to make it a pretext for assigning prose to them as their province, and denying them the poetic faculty. Their clarity is not, however, purely abstract. It is a veritable light, shining in the dominant vowels, illuminating the best and only noteworthy verses of the troubadours. Some examples must be cited of the success often achieved by any poet who took happy advantage of the genius of the language.

In the old romances we read that:

> Bele Erembors a la fenestre au jor
> Sor ses genolz tient paile de color.[2]

or that:

> Bele Yolanz en chambre koie
> Sor ses genoux pailes desploie
> Coût un fil d'or, l'autre de soie.[3]

In the *Chanson de Roland* there is the following description of sunlight streaming upon an army:

> Esclargiz est li vespres et li jurs;
> Contre l'soleil reluisent cil adub;

---

[1] The analysis of these characteristics is taken from E. Legouis, *Défense de la poésie française à l'usage des lecteurs anglais* (London, 1912).

[2] Fair Erembor at her window in daylight
Holds a coloured silk stuff on her knees.

[3] Fair Yoland in her quiet bower
Unfolds silk stuffs on her knees,
Sewing now a thread of gold, now one of silk.

> Osbert e helme i getent grand flambur,
> E cil escut ki bien sunt peint a flurs,
> E cil espiet, cil oret gonfanun.[1]

and this one of Durandal, Roland's sword:

> E Durandal, cum ies clere et blanche.
> Cuntre soleil si reluis et reflambes.[2]

Chrestien de Troyes has dazzling passages, and there are the following two lines from Marie de France:

> Fils d'or ne gette tel luur
> Cum si chevel cuntre li jur.[3]

There is lively, splendid colour in these lines. After the Anglo-Saxon verses it is almost blinding. Yet itself pales if it be compared with more southern poetry, where profusion of sonorous vowels makes a red and yellow vividness. For the Englishmen who knew them, the verses of such as Bernard de Ventadour had even more colour than those in the *langue d'oïl*:

> Tant ai mon cor plan de joja
> Tot me desnatura;
> Flors blanca, vermelh e bloja
> Me sembla la froidura.[4]

The peculiarity of the *langue d'oïl* was less colour than sheer light, white light or the transparency of water flowing over rock, or of a pure fountain playing on a bed of fine sand. It is a question whether any language has ever been as well endowed as French with native sounds to suggest this clarity that has neither fire nor colour. Perhaps it is the surprising dominance of the *é* over the *a* and the *o*, those more obtrusive vowels of the South. The word *cler* (clear), which expresses the sensation, is itself an admirable achievement, and its worth was so well understood by the old French poets that they made it the favourite of their vocabulary, and it gives

[1] The day has cleared up;
The arms shine in the sun;
Hauberk and helm throw forth bright flames,
And the shields finely painted with flowers,
And the spears, and the golden banners.

[2] Eh, Durandal, how clear and white thou art!
So bright dost thou blaze in the sun!

[3] No golden thread shines so bright
As her hair against daylight.

[4] So full of joy is my heart
That it changes all nature for me;
To me the very winter seems
A flower white, ruddy, and blue.

atmosphere to their poems.   The predilection was shared by
Roland's singer, in whose epic it would be interesting to count
the lines in which the word occurs, always placed so happily
that it makes a picture:

> *Clere* est la lune, les esteiles flambient. . . .
> Tresvait la noit, e apert la *clere* albe. . . .
> Contre le ciel en salt li fous tuz *clers*. . . .
> Parmi la bouche en salt forts li *clers* sancs. . . .[1]

This whiteness is everywhere in the verses of Chrestien de
Troyes, as well as in the old romances and pastorals:

> En un vergier, lez une fontenelle
> Dont clere est l'onde et blanche la gravele,
> Siet fille à roi, sa main à sa maxele;
> En sospirant son doux ami rapele.[2]

It was from the perception of this light and the effort to
reproduce it that the most beautiful verses of the English
language, as renewed in the fourteenth century, were born.
It is not only curious, but also highly significant, that the
English poets adopted the word *clere* anew, and used it hardly
less than their French predecessors and for like effects.   Thus
Chaucer, in his delicious address to the Virgin:

> Continue on us thy pitous eyen *clere*.

And he begins his most lyrical song with the line:

> Hyd, Absolon, thy gilte tresses *clere*.

He says of the bells hanging on the monk's bridle that they
'ginglen clere,' and everywhere, with this word and many
others having the same effect, he gives the impression of a
changed atmosphere, one which is more luminous and happier,
which, in a word, is French.

(2) It would certainly be wrong to attribute this omnipresent clarity to language only.   The aptitude of the writers
to seize a luminous detail is as manifest as that of the language
to express it and give it value.   Something in their taste for
well-lit pictures was the outcome of their joy in life, their
pleasure in blue sky and sunlight.   They never missed an

---

[1] Bright is the moon, the stars shine out. . . .
The night passes, and the clear dawn appears. . . .
The bright spark springs up to the sky. . . .
From the mouth springs forth the clear blood. . . .

[2] In an orchard, near a springlet
Whose water is clear and gravel white,
Is a king's daughter sitting, with her hand to her chin;
Sighing she calls her sweet love back.

opportunity to shed light upon a picture. *Roland*, which is a song of disaster, is a series of brilliant touches. Clear light falls from the heavens by day and by night. It streams over armies ready to commit slaughter. Colour bursts upon the 'banners, white, blue, and vermilion' (*gonfanons blancs et blois et vermeils*). Nothing is more luminous than Roland's portrait: with clear and laughing face (*le vis cler et riant*), ready for the fight, mounted on Veillantif and with his arms in good state, he whirls the handle of his lance which points skywards, and has streaming from its end a pure white pennon, with a golden fringe which strikes the hero's hands. There is no bright spot so small that the poet does not notice and acclaim it. He sees a warrior's 'spurs of fine gold,' another's 'golden and beflowered shield,' the gems 'flashing' upon the helmet of the emir, whose white beard is like 'blossom,' 'blossom in April,' or 'the blossom of a thorn.' He has picked up the point of light which the teeth of the Ethiopians make in their black faces:

> Ne n'unt de blanc ne mais que sul les denz.[1]

He admires the sparkle of the beaten metal of armour. Even horrors take on a sort of beauty for him. The mounted warriors wade, up to their bodies, in 'vermilion blood' (*en sanc vermeil*). When a hard blow had been dealt, 'vermilion blood gushes forth up to the arms' (*li sancs vermeilz en volat jusqu'as braz*). The 'clear' blood (*tout cler*) of the dying Oliver springs radiant (*raiet*) out of his body. Thus dazzling pictures are made of the most terrible wounds. The iron of a lance, transfixing a body, hangs it with brilliant pennons:

> El cors li met tote l'enseigne bloie.[2]

And we pass continually from this exterior luminosity to the sunshine of the heart which gives light from within. There is close association between the ideas of shadow and of evil. The devils inhabit the land of Valnaire (Black Valley), where all the stones are black and the sun never shines. A gloomy and sad countenance is an index of crime, as in the Saracen Abisme:

> Plus fel de lui n'out en sa cumpaigne. . . .
> Unkes nul hume ne l'vit juer ni rire.[3]

---

[1] No whiteness have they, save on their teeth.
[2] Thrusts the whole blue standard through his body.
[3] No feller than he was in his company. . . .
No one ever saw him play or laugh.

On the other hand, every one of the righteous has gaiety for his sign, and turns, like Charles, his face to the rising sun:

Turnet sun vis vers le soleil levant.

The games of the French are gay and played in the open air, 'beneath a pine, beside an eglantine.' They sit on 'white silk stuffs.' There is noisy, frivolous merriment among them. Ganelon says of Roland that 'for a single hare he winds his horn all day':

Pur un sul lievre vait tut le jur cornant.

Archbishop Turpin's exuberant merriment and his contempt for the monk who spends his time praying rule out every idea of a lugubrious, forbidding religion. Even the love of fighting is no gloomy appetite for slaughter. It is love of movement, noise, colour, and glory. At the end of their life of warfare the fighters have a glimpse of the paradise where they will rest 'among holy flowers' (*en saintes fleurs*), 'crowned and decked with flowers' (*couronnés et fleuris*).

It is true that these men know sorrow:

Mult ad apris ki bien conoist ahan.[1]

These French shed tears easily. They weep and they swoon as Beowulf did not. Just because they get so much joy out of life, they have cause to regret it. They complain, too, of exile from their country:

Tere de France, mult estes dulz païs.[2]

Friend mourns friend. Roland mourns Oliver with impassioned tenderness. Words fail the Beautiful Aude when she learns the death of Roland, and she can but die also. Generally, however, the men are men of action. Never, like the Anglo-Saxon heroes, do they give the impression that the mainspring of life, which is love thereof, is broken. Soon they leave their mourning and make another beginning, once more 'brush forward on their coursing steeds':

Brochent avant sur leurs destriers courants.

Such was the great revelation of early French literature to the Anglo-Saxons. It was the contribution which a race in love with light and life, believing itself God's people, made to a race languishing not indeed for lack of heroism, but for lack

[1] He has learnt much who knows grief.
[2] Land of France, thou art a most sweet country.

of clear light overhead and of faith in itself and the future. Beowulf, a victor, spoke as he left the earth words full of the Christian consciousness of the nothingness of earthly things. The conquered Byrhtnoth died proudly, but without a hope for his country.

The poets of Anglia had called sinister landscapes and lugubrious scenes into being with a strength of characterization and atmospheric truth before which the corresponding passages of the French trouvères sink to insignificance, for instance the attempts of the author of *Roland* to describe the fearful portents which announce the death of his hero. In his cold and unimpressive catalogue of horrors, he uses words too slight for the images they would convey. But when, at Hastings, a primitive fragment of verse rings out in Taillefer's song, movement, gaiety, and light enter English literature. Half the gifts and aptitudes of English poetry have then their beginning. Taine's theory that all English poetry derives from Anglo-Saxon and all English prose from Franco-Norman is therefore inaccurate. Taine sees in old French poetry only the elements which degenerate to 'gossip and platitude.' It is made up, for him, of dull stories, mere statements of fact which 'never wait for poetry and painting.' He even says of the poet of *Roland* that there is 'no splendour and no colour' in his story. It is a strange opinion for one who had read *Beowulf* immediately before *Roland*, a poem compact of gloom before one woven of clarity. Taine's estimate can only be explained by supposing that he was unconsciously under a Romantic influence which caused him to confuse poetry with sadness and murkiness, prose with clarity and lightness of heart. He reserves the word poetic too exclusively for happenings during a dark night in which nothing is heard distinctly, only the tramping of feet and cries of rage or pain. To follow him closely would be to reject all the poetry of southern countries, that of Italy and even that of Greece, as no more than measured prose in comparison with the sombre and often formless effusions of the Germanic and Scandinavian tribes.

(3) Taine is, however, right when he adds that the style of *Roland* is 'bare, without images.' This bareness is one of the most marked features of old French poetry. To turn to it from the poems of the Anglo-Saxons is to receive, among other general impressions, that of having left violence for calm. To an ear still a little deafened by the Anglo-Saxon clamour, the voice which speaks quietly or sings in a gentle undertone at

first seems weak. Some time is needed before the charm of softer, more modulated tones can be savoured. The surcharged, ejaculatory rhetoric of Anglo-Saxon poetry gives an appearance of singular poverty to a language which is really new, in which words have as yet no past and figures and periphrases have still to be born.

From the time at which it is first known, Anglo-Saxon is a traditional language with a style already inclining to decadence. It possesses the accumulated wealth of a long life. Its remoteness from the object or idea it expresses is seen in the very sumptuosity of the decoration. The literary ornaments are so many veils, which prevent contact with things rarely denoted by their simple name. The French of the eleventh century, on the other hand, starts naked as it was born, without heirlooms or the pomp of inherited rhetoric. It may be said to have created its splendour out of nothing, only by its own radiance. It is slight as a river at its source, transparent as the water which gushes from a rock, but vital as that which has space and the future before it. It takes its words straight from the vulgar tongue, uses only the same terms as everyday prose. It has no solemn or strange periphrases with which to make its effects. All it can do is exactly to choose the best of the common words, and to combine them in harmonious and varied groups. To move and captivate, it must have facts, the interest of a story, or else, for more lyrical compositions, the naked beauty of feeling and idea. It is by these signs that the infancy is recognized of a literature which may one day have great fortunes and make a tradition, but which has as yet no heritage to help or hamper it.

The same is true of the future poetic language of England. It made hay of all its former opulence. But after the long winter which ensued on the Norman Conquest, it had a season of renewal. It sprang again to life, bereft, stripped naked, prosaic, pedestrian, glued to facts, careful only for the accuracy after which it long tried vainly, yet with honest concentration on this modest aim. And when, at the advent of Chaucer, the language of English poetry had completed its initiation, the fine slightness and bareness of its framework were still distinctly perceptible beneath the poet's graceful images and his movement, his sprightliness, and his varied colours. Poetic language had begun again at the very beginning in order to make itself what it was, and what it still is.

(4) A merit of old French poetry from which the English

reaped abundant advantage has still to be noticed. The
French trouvères have, not without reason, been reproached
for monotony and long-windedness. But to turn to them
from the scops is to be struck, perhaps equally, by the almost
endless variety of their themes and their moods and by the
large number of the works in which they have resisted the
temptation to gossip, and successfully found for their conceptions an artistic frame, sometimes bare and severe, sometimes
prettily decorated, but proportionate to their matter, so that
subject and form are happily balanced.

After reading the chief Anglo-Saxon works, it is easy to
imagine the surprise with which some Englishmen gradually
learnt to know the fertile and artistic literary productions
of their conquerors. One has but to take the omnipresent,
uniform alliterative line, which magnified all subjects alike,
whether great or small, gave them all the same lyrical and
epic tone, and to place it beside these varied French verses,
ranging from the alexandrine to the monosyllabic line, beside
their endless combinations of assonances and rhymes, which
between the two extremes of the long *laisses* of the *chansons de
geste* and the short, sparkling stanzas of the songs, run through
the whole gamut of strophes, and are able, with their odd and
even rhythms, to reproduce every step and gait, to translate
the finest shades of feeling, from heroism to impertinent
frivolity.

There are, for instance, French lives of the saints, primitive
poems, of which the *Life of Saint Alexis* is the noblest that
remains. To whosoever has read some of the amorphous,
tormented hagiology sung by the Anglo-Saxons, it is a surprise to come upon the calm stanzas on one assonance of *Saint
Alexis*. From the first they give the impression that a new
world has been entered, in which grave and deep religious
feeling is so allied to the simplest and surest art that the result
can only be called perfection. Every part of the story, every
corner of the picture, is, without effort, enclosed in a stanza.
The story proceeds without hurry or jar. Emotion seems to
be evoked not by the words, but by the details, that is, the facts,
which are presented without emphasis, in an order so luminous
that it has the effect of the inevitable.

In *Roland* it is the dash which is admirable. The long *laisses*,
the chained assonances of decasyllables, succeed each other, as
do the charges of the Frankish and Saracen knights in the
interminable fight. If after each there is a pause, the next

starts with the same gait and covers another stage. The assonance constitutes the uniformity in the lines of the *laisse*, so much alike that they are a distinct and coherent group, but the association is freer than that effected by rhyme, and each line retains an undefinable but sufficient individuality. Nothing could be more alert and ongoing than these disciplined masses which 'brush forward on their coursing steeds,' moved by one impulse, lit up, here and there, by the sonorous clarity of the syllables—'Halte-clère, Joyeuse'—as by the brandished swords of galloping horsemen.

The heroic age and the great *chansons de geste*, in which the *laisses*, the chained assonances, lend themselves to grandiose expression, as in the description of the fight between Roland and Oliver (*Gérard de Vienne*), or to metrical eloquence, as in Charlemagne's apostrophe of his barons (*Aimeri de Narbonne*), was succeeded by the age of romances, which was neither free from convention nor innocent of diffuseness and platitudes, but which made its own contribution of new graces. After the decasyllabic or alexandrine line came the line of eight syllables, and the distich superseded the *laisse* or stanza. Everything speaks of smaller ambitions, a feebler inspiration. It is a decline to the petty, to a prettiness, sometimes exquisite, which attains to a perfection of its own in many passages of Chrestien de Troyes's considerable works, in the short lays of Marie de France, and in the first half of the *Roman de la Rose*. But the same verse-form lent itself well to satire, to the fable and the fabliau, and with its serried rhymes was a good medium for Renart's ironies, for the highly flavoured stories of conjugal misadventure, and for Jean de Meun's encyclopaedic satire.

Always there were, not indeed below, but round about these different works, countless songs, romances, and *pastourelles*, at first and at their most beautiful in free verse and varied rhythms, but passing, gradually, to a formal lyricism, increasingly stereotyped in metre and sentiment. Although the surviving examples of these old romances are all too few, there are enough of them to show that they had the very qualities which have been denied or too grudgingly allowed to the old French poets. A strangeness, together with the vagueness of the refrains, refutes the charge of lack of mystery, excess of dry light, and exaggerated regularity. Sometimes there is the charm of delicious, fanciful unreason (*Volez vos que je vos chante ?*), or, in a few stanzas, an emotional drama of inexhaustible melancholy (*Gaiète et Orior*). More often, in the *Reverdis*, the *jeu-partis*, the tensons, the rondels, the *ballettes*, there are rhythms light as a bird, so winged and so singing that as one reads them one hears a tune:

> Por coi me bat mes maris,
> Laisette! [1]

Every verse-form, every arrangement of rhymes, and every stanza afterwards used in English poetry is to be found here in seed or in flower. Henceforth English, like French, poetry had a variety of forms proportionate to its variety of subjects.

It should be added that the change in the verse was not merely exterior. Its inner character was from this time modified. The principal accent came to fall where it fell in French, before the caesura and on the rhyme. The culminating points became the end of the line and the end of the hemistich. The line rose towards its rhyme, instead of falling, as formerly, from the initial alliterations. The pleasure of echoing and recalling sounds gave to vowels an importance in the line at least equal to that of consonants. Words, even Germanic words, were for long severely constrained in order that they might be bent to the exigencies of a foreign rhythm not made and hardly fitted for them. Even to-day the traces of this struggle have barely disappeared. French poetry captivated the Anglo-Saxons to such a point that it changed their ear, and made them delight in accents recurring at fixed intervals and similar and echoing terminations—in syllabism, measure, and rhyme.

2. *Anglo-Norman Literature*.[2]—It was essential to recall the chief characteristics of French medieval literature, in general, without limitations of time or province, because the whole of this literature was, as long as it lasted, known and loved by the Normans, and much of it was gradually translated or imitated by the English. Three centuries after the Conquest, the aesthetic character which we have noticed in this literature reappeared, almost in its entirety and with hardly any admixture, in Chaucer's English works. It behoves us now, however, exactly to determine the special contribution of the

---

[1] Why does my husband beat me, alack the day!
[2] G. Lanson, *Histoire de le littérature française*, Parts I and II; Gaston Paris, *Littérature française au moyen âge*, *La Poésie du moyen âge* (2 series), *Poèmes et légendes du moyen âge*; J. J. Jusserand, *Histoire littéraire du peuple anglais*, Book II, Chaps. II and III; W. H. Schofield, *English Literature from the Norman Conquest to Chaucer*, Chap. III (excellent bibliography); J. Vising, *Anglo-Norman Language and Literature* (Oxford Univ. Press, 1923).

Normans to old French literature. To have confined ourselves to what they alone produced would have been manifest
error, for the works which had most influence on early English
poetry—the larger part of the chivalrous romances, the great
allegories, the *Roman de Renart*, the fabliaux, the free and the
formal lyrics — are of continental origin. Their particular
contribution, and especially that of the Anglo-Normans,
must, none the less, be distinguished and characterized, in
order to understand the minds of the conquerors, that is, of
the people whose literary tastes and needs were to make the
most direct impression on the unified nation which sprang of
their fusion with the vanquished.

The Norman element is, before the Conquest, difficult to
unravel from the mass of French literature. What is certain
is that the Normans had already severed every tie with the
language and poetry of the Scandia whence they emanated.
They may have kept the adventurous and warlike character
of their Scandinavian ancestors, but marriages, the influence
of their new surroundings, and their conversion to Christianity
had gallicized them swiftly and fundamentally. From the
eleventh century onwards, Normandy had a high repute for
clerical science and piety, solid orthodoxy, and the beauty of
her religious buildings, which are intermediate between the
Romanesque and the Gothic. Rouen was a lettered, artistic,
and religious capital city in which mystery-plays were already
being performed. The Normans did more than any other
people to propagate the cult of the Virgin, and to introduce
the feast of the Immaculate Conception which was long forbidden by the Church. In spite of this, their ties with Rome
were very close; their clergy were, on the whole, orthodox
and rational. In the matter of poetry, they found the epic
ready-made when they settled in France. 'They hardly
seem,' says Gaston Paris, 'to have taken a personal part in
the epic movement which was going on around them.' But
they had a passion for this kind of poetry, for instance for the
Chanson de Roland, which is not theirs but which they preserved, and whence some primitive fragment is said to have
been sung by Taillefer before the army at Hastings. Their
highest claim to be poets would be found in the *Vie de Saint
Alexis* by Tedbald de Vernon, if the origin of this work were
certain.

They landed on English soil, and for more than a century
their language showed no essential difference from French.

The Norman and Angevin kings remained intellectually continental and French until they lost Normandy and Anjou in 1204. Many of the best French writers of the time lived at their court; many of the principal works of the twelfth century were composed there. The reign of Henry II (1154–99) marks the zenith of this literary glory.

Already, however, it is possible to see that the trouvères born in Great Britain, or called thither from the Continent, were under a special influence. Public taste dictated the matter and the form of their writings unless these had a political inspiration. They are nearly all chroniclers, by their subjects and their style. This is true of Gaimar with his *Lestoire des Engles*, Wace with his *Roman de Brut* (Brutus) and *Roman de Rou* (Rollo), Benoît de Sainte-More with his *Lestoire e la généalogie des dux qui unt esté par ordre en Normendie*, his *Roman de Troie*, and his romance of *Aeneas*, Eustace or Thomas de Kent with his *Alexander*, Garnier de Pont-Saint-Maxence with his *Vie Saint Thomas le Martir*.

Many of Taine's reproaches, which are too general because he extended them to all French poetry, would be better founded if he had limited their application to the Anglo-Normans. On the whole, Anglo-Norman verse does not deserve to be called very poetic. Almost all the verse certainly known to have been written by an Anglo-Norman poet, or a French poet at the Anglo-Norman court, has an indisputably prosaic character. It falls short in sensibility, in enthusiasm, in the search for beauty. It is made up, for the most part, of versified chronicles and didactic treatises. The Anglo-Normans were dominated either by intellectual curiosity or by utilitarianism. The epical and lyrical metres of their predecessors were almost exclusively succeeded by an octosyllabic line, which uses rhythm and rhyme only to aid memory, and since to the constraint of verse it adds none of its rightful pleasures, it often awakens regret for prose.

The conquest of England inspired the trouvères not with epics after the style of *Roland*, but with metrical chronicles. The battle of Hastings in the *Roman de Rou* has an almost equally surprising effect if it is read after the description of the fight at Maldon in which Byrhtnoth died, or after that of the battle of Roncesvalles where Roland met his death. The legendary glory of Roland and the epic heroism of Byrhtnoth alike are gone. Wace's very long story is copious and well-informed history and nothing more. It states the happenings in the camp from hour to hour, from the eve to the morrow, reproduces the very words of the combatants, records the tactics of the two leaders, and describes the details of their armour, and the most trifling incidents of the battle. There is certainly no lack of heroic motifs, for instance the successive refusal of Raoul de Conches and of Walter Giffart to bear the duke's standard, because they wish to fight themselves. There is lively presentment of the tumult of the battle—'Moult oïssiez graisles sonner.' But there is little poetry. The narrator may love fine sword-play and the din of the mêlée, but he no more loses his head than Froissart in the story of Crécy. He knows how to classify the enormous mass of information he has collected and to sift evidence. Throughout, his octo-syllabic couplet trots forward at an even pace, and he holds the reins with the steadiest hand.

Wace's characteristics recur, more or less, in all the Anglo-Norman poems of the great period. The contrast is less, but still striking, between the purely French romances of Chrestien de Troyes and those of Benoît de Sainte-More who lived at the court of Henry II. Chrestien turns to romantic and picturesque use all the historical remains in the legends which are his material. His aim is to please by strangeness of adventures and graces of style. But Benoît, who is first of all a chronicler, gives a pseudo-historical air even to his inventions. He is spirited but not poetic.

Many of these Anglo-Norman writings are, for that matter, real history, and even such of them as are fabulous or legend-ary pretend to truth. The aim of several is to satisfy the ingenuous curiosity of readers who wished to know foreign nations, to explore the present and the past. Other poems, of yet more positive design, attempt to weld together the legends scattered throughout the land of Great Britain, and thus to facilitate the fusion of its conflicting races. Their authors would have rallied, on English soil, divergent hostile patriotisms, united Britons, Angles, and Normans in the praises of the country they all inhabited, in which all that was and had been was equally dear. The great island had never received such homage as was tendered it in the *Brut* (Munich MS.). Praise, characteristic of the author's practical mind, runs through these verses in which the country is reviewed as by a conscientious geographer: its orography and hydrography, its mineral and agricultural wealth, the history of its population— all pass, in good order, before one whose admiration never modifies his cool judgment. And nothing is more striking than the smiling aspect, the plenty, this alert observer discovers in the country which Anglo-Saxon poetry had wrapped in fog and horror. It is almost comfortable already. The surrounding sea is no longer 'the path of the storm,' but the wide, convenient highroad of an easy foreign trade.

Anglo-Norman is thus distinguished from French literature by a more marked didactic and utilitarian tendency, and by a weakened aesthetic character. This is not surprising if it is remembered that its first mission, on entering a country which had relapsed into ignorance and was populated by enemy races, was to instruct and to unify. Inevitably the native purity of the French language was very soon adulterated in an island in which it was cut off from its roots among the people. The mother-tongue of the settlers in a foreign land is always thus corrupted or stiffened. It becomes a written, bookish language, preserved with effort and artificially, or, as a spoken tongue, it is contaminated by contact with speech which differs from it profoundly, and suffers from the outset an accretion of many words disfigured by their passage through foreign lips. Thus foreign geographical terms, and expressions referring to local customs which survived the Conquest, adhered to Norman-French. The momentary brilliance of Anglo-Norman letters was, therefore, mainly due to the continental writers attracted to the court of the kings of England, and literature was kept alive among the Anglo-Normans, properly so called, only in so far as it was useful. As for the English who practised writing in the language of the conquerors, they could not but aggravate the artificial or incorrect character of this literature in a tongue which was not their own.

The consciousness of these inevitable lapses inclined the more intelligent of Anglo-Norman writers in the twelfth and thirteenth centuries to turn to Latin.[1] It is true that Latin was then attracting a large number of clerks and literates throughout Europe, who were thus lost to the cause of progress in the vulgar tongues. But this loss was felt in Great Britain more than anywhere else, and literature there may be said to have been beheaded—it lost its leaders—for the sake of Latin, the only common language in a country where Babel reigned.

[1] J.J. Jusserand, *Histoire littéraire, etc.*, Book II, Chap. III; W. H. Schofield, *English Literature from the Norman Conquest to Chaucer*, Chap. II; Helen Waddell, *The Wandering Scholars*, 1927.

It was not only the clerks who wrote Latin, nor did they con-
fine its use to religious treatises. It was employed in this age
in works of every kind, serious and frivolous, learned and
popular, many of which greatly surpassed the writings in the
English of the conquered or the French of the conquerors.
William de Jumièges's *History of William I*, Ordericus Vitalis's
Ecclesiastical History, William of Malmesbury's *Chronicle of
the Kings of England*, and Henry of Huntingdon's *Annals* are
the principal monuments of the serious part of this literature
in Latin,[1] and of the fantastic, mystifying works, the best
known is Geoffrey of Monmouth's *History of the Britons*.
The best examples of the works apparently more frivolous,
but also more truly literature, are the letters and stories of
Giraldus Cambrensis, the Latin jests and miscellaneous profan-
ities of Walter Map, and Nigel Wireker's *Speculum Stultorum*
or comic adventures of the ass Brunellus.

From what has been said, it follows that the study of literary
monuments of the time should extend from French to Latin, if
all and the highest intellectual activity of the inhabitants of
Britain after the Norman invasion is to be understood. If the
aesthetic elements which were to fashion renascent English
literature are to be analysed, it is necessary to go further,
to study not only the Latin of England, but also all the
Latin, whatever its origin, of the religious offices which
sounded week by week in the ears of the faithful, and had
plainly an influence on the English verse-form in process of
evolution.[2] When medieval Latin poets finally gave up
attempting to reproduce the prosody of antiquity, when they
wrote Latin verses with a purely accentual rhythm, and took
advantage of the numerous similar endings of words in Latin
to enrich their productions with sonorous rhymes, they provided the vernacular poets with models of versification. It
was, in fact, they who first fully realized the resources of
the new versification, and fully exploited its potentialities for
the solemn and the comic. In no language was there for a
long time anything to match the perfection of the hymns of
the Church which were repeated throughout Christendom,
Jacopone's *Stabat Mater* or Celano's *Dies Irae*. Nor was there
anything to equal, for comic effect, the sonorous, single-

---

[1] Stephen Gaselee, *An Anthology of Medieval Latin* (prose and verse, 1925);
The Oxford Book of Medieval Latin Verse (1937).
[2] G. Saintsbury, *History of English Prosody*, vol. i; idem, in *Cambridge
History of English Literature*, vol. i, Chap. XVIII.

rhymed quatrains of the Goliards, or unfrocked clerks, such as those attributed to Walter Map:

> Meum est propositum in taberna mori:
> Vinum sit appositum morientis ori,
> Ut dicant, cum venerint, angelorum chori:
> 'Deus sit propitius huic potatori.' . . .

These Latin verses, which the faithful conned in church or drinkers trolled in the taverns, could exercise a considerable influence on English poetry from the time when the Anglo-Saxon line was finally abandoned, and new paths were explored for a metre which should be at once accentual and rhymed. The Anglo-Saxons had been able to translate much Latin quantitative verse without modifying their own prosody, for there was no common measure between the two verse-forms. But from this time Latin rhymed verse was allied with French verse to undermine and overthrow the Anglo-Saxon form. English poetry was to aim henceforth, though vainly for generations, at analogous effects of high lyricism, jollity, and swing.

Before dealing with poetry in English, we must mention another force which had important and lasting influence on it, and reached it first through the French and Latin of the conquerors. There is in Anglo-Norman literature, on the whole so practical and prosaic, one region in which sentiment and the marvellous are paramount. They exist, it is true, only in the subjects, and do not affect the even calm of the writers' tones. Yet they are there whenever a chronicler, pursuing his curious search for stories, has heard and wishes to repeat some Celtic legend.[1] It must continually have happened that the Normans became aware of the tales which had been traditional among the Britons around them since their glorious days and were the depository of their hope of revenge, and also of the fair dreams of adventure and love by which their imaginations were charmed. If some of these poems reached England from Armorica, through the medium of continental French poetry, there were others which passed straight from the Britons in Wales to the Anglo-Normans.

Was this Celtic influence, which is always a little mysterious and indeterminate, now exercised for the first time? Probably not. In Anglo-Saxon times the neighbourhood of the vanquished Britons had already had its effect. History no longer admits that the Britons suffered mass extermination at the

[1] G. Saintsbury, *Flourishing of Romance and Rise of Allegory*, 1897; E. Faral, *La Légende arthurienne des origines à Geoffrey de Monmouth*, 1929.

hands of their Germanic conquerors, but teaches that as well
as the Irish, untouched within their island, and the still
independent Britons of the western and northern mountains,
there were many survivors of this race in the centre and the
south who were merged in the conquering people.   We have
seen that the conversion of the Angles to Christianity was
the work of the Church of Ireland, and that Bede, though
an out - and - out Romanist, emanated from a monastery
founded by Celts and animated by their spirit.   Anglo-Saxon
hagiography is partly of Celtic inspiration, and there is a
great resemblance between the life of the Irish saint
Brandan and those of the Anglo-Saxon saints Cuthbert and
Guthlac.   Even the half-pagan poetry of the Anglo-Saxons is
often much akin to what is nowadays called Celtic mystery
and strangeness.   The romance of *Beowulf* opens with a prologue on the mysterious origin of the hero which is singularly
like the story in the British cycle of the apparition of Arthur.
However, on the one hand, the defeat of the Church of Ireland
by the Church of Rome, and, on the other, the exclusive, in-
curious character of the Anglo-Saxons, seem to have put very
strict limits to their poetic debt to the Britons.

All this was changed at the coming of the Normans.   For
the first time, the proscribed Saxons felt themselves the
brothers of the Welsh whom they had formerly despised
and persecuted.   The Normans, meanwhile, were the first to
effect a fusion between these races, and they did it by violence.
In the reign of Henry I they made a cruel and bloodthirsty
conquest of Wales, hitherto independent.   For two centuries
this subjugation was nothing like final, but the contact, so
early established by measures of force, made the Anglo-
Normans curious about their adversaries.   Hence works were
written which at first were hardly literary in themselves, but
which were important for the echo which they found in French,
and even more in English, literature.

The first of these works in date, and the one most fruitful
of consequences, was the Latin *History of the Britons* which
Geoffrey of Monmouth wrote before 1147, and dedicated to
the son of Henry I.   The author had been brought up in a
Benedictine monastery near Monmouth in Wales, of which
place he was archdeacon when he wrote his book.   He poses
as a truthful chronicler, and claims to translate an old and
unknown British book.   He had, in fact, no precursors, save
Gildas (sixth century), who does not mention Arthur, and

Nennius (tenth century), who says very little about him. Moreover, exploration of the Celtic literatures has yielded nothing except what is later than Geoffrey and imitated from him.

Thus Geoffrey is, in large part, the creator of the Arthurian legend. His book is a work of imagination in disguise, and it is impossible to say to what extent tradition helped him. But it was certainly with an historian's gravity that he wrote out his fables.

Following Nennius so far, he makes Brutus, the father of the Britons, into the great-grandson of Aeneas, who came to Britain and there founded Troynovant, or New Troy, afterwards called London.

But the most curious parts of his story are those which concern Arthur, represented as the heroic defender of the Britons, and Merlin, whose prophecies he collects. Arthur appears as the conqueror of the Anglo-Saxons, the Picts, and the Scots. He brings Ireland, Iceland, Scandinavia, and Gaul under his imperial rule, enters into conflict with the Roman emperor, triumphs over him, and makes the Romans his slaves. Ever victorious, he lives until the end of the seventh century.

In spite of the protests of several clerks, Giraldus Cambrensis among others, Geoffrey's fables were accepted. They were assimilated first by the Normans and then by the Anglo-Saxons. Both peoples were presently enthusiastic for the British hero, their racial enemy, and adopted him as a glorious ancestor. The illusion was singular, but it had its part in weakening racial hatred and giving birth to English patriotism.

Geoffrey Gaimar, a mediocre Norman trouvère, was the first to turn this story into French verse. He shows Arthur, after his victories, summoning a meeting of the kings at Caerleon— the City of the Legions—and there crowned in splendour, and thus he gives the first suggestion for the legend of the Round Table. Other Celtic legends gathered about the early nucleus. Marie de France contributed to them in lays written at the court of Henry II. Allowing for the part of Chrestien de Troyes, the conclusion is that the British cycle was evolved principally by the Anglo-Normans, and that Walter Map, who was half-Norman and half-Welsh, presumably welded together the Arthurian legend and the legend of the Holy Grail. He is credited with giving the cycle its religious and moral character, in that he represented Guinevere, Arthur's wife, as an adulteress, and her lover, Lancelot, as unworthy, by his sin, to accomplish the quest of the Holy Grail, which was reserved for his son, Galahad. The *Queste del Saint Graal*, *Lancelot du Lac*, and *Mort d'Arthur* are attributed to Walter Map.

The powerful imaginative leaven of this story, the most beautiful and varied of all those in the minds of the English when they again began to write, must not be forgotten. It was a story all the more stimulating to them because it was set in their own country, and they believed it to be national.

3. *English Literature from 1066 to 1350.*[1] *Changes in the Language.*—Small though the aesthetic value of Anglo-Norman literature may be, it is great in comparison with that of the contemporary literature in English, labouring, as this did, under the disadvantages of a despised language, loss of tradition, and lack of culture. It was a literature written by half-literate men for an ignorant people. The three centuries after the Norman Conquest produced writings which show the gradual transformations undergone by the old language, and are therefore full of interest for the philologist, but which offer hardly anything to the amateur of literature. He may be touched by the very awkwardness of these attempts at literary composition, but he esteems them merely as rude translations, inharmonious verses which hesitate between alliterative rhythm and the cadence of the rhymed line, and alternately obey and ignore the laws of syllabism. All this licence would have horrified the scops and it gave the trouvères good matter for ridicule.

The reconstruction was slow, but the ruin of Anglo-Saxon rhetoric was prompt, almost, indeed, instantaneous. It had two principal causes, the repeated efforts of English writers to translate the works of French poets, often to translate them literally, and the wide and deep changes swiftly wrought in the speech of the vanquished people by their lack of culture and by the contaminating influence of the language of the conquerors.

Several modifying processes affected Anglo-Saxon.[2] The vocabulary suffered the rapid and final loss of a considerable number of words, of nearly all those proper to the old poetic

[1] Jusserand, op. cit., Book II, Chap. IV; Schofield, op. cit.; J. E. Wells, *Manual of the Writings in Middle English* (New Haven, 1916–51); J. Hall, *Early Middle English* (Oxford, 1920); K. Sisam, *Fourteenth Century Verse and Prose* (Oxford, 1921); R. M. Wilson, *Early Middle English Literature*, 1952.
[2] H. Bradley, in *Cambridge History of English Literature*, vol. i, Chap. III; idem, *The Making of English*, 1904; O. Jespersen, *Growth and Structure of the English Language*, 1906; H. C. Wyld, *The Historical Study of the Mother Tongue*, 1906; R. Huchon, *Histoire de la langue anglaise*, vol. ii, 1931.

style, and it received, in exchange, French words which penetrated it slowly and gradually.   By degrees English came to
borrow the words which denoted the customs and ideas imported from Normandy—the learned terms of warfare, hunting,
and falconry, words which referred to chivalry, scientific and
legal language, courtly speech, abstract and technical terms,
and those connected with art and luxury.   Thus was constituted the modern English language, in which words of French
origin or words based, in imitation of French, on Latin or
Greek, are much more numerous than Germanic words,
although these, in current speech and frequency of use, are
to the others in the average ratio of ten to one.

At the same time, there was a modification of the form and
the pronunciation of such Anglo-Saxon words as subsisted.
Most often they were contracted: unprotected by any culture
and assailed by deforming foreign attempts to pronounce
them, they tended to keep only their essential, that is, their
accentuated, syllable.   They were like a besieged fort, holding
only the central tower, abandoning the outer works.   There
resulted an increase of the monosyllables which are so
numerous in modern English.

Degradation overtook, in particular, the terminations in
use among the Anglo-Saxons.   The Norman Conquest affected
them in two ways: first, it suppressed or weakened many of
them, and thus accelerated the progress of the English language to its present analytical state, in which relations
previously indicated by inflections are shown by distinct
words; secondly, it helped to determine the choice for survival
of certain inflections out of the number of those customary
among the several peoples of Anglia, Mercia, and Wessex,
whose differences were reproduced in the chief Middle English
dialects, those of the north, the centre, and the south.   While
endings of words were indeterminate and at rivalry, the
language of the conquerors sometimes had the additional
weight which made it the arbiter of victory among them.
This is the best explanation of the extension to all declensions
of the plural in *es* or *s*, at first used only in one of the declensions
of the noun.

French grammar contributed several of its uses.   Anglo-
Saxon formed the comparative and superlative of adjectives
by inflection, but French introduced the use of the adverb
also, so that, while the Germanic form was retained for monosyllables, mostly of Saxon root, the analytical form came to

prevail for polysyllables, which were mainly derived from the French. Similarly, possession, formerly expressed by the genitive case, was expressed henceforth either by the genitive ending or by a preposition.

Anglo-Saxon, as a whole, was gradually simplified to modern English, a language of singularly few grammatical complications. Genders, arising out of the form of words or obscure and forgotten traditions, needed too delicate treatment to allow them to remain intact in a country of mixed population, and they were logically distributed according to sex, the neuter being reserved for all words in which there is no idea of sex. Only vestiges of the old grammar were left—the few present irregularities of the verb and the noun, and the genitive case, the only one which has survived. The article and the adjective became invariable. Pronouns and auxiliaries were introduced to mark in the verb persons and tenses which had been expressed by inflections.

Thus a regular syntax, in which inversion and ellipses were only exceptionally allowable, was introduced. The poetic language lost closeness, freedom, and some elements of the picturesque, but the language as a whole gained lucidity and precision.

The final result of these transformations was not felt until the sixteenth century. In the meanwhile inflections kept a semblance of life, the varied, sonorous vowels first giving place to a uniform *e*, often arbitrarily used, which was perceptible to the ear at the beginning of the period in question, but was swiftly tending to purely orthographic existence. Philologists give the name of Middle English to the language of this long period of transition.

We are not here concerned to describe the slow and deep-reaching evolution in detail, and must be content with a mere sketch, instead of a complete picture. At first, French and English naturally kept separate. The conquerors spoke French, the vanquished Anglo-Saxon, which lost the dignity of an official and of a literary language. French became the language of the court, the schools, and the law-courts, and, alternately with Latin, of the Church and of science. Its use spread among the burghers and among the landed gentry, who were largely Norman. It was only when they found themselves confined to Great Britain, after the loss of Normandy by John Lackland in 1204, that the conquerors began to pay any attention to the native language. Then it was that insular patriotism was born in the Norman, now cut off from the Continent, and as his preoccupation with the people among whom he lived increased, he learnt their speech. The simplifications of English of which we have spoken, the sort of compromise effected between the two languages, made it possible for the two races to understand each other, more or less. The words which the Normans found most difficult, in meaning or pronunciation, were gradually dropped and replaced by their own words. The whole of the thirteenth century is filled with these changes, which were accomplished in silence and by degrees, and which were hallowed by the custom of the fourteenth century. The Normans had, by this time, in great part abandoned French, and the native people had brought their language to a point at which it had lost the crabbed visage of its birthplace. Henceforth English reigned alone: in 1350 it took the place of French as the language of the schools; in 1362 it became that of the law-courts; and in 1399 it was used in Parliament for the first time by Henry IV. In the same period prosody, which for long had wavered between one and the other of the two traditions, attained to perfect balance with Chaucer, who combined respect for the native tones of his fellow-countrymen with obedience to the essential laws of French versification. Whatever be the individual merits of the poets who preceded Chaucer, they do no more than mark the steps to that honourable place where he is enthroned as the first great metrical writer of his country.

4. *Literature in English. The Religious Writers.*—A hundred years of complete silence followed the Norman Conquest, and when a few writings in the native language reappeared towards the end of the twelfth century, they were mainly works of piety. To a disinherited people, no longer able to read, the essential Word, which helps man to work out his salvation, had to be carried first. Homilies, sermons in prose and in verse, translation of the Psalms or parts of the Bible, rules for a devout life, lives of the saints, and prayers—these fill the pages which form the mass of what may be called English literature until about the middle of the fourteenth century. They are at first almost the whole of this literature, and they are its predominant part until this period ends. Inevitably, their only local element is language. As regards their matter, they are transcriptions, often literal, from Latin or French. If the passage of generations somewhat modified

their religious sentiment, these were changes which affected all
Europe, and sprang not from conditions in England, but from
the widespread fluctuations of piety in the Middle Ages. The
asceticism of cloisters, the growing tenderness which mingled
with the devotion to the Virgin Mary, and the exaltation which
was imbued with chivalry and mysticism, were reflected, in
turn, in these English works.

Whenever they are specifically English, they owe it to the
very popular character of their public. The problem was to
gain the ear of an oppressed, poor, and ignorant people, and
more than elsewhere it was therefore necessary to use a very
simple language and to multiply explanations and concrete
details. Sometimes, also, the choice of the subject and the
mood of the story were determined by a gentle pity for the
miserable state of the faithful. Again and again, an author
excuses himself for using a language so much despised as
English, saying that he has wished to write for men who know
no French and have no edifying books. He knows that his
style is bad, that his rhymes are weak, but he believes himself
justified by his aim. It is chiefly the progress in form which
to-day has interest for those who go through this starved
period of English literature.

The earliest in date of these religious writings, the *Poema
Morale* [1] which in its original form goes back to about 1150, is
a grave exhortation to Christians to turn aside from the paths
of this world and to enter those of devoutness and salvation.
The preacher begins with self-accusation—he has reached old
age without giving enough of his thoughts to God. He begs
men to remember the day of judgment, to keep the thought
of hell and paradise ever before them. Let them leave the
broad road which leads to hell and take the strait path to
heaven.

The feeling animating the poem is sincere and sometimes
ardent, but severe and sad. While the conception of paradise
is mainly spiritual, hell is depicted with all its arsenal of
material terrors. Souls are tortured by fire and cold in turn:
burning, they think that to freeze is felicity; freezing, they
sigh for the flames. Although the Old and New Law are said
in one passage to be comprised in love for one's neighbour,
charity is not preached except as the means of salvation.
The asceticism of the cloister is predominant, and the individu-

---

[1] Text in Morris and Skeat's *Specimens of Early English*, vol. i. English
translation by Gasquet (1905).

alism of the Christian who must esteem himself above his kin.
'Nor let wife hope in husband, nor husband in wife.   Let
each man live for himself throughout his days.'

The novelty of this poem is not doctrinal but formal.   In
style and versification, these four hundred lines of seven accents,
in sections of four and three, are an innovation, and the form
had a high destiny, for it was adopted by most of the popular
ballads.   Since the rhythm is iambic, the line is, at the same
time, roughly syllabic.   Almost every one of these lines, which
are rhymed in couplets, contains a maxim, sometimes well
turned and in the nature of an antithesis, so that it is easy to
remember.   The sententious style contrasts with the epical
manner of the Anglo-Saxons.   The old phraseology has gone,
and has been replaced by a simple language, without images
and bare and precise, but animated by some homely comparisons, at once exact and prosaic:

> Each man with what he hath may buy him heaven,
> Both he that hath more and he that hath less,
> This one with his penny, the other with his pound,
> 'Tis the most wondrous bargain that any man found.

We feel ourselves not far removed from the couplets of a
Defoe, blunt and practical, in which there is the same lack of
poetry and the same skill in speaking straight to simple
people.

There is no originality of matter in *Ormulum*,[1] a mere translation and paraphrase of some forty of the Gospels read at Mass,
which was written about 1200 by the monk Orm, a native of
north-east Mercia.   This author's most salient characteristic
probably is the respect for ancient tradition which made the
commentaries of the Venerable Bede his inspiration.   But the
form of his work is entirely new, and remained an isolated
phenomenon of literature.   The seven-accented line with a
fixed caesura $(4 + 3)$ is used as in the *Poema Morale*, but is
unrhymed, is made on the pattern of the quantitative Church
verses, ends with a redundant feminine syllable, and is completely regular as regards the place of its accents and the
number of its syllables.   It is like a first essay in blank verse.
Regularity is its only merit.   The author is afflicted with
pedantry and purism to a singular degree.   He invents a new
spelling, best illustrated in his redoubling of the consonant after
every short vowel.   Deliberate and diligent, spending all his

---

[1] Holt edition (Oxford, 1878).   Extracts in Morris and Skeat, op. cit., vol.i.

energy on form, Orm marks the beginnings of the desire to subject the universal indiscipline of the language to rules.

There is more poetry in some of the contemporary prayers.[1] The *Prayer to Our Lady* has warmth and emphasis, although its rhythm is uncertain; and in a few effusions of the early thirteenth century there is the tender mysticism of a Hugh of Saint-Victor, for instance in the *Luve Ron* of Thomas of Hales, which contains the first truly artistic and poetic stanzas in the new language. It is with Villon's accent and in verses as rhythmical as his, that the poet speaks of the transitory nature of earthly joys, and with an emotion already romantic that he enumerates the illustrious heroes and ladies of the past:

> Hwer is Paris and Heleyne,
> That weren so bryht and feyre on bleo,
> Amadas, Tristram and Dideyne,
> Yseude and alle theo,
> Ector with his scharpe meyne,
> And Cesar riche of worldes feo?
> Heo beoth iglyden ut of the reyne,
> So the shaft is of the cleo.[2]

The *Ancrene Riwle*,[3] the best specimen of the prose of this time, is equally suave. It consists of rules for the ascetic life given by a prelate to three anchorites, women who have decided to live not in a convent, but in a solitary dwelling near a church. There is new sweetness in these artless and minute instructions. The atmosphere is that of a period in which devotion to the Virgin is supreme, and the consciousness of feminine nature has entered even asceticism. This Rule also exists in Latin and in French, but the English does not seem to be a translation.

The pious writings of the early fourteenth century are more alert in style, and can be vivacious, gay, and charming. The *Life of Saint Brandan*,[4] a translation from the French, introduced

---

[1] F. Furnivall, *Early English Poems and the Lives of the Saints*, 1862.

[2] Where is Paris and Helen,
That were so bright and fair of face,
Amadis, Tristram and Dido,
Isoud and all they,
Hector with his sharp strength,
And Caesar rich of world's wealth?
They are gone out of the realm,
As the shaft is off the cliff.

[3] Ed. by S. Morton (Camden Society, 1853); by Mabel Day (E.E.T.S. 1952). Modern English translation in Medieval Library, vol. xviii, 1926, and by M. B. Salu, 1955.

[4] *The Early South English Legendary or Lives of the Saints*, ed. C. Horstmann (E.E.T.S., vol. lxxxvii).

the English to the enchantments and marvels and the optimism of the beautiful Celtic legend. The *Life of Saint Dunstan*, which is attributed to Robert of Gloucester, is full of homely touches and cordial light-heartedness. These rude and artless verses have a comic liveliness which compensates for their unrelieved prosaic character, for instance, in the scene in which the saint, busy at his little forge, receives a visit from the devil in the guise of a pretty woman who smilingly talks nonsense to him. The saint is not taken in, but puts his pincers in the fire while she is speaking; then suddenly, when they are red-hot, pinches the devil by the nose, so that he flees, writhing and howling:

> As well for the Devil to have been at home, and wiped his nose,
> He never hied him thither more, to heal his cold.

At about the same time, in 1303, a Gilbertine monk, Robert Mannyng of Brunne, in Lincoln, undertook to translate, under the title of *Handlyng Sinne*,[1] the *Manuel des Péchés*, which one of his fellow-countrymen of the previous century, traditionally known as William of Wadington, had written in the French of England, the debased language for which he excused himself by pleading his birth:

> De le françois ni del rimer
> Ne me doit nul homme blâmer
> Car en Angleterre fus né
> Et nourri, ordiné et élevé.[2]

Wadington, in forty-four stories, had shown the paths of sin. Mannyng by turns follows, neglects, and adds to this model, showing more independence than was customary. Although he uses the octosyllabic line with great licence, his verse is much more rhythmic, alive, and vigorous than that of his Anglo-Norman prototype. He has, moreover, sacrificed a fair number of dull, theological dissertations to the forcefulness of his narratives. He adds a dozen stories of mainly local origin. His object is amusement as much as edification. He is an observer of the customs of his time and paints them in lively colours. He inclines to satire, and he makes frank attacks on the landlords, anticipating *Piers Plowman*, and does

[1] Edited by Furnivall (Roxburghe Club Publications, 1862, and Early English Text Society, vol. cxix). *See* E. J. Arnould, *Le Manuel des Péchés* (Paris, 1940).

[2] For my French and my rhymes
No man should blame me,
For I was born in England,
And there bred and brought up.

not spare the clergy, whom he blames for laxity, luxury, and
frivolity. A true monk, he has little indulgence for women,
and makes them responsible for the sins of men.

But his real merit is that he can tell a story well, clearly,
with go, and with a certain agility hitherto unknown in England. To invent was not his part. When he does not copy
Wadington, who himself had said of his book: 'Rien del mien
ni metrai,' he draws on the common treasure. His stories are
always interesting, in spite of their childishness and strange
moral standpoint. They are very like the stories peddled by
the Franciscan friars, to stimulate the curiosity as much as the
devoutness and charity of the people.

The demand for pious stories was abundantly supplied by a
collection of twenty-four thousand lines of verse, the *Cursor
Mundi*,[1] which dates from about 1320. It is an embellished
version of the New Testament, in the Northumbrian dialect,
and an octosyllabic metre more regular than Mannyng's. Its
aim is to interest the people in the Bible stories, thus providing
a counter-attraction to the romances. 'Most books are written
for the French,' says the author, and declares that he speaks
to Englishmen. His poem may be described as the matter
of the dramatic mysteries in narrative form. The Bible is
not its only source, for its unknown author has recourse also
to the *Historia Scolastica* of Peter Comestor, and does not
hesitate to draw on many other French and Latin writers of
the previous age. His copious verses are often picturesque,
and are full of humanity, and that they enjoyed a great popularity is proved by the number of manuscript copies in which
they have reached us.

A work of more local significance is that of the hermit
Richard Rolle of Hampole.[2] For one thing, this writer is
the only one of his time whose life is known to us in some
detail. His reputation for sanctity was well established when
he died, for the Cistercian sisters, whose convent was near his
hermitage, expected his canonization so confidently that they

---

[1] Ed. R. Morris (E.E.T.S., lvii, lix, lxii, lxvi, lxvii, xcix, ci).
[2] *The English Writings of Richard Rolle*, ed. H. E. Allen (Oxford, 1931).
Selected Work of Richard Rolle, modernized version, ed. G. C. Heseltine, 1930.
See study by H. E. Allen, *Writings Ascribed to Richard Rolle . . . and Materials
for his Biography*, 1927. Rolle's fame is attested by the number of contemporary or near-contemporary manuscripts of his works (some 150) now in the
libraries of Europe, a number far larger than that of any other medieval English
writer, Wyclif and Chaucer included.

had an office written in his honour, together with his life in Latin.

He was born in Yorkshire about 1290, studied theology at Oxford, and at the age of nineteen fled, in fear of temptation, first from the university and then from his family, who thought him mad. He became a hermit. The fame of his sanctity spread through the neighbourhood and men came to visit him, but even while he was answering questions, he went on writing his meditations, and 'what he said differed from what he wrote.' He is the most diligent religious writer of his time. Such was his absorption in contemplation, that his friends could divest him of worn clothes, mend them, and put them on him again without attracting his notice. Enthusiastic and visionary, mystical and fervent, he is a connecting link between the orthodox saints, of whom he is the last, and the Protestant visionaries—Fox, Bunyan, Wesley, and their like—whom he resembles in certain particularities of his life. He is tempted by the devil in the semblance of a girl he had once loved. He is haunted by fear of death and hell. He has moments of tenderness so exalted that his prose halts, for instance in his *Nominis Jesu Encomion*:

Therefore Jhesu es thy name. A! A! that wondyrful name! A! that delittabyll name! This es the name that is abown all names. . . . I gede abowte be covatyse of reches and I fande noghte Jhesu. I rane be the wantonnes of flesche and I fand noghte Jhesu. I satt in companyes of worldly myrthe and I fand noghte Jhesu. . . . Therefore I turnede by anothir waye, and I rane abowte be poverte, and I fande Jhesu, pure borne in the worlde, laid in a crybe and lappid in clathis.

It was long believed that Richard Rolle had written *The Pricke of Conscience*.[1] It is now practically certain that this poem merely belongs to the same time and place, though it may have been written under his influence. Rolle's literary achievement loses nothing by the exclusion from his canon of that didactic poem. Wordy and mediocre, never without the taint of the scholastic and the puerile, its wide popularity nevertheless makes it worthy of study. About 1340, when Wyclif was already sixteen years old and about to drive a breach in the system of strict Roman discipline, its anonymous author extols it with the most rigid orthodoxy. His aim is to give an impulse to devoutness, by first showing forth the miseries and vicissitudes of this world, and then depicting the after-life, of which his presentment is as concrete and grossly material as was usual among the preachers of the day.

[1] Ed. in *Yorkshire Writers, Richard Rolle of Hampole*, 2 vols. (1895–6). Over one hundred manuscripts (as well as Latin versions) are extant.

Diseases are among the pains of Purgatory—dropsy, gout, ulcers, boils, paralysis, quinsy, leprosy—and so is fire, the heat of which is graduated according to the gravity of sins. Great sins burn like wood, small sins like straw, those of middling import like hay. He emphasizes the value of prayer, alms-giving, fasting, and Masses as means of relieving the souls in Purgatory. At this moment of history, it is curious to come upon his unhesitating declaration of the efficacy of pardons bought from the pope or the bishops, who hold the keys of the treasure of the Church, purchased for her by her doctors, saints, and martyrs. The pains of his Hell are heat, cold, dirt, evil smells, hunger and thirst—the damned drink fire and suck vipers' heads to quench their thirst—and also darkness, the sight of devils, vermin, the blows of red-hot hammers wielded by demons, tears of fire, shame, red-hot chains, and despair. No idle tale overtaxes this author's credulity. One could wish, for his own sake, that many of his grave explanations had been written in jest. There is, for instance, his prescription for discovering the sex of a child in the act of birth: if its first cry be *A* it is a boy, if *E* a girl; for was not Adam's initial *A* and Eve's *E*? Whether a hermit or not, he was a little too credu-lous, behind even his own generation. He awakes a longing for the rough good sense of Langland and Chaucer's merry scepticism. And he makes us sigh also for Chaucer's art, as we read the ten thousand octosyllabic lines that versify his visions and display the childishness of his matter, unrelieved by any merit of form. These are poor verses. He himself confesses that he has no regard for the beautiful,

> For I rek noght, thogh the ryme be rude,
> If the maters thar-of be gude.

The Pricke of Conscience marks the decline of religious poetry in the first half of the fourteenth century.

5. *Secular Poetry from 1200 to 1350.*—A little later than religious poetry, yet side by side with it and growing rapidly from age to age, a secular literature developed which was founded exclusively on French works. It was, as was natural, predominantly chivalrous, and was inspired by French roman-tic poems. It has, therefore, very little originality of matter, but it betrays national instincts in a preference for subjects and heroes connected with the land of Britain. Large parts of every one of the romantic cycles of chivalry were turned into English in order that minstrels might tell them to the

people, but from the beginning the British stories were most valued, and gave the native poets matter for their most popular, and here and there also for their most original, songs.

In the last quarter of the twelfth or in the first years of the thirteenth century Layamon, a priest of Ernley, on the Severn and near the Welsh border, put Wace's *Brut* into English verse for the benefit of his fellow-countrymen.[1] Wace, with the curious mind and the detachment of an Anglo-Norman trouvère, had followed Geoffrey of Monmouth's fabulous history of the Britons, and had therefore glorified that people at the expense of their Saxon adversaries. And Layamon, or Laweman, a pure German by race and tongue, faithfully repeated this story, as though he were ignorant of his own origin. His sympathies are all with the Britons; the Saxons are for him barbarians whose victories grieve him sorely and whose defeats delight him. It is not astonishing that he has scandalized modern English historians, almost to the point of being dubbed traitor. Freeman, the historian of the Norman Conquest, cannot enough despise this Anglo-Saxon who betrays his race, whose national heroes are not Alfred and Hengist, but Brutus, the descendant of Aeneas, and the famous King Arthur. None the less, Layamon's patriotism is as ardent as it is mistaken. His error draws attention to the fact that the two races who had been enemies were already inextricably fused. They constituted a new unity which was already the English nation, and had England for its place and symbol. It is because he sees the Britons as legitimate owners of England that Layamon makes common cause with them against the Saxons, whom he regards as invaders, and there is not a doubt that when he speaks of the Saxons he is secretly thinking of the Normans, the oppressors of his fellow-countrymen.

Layamon is, on the whole, a faithful translator. He contributes nothing new except certain passages of the Arthurian legend. These principally reflect the developments of this legend in the half-century which separated him from Wace, yet he deserves honour for first revealing some of the most poetic touches in the story. Living, as he did, on the Welsh March, he may have had direct access to traditions of which his forerunners were unaware. Most of his additions are, however, accepted nowadays as either based on a text of Wace

[1] *Layamon's Brut*, ed. with translation by F. Madden, 1847. Extracts in Morris and Skeat, *Specimens. Selections*, ed. by J. Hall (Oxford, 1924).

other than that printed, or borrowed from the lost *Chronique rimée* of Geoffrey Gaimar.

Nevertheless, Layamon is no mere translator. He cannot be classed among the trouvères, with their curiosity and the simple amusement they found in their own fine tales. He is a scop, and has kept something of the epic mood and the wild, impassioned note of Anglo-Saxon poetry, together with part of its vocabulary, a rhythm which still hesitates between rhyme and alliteration, and certain traces of the ancient mythology and the sombre, ancestral enthusiasm for war. He is, moreover, the first writer to weave about King Arthur a fairy lore of which there is hardly a word in Geoffrey of Monmouth or in Wace. He is more at his ease than they in the realm of the marvellous. When he tells the story of the passing of the king we seem to be listening to Malory:

> When these words were spoken,
> There came thither wending,
> A little boat moving,
> On the waters it floated,
> And two women in it,
> Wondrously formed;
> And lo! they took Arthur,
> And swiftly they bare him,
> And softly him down laid,
> And forth 'gan their sailing
> Then was it accomplished
> What Merlin said whilom,
> That great woe would follow
> On Arthur's forthfaring.
> Still think the Britons
> That Arthur yet liveth
> And dwelleth in Avalon
> With the fairest of all elves;
> Still wait the Britons
> For Arthur's returning.

Very far from attaining to Wace's easy fluency, correctness, and courtliness, Layamon, awkward and blunt, yet has a plebeian way which is not unpleasing. He recurs to the massive ironies of the Anglo-Saxon epic. Thus he tells how the British king Uther, with Arthur's help, defeated his brother Pascent, who together with Gillomar, the savage Irish invader, attempted to dethrone him. At the moment when Uther has wounded Gillomar to death and Arthur has slain Pascent the poet's voice has the very tones of the *Ode of Brunanburh*:

> On the head he smote him
> So that he down fell,

In his mouth his sword thrust—
Uncouth his dinner—
So went the sword's point
In the earth beneath him.
And then spake Uther,
'Pascent, now lie there,
Now hast thou Britain,
To thy hand hast won it.
So is now hap to thee;
Therein death hath come to thee;
Dwell shalt thou therein
With thy fellow Gillomar,
And well enjoy Britain.
To you I deliver it;
Ye twain may presently
Dwell in the land with us;
Nor dread ye ever
Who food will give ye.'

Such passages, occurring in a chivalrous romance, show the transitional character of Layamon's curious version of the Arthurian story. He was at once the last of the scops and the first of the English trouvères.

The works which came after his were principally rhymed chronicles, translations which include nearly all the cycles and are interesting mainly when they have a national character. Popular sympathy was to gather later about Robin Hood, the outlaw and unmatched bowman, a Saxon, proscribed by the Normans, who lived in Sherwood Forest with Maid Marian, his love. Meanwhile the English people were beguiled by the prowess of Bevis of Hampton, or they followed in amazement the improbable adventures of Sir Guy of Warwick, who left his wife, the fair Felice, that he might deserve her by his exploits, and who went to Palestine, slew the giant Colbrand, and died as a pious hermit.

These romances were hardly more than copies of French or Latin books. There is more originality of plot, manner, and spirit in the romances of *Havelok* and *Horn*, which were in-spired by Scandinavian legends.[1] Both had already been told in French by the indefatigable trouvères, but the versions of the two unknown English poets are independent, attractive, and in some ways superior. They have a distinct manner due to a different public. For there was something rough and popular about the audiences of the English minstrels.

[1] W. W. Skeat, *Havelok*, 2nd ed. (Oxford, 1915); F. Holthausen, 3rd ed. (Heidelberg, 1928); J. Hall, *King Horn* (Oxford, 1901). Translations by L. A. Hibbard, 1911. See Hibbard, *Medieval Romance in England* (Oxford, 1924); W. H. French, *Essays on K. H.* (Ithaca, 1940). See also p. 97.

They would have wearied of long traditional descriptions of magnificent ceremonies and sumptuous halls, of unending analysis of courtly love. They wanted a quicker moving story, a franker sentiment, and homelier realism in descriptions.

These two romances appeared in their English form towards the end of the thirteenth century. French chivalrous poetry was beginning to exhaust itself with repetition, and to give place to prose as a medium for reaching a public which had almost ceased to seek anything in literature except the element of the curious in adventures. But the romances had only just reached the people of England, whose minds were less cultivated, simpler, and more susceptible to the charm of rudimentary poetry.

After his *Lestorie des Engles* Gaimar had written the *Lai de Haveloc*, the title being a corruption of the name of the Dane Anlaf Cuaran, who fought at Brunanburh. The English poet, while seemingly unaware of Gaimar, yet does not derive immediately from the original legend, for the usual outline of the French romances has plainly influenced his style. Its beginning recalls the popular story which was to be crystallized in the famous ballad of the *Babes in the Wood*.

Goldburh, daughter of Athelwold, the good king of England, is left an orphan and the ward of her uncle Godrich, Earl of Cornwall, who has promised to marry her to the best man in the kingdom, but who really is envious of her throne and thinks of ridding himself of her. As for Havelok, son of the Danish king Birkabeyn, he is in the power of the wretch Godard, his guardian, who delivers him to the poor fisherman Grim to be put to death. Grim spares the boy, who reaches England, where he is long a wanderer but is at last hired as scullion by Princess Goldburh's cook. Thus humbly placed, he amazes the countryside by his strength and his exploits, and Goldburh's uncle ironically marries her to him, as the best man he knows. But Goldburh recognizes the youth's royal birth by the light which issues from his mouth and by a sign, the red cross he bears on his shoulder. With the help of a vassal who has remained faithful, Havelok reconquers Denmark, then wrests England from Godrich. Godard is dragged over stony soil by an old mare and then hanged, and Godrich is burnt alive. Thus all ends for the best.

Love plays an insignificant part in this romance in which adventure dominates. But the simple and artless narrative throws the element of the pathetic into full relief. In the beginning, when Godard's atrocities are related, we are a little reminded of Ugolino's tower, or of the prison in which Hubert makes ready to burn out little Arthur's eyes at the order of King John. Godard goes to visit his nephew Havelok and his two nieces in the dungeon in which he has cast them to die of cold and hunger. He kills the two little girls there, but his heart fails him so that he cannot finish the business. The miserable hut of the fisherman Grim, his dialogue with his wife Dame Leve, the fisherman's revulsion of feeling when he sees that the boy is of royal race, the mixture of pity, reverence, and self-interest which decides him to spare and even to serve the child whom he had sworn to kill—these scenes and others are so vigorously realistic as to appeal to every class of reader, and interest the simplest of them.

Havelok is a narrative in octosyllabic couplets, approximately correct. *Horn*, with its very short lines, not syllabic but accentuated, has the form of a lay intended to be sung. Love, which is hardly mentioned in *Havelok*, is dominant in *Horn*. Thus *Horn* is particularly interesting as being transitional between the romances of the twelfth and thirteenth centuries and the romantic ballads of the later period.

According to the trouvère Thomas, who wrote *Horn et Rimenhild* in the twelfth century, Horn was the son of Havelok and Goldburh, the hero and heroine of the preceding romance. The two stories have in common their Scandinavian origin, but the later of them has much the larger share of the marvellous and the exotic.

There is a great difference between Thomas's version, with its five thousand alexandrine lines and long single-rhymed stanzas, and the lively English poem, which has fifteen hundred brief lines of two accents, so that it is about seven times shorter than the other. Its adventures are hardly less numerous, but the descriptions introduced on the slightest pretext have disappeared. Thomas never loses an opportunity to describe, whether holidays, feasts, ceremonies, fights, persons, or clothes, and he fully analyses sentimental feelings. But his pictures and his analyses are alike conventional in type, and it is only because of the courtliness and refinement which he shares with all his school that the English poem awakens any regret for their tedium. There is much more go and energy in the English *Horn*. When we hear it, we do not feel that we are listening to a trouvère with his poetical recipes and his ready-made developments of a situation. In spite of its improbabilities, the balder story comes nearer to the frank, manly tone of the epic.

Horn, the son of the king of Suddene, is a child when his father is slain by the Saracens, who land on the coast and waste the country. But Horn is so handsome that the Saracens cannot make up their minds to kill him, and with twelve other noble boys they put him on board a ship without sails or oars. The current bears these children, safe and sound, to the land of Ailmar, king of Westernesse. Under this king's care Horn is well treated and taught, and wins love from every one, but especially from Rymenhilde, the king's daughter, who gives herself to him. When their love is discovered, Horn is banished from the kingdom by Ailmar. He asks the girl to wait seven years for him, after which time she may, if he has not returned to her, marry another. She gives him a ring which is to remind him of his love and endow him with strength to withstand every trial. The seven years are filled with adventures and prowess. At their expiry, Ailmar compels his daughter to accept the hand of Madi, king of Reynes. Horn, whom she warns, hastens to the palace and reaches it on the wedding-day. He enters, disguised as a pilgrim, and his face smeared with black, so that he is not recognized, but is taken by every one for a beggar. The bride is beside herself with grief and disfigured by tears, but she goes through the rites of a wedding-day. The scene of her recognition of her lover gives an idea of the swiftness and simple pathos of this poem. When she omits to pour out wine or ale for the supposed pilgrim, he asks her for a drink, because 'beggars are thirsty,' and while she is serving him he alludes obscurely to the past, turning her heart to ice since she fancies him a messenger sent to announce her lover's death to her. For some time he encourages her in this mistake, even giving her, as a last memorial of him she had loved, the gold ring which had been her own present. Thereupon she exclaims:

> 'Heart, now thou burst,
> For Horn hast thou no more
> That thee hath pained so sore.'
> She fell on her bed,
> There her knife is hid,
> To slay therewith her loathed king
> And herself, both,
> On that same night,
> If Horn come not might.

To heart knife she set,
But Horn anon her let,
His shirt-lap he can take,
And wiped away that black,
That was on his neck,
And said, 'Queen, so dear,
I am Horn, thine own.
Nor canst thou me not know.
I am Horn of Westernesse,
In arms thou me kiss.'

There are no subtle analyses in *Horn*, but it has what is better, the undisguised voice of passion.

Havelok, and even more *Horn*, show how much borrowing from French chivalrous poetry went on at this time, and how original English poetry was beginning to be, even when it borrowed.   There is the same mixture of imitation and independence in the other poetic forms acclimatized in the same period.   As early as the middle of the thirteenth century, a curious poem was written in eighteen hundred octosyllabic lines, *The Owl and the Nightingale*.[1]   It is one of the *disputoisons* or tensons, held in so much honour by the poets of Provence and France, an allegorical debate between an owl and a nightingale who discuss the rival merits of their song.   Finally they decide to submit the dispute to 'Maister Nichole of Guldeforde. . . .   He wuneth at Porteshom, at one tune in Dorsete. . . .' The solution is proposed by the nightingale and accepted by the owl, who knows that if, in his youth, Master Nichole loved the nightingale and 'other wighte gente and smale' overmuch, he has grown older and wiser.   Master Nichole has often been cited as author of the poem, but since it praises him he was more probably the author's friend.

This poem is older than *Havelok* and *Horn* by half a century. It is the first work in English which is written correctly and under French influence, and which, therefore, shows that the foreign form had been so assimilated as to allow native words to be fitted to it pleasantly as well as exactly.   It is true that it does not attain to beauty: it has a stiffness, as of a language not yet supple, and it is weighted by many tedious passages and repetitions.   But the style is lucid, there are lively touches, and an attempt is made to use rhyme for emphasizing points and outline.

[1] Ed. J. W. H. Atkins (with translation, Cambridge, 1922); J. E. Wells (Belles Lettres Series, Boston, revised ed. 1909).

The scene is well set: the picture of the flowery hedge in which the nightingale sings, and of the ancient, ivy-grown trunk on which sits the owl, is clear. The opponents are made to join issue cleverly. Later the fable does indeed unmask itself rather too completely. The adversaries evince a litigious acrimony, more appropriate to the law-courts than the woods. They are veritable litigants and forget too easily that they are birds. It is soon evident that the nightingale, with his voice 'of harpe and pipe,' stands for careless youth, the owl, with his mournful cry, for the wisdom of old age. Both are pious, but while the nightingale hymns a rapturous piety, thinking to win heaven with songs, the owl insists on the need for gravity, self-examination, and good works. The poet is inclined to side with the owl, but on the whole his dramatic impartiality is sufficiently indicated, and Master Nichole's verdict is left doubtful.

Although it has less lightness and charm, is harsher and heavier and more carefully moral, *The Owl and the Nightingale* is very like some pages of old French poetry. But this time it seems that we are concerned with an original work. The markedly iambic line, much accentuated and made up almost entirely of monosyllables, tends to diverge from the French while it imitates it. The metrical line is more robust and less fluent than its French models, more beset with consonants and poorer in vowels.

This poem, in the middle of the thirteenth century, was isolated, but in the early years of the next century the various forms of a poetry no longer exclusively religious or chivalrous were multiplied. With the fourteenth century the satirical spirit entered English in adaptations of the fabliaux, some of them so lively that they herald Chaucer. Such is the fable of *Dame Siriz, or the Weeping Bitch*,[1] in which a self-styled witch, a true Macette, favours a clerk's love-suit to a merchant's wife. The burgher woman is unmoved until the witch appears before her, leading a little bitch to whom she has given pepper and mustard to make it weep, and whom she declares to be her own daughter, metamorphosed for having rejected the advances of a clerk. Clerks are, she says, redoubtable persons. And the frightened burgher's wife thereupon lets her lover have his will of her.

Here disrespect for morals knows no restraint. Nor does it in the *Roman de Renart*; and it is with same mocking spirit

[1] G. H. McKnight, *Middle English Humorous Tales in Verse* (Boston, 1913).

and pleasure in beholding the tricks of the unscrupulous that a poet relates, in *The Fox and the Wolf*,[1] the amusing cunning of a fox who falls carelessly into a well, and induces the wolf, after due confession and sermon, to pull him out and take his place there. Here, indeed, only language shows that poet and public are not French.

We have the same impression when we read the few extant songs of the period. Some, dating from the reign of Edward I (1172–1307),[2] far surpass in lyrical charm the verses we have examined, and their inspiration and form are entirely French. They have the French way of evoking pictures of spring and flowering gardens, and these clichés take the place of the sombre, northern suggestions of the Anglo-Saxons. But the literary novelty of the language can lend to this poetry a sincerity and pathos which are absent from the outworn and conventional French verses of the same age. Thus, in the graceful song *Alison*, a refrain on the French model supports a stanza of mixed three- and four-accented lines, which has skilfully arranged rhymes, some of them repeated as often as five times:

> An hendy[3] hap ichabbe y-hent,[4]
> Ichot[5] from hevene it is me sent,
> From alle wymmen my love is lent,[6]
> And lyht[7] on Alisoun.

In the song *Springtime* the misery of passion is portrayed. The lover sees joy everywhere around him, in the sky, among the birds, among the very worms—'worms woo under clods'— among lovers who secretly whisper, and among women 'who wax wonder proud, so well it will them seem.' But for lack of the only love he desires, he 'this joy-weal will forgo, and in the wood be banished.'

Elsewhere freer and more native rhythms give out a yet more spontaneous note:

Sumer is icumen in.	Summer is come in.
Lhude sing cuccu.	Loudly sing cuckoo,
Groweth sed and bloweth med,	Groweth seed and bloweth mead,
And springth the wde nu.	And springeth the wood new.
Sing cuccu.	Sing cuckoo.

---

[1] G. H. McKnight, *Middle English Humorous Tales in Verse*. Translation by J. L. Weston in *The Chief Middle English Poets* (Boston, 1914).
[2] E. K. Chambers and F. Sidgwick, *Early English Lyrics* (1907).
[3] Gracious.   [4] I have caught.
[5] I wot.   [6] Given away.
[7] Alighted.

Awe bleteth after lomb,	Ewe bleateth after lamb,
Lhouth after calve cu.	Loweth after calf the cow.
Bulluc sterteth, bucke verteth,	Bullock starteth, buck verteth,
Murie sing cuccu.	Merry sing cuckoo.
Cuccu, cuccu.	Cuckoo, cuckoo.
Wel singes thu, cuccu,	Well singest thou, cuckoo,
Ne swike thu naver nu.	Nor cease thou ever now.

We quote also the simple refrain of a poem of courtly love which has otherwise nothing of the popular:

> Blow, northern wind,
> Send thou me my sweeting,
> Blow, northern wind, blow, blow, blow!

Folk-songs of this type reappear only at the end of the six-teenth century, for they were long overlaid by a more formalist poetry. But at this time the numerous and exact descriptive touches bear witness to a more marked feeling for nature than is perceptible in most of the contemporary French songs.

But it is perhaps in the political songs,[1] made from the middle of the thirteenth century onwards, that the native genius shows itself most unmistakably. Elsewhere imitation is the rule and themes are borrowed wholesale from foreign sources. But the political songs are inspired by events within the country; they express aspirations, anger, loves, and hates which are specially English. At first, it is true, they were written in Latin or French: they originated with the clerks and were meant for the ruling class. But very soon the min-strels began to compose them for the people, and therefore in English. It is noteworthy that the earliest of these satires appeared during the Barons' War, when the nobles ranged themselves about Simon de Montfort to give royalty check. The whole English people were moved by this great quarrel, and the support of the popular or Anglo-Saxon element was indispensable to the audacious campaign of the rebel peers. In 1264 a song on the battle of Lewes ridiculed Richard of Cornwall, the brother of King Henry III:

> Richard that thou be ever trichard,
> Trichen shalt thou never more.

Presently the voice of social satire was heard in the land. In tones that are harsh and often coarse, which must have been echoed by common men up and down the country, the vices of the nobles, the State, and the clergy were denounced. Song

[1] T. Wright, *Political Songs of England from the Reign of John to Edward II* (Camden Society, 1839); *Political Poems and Songs . . . Edward III to Richard III* (Rolls Series, 1859–61).

sided with the people against their governors, for instance in the *Song of the Husbandman*, which complains of the burden of taxes and the oppression of bailiff and woodward. Song rose even against the king when he was tyrannous and, like Edward II, dissolved his parliament to save his favourite. The repetition of rhymes at short intervals crystallized in the memory some rough truths which served as rallying cries to the multitude:

> For might is right,
> Light is night,
> And fight is flight,
> For might is right, the land is lawless,
> For light is night, the land is loreless,
> For fight is flight, the land is nameless.

Another poet anticipated Langland in his denunciation of all the vices of society: the law, the Church, the priest, the friars mendicant—all had been alike corrupted by love of money:

> And if the rich man die that was of any might,
> Then will the Friars for the corpse fight,
> It is not all for the calf that cow loweth,
> But it is for the green grass that in the meadow groweth,
> > So good.

The Knights Hospitallers were no better, nor were the nobles, the physicians, the traders, the bakers. The honest and pious poet is indignant against every kind of fraud.

It was easy for this entirely national poetry to become patriotic. The English attentively followed foreign events. France was now their enemy, and there was great rejoicing when the news came, in 1302, of the defeat of the French chivalry by the burghers of Flanders:

> Listen, lordings, both young and old,
> Of the Frenchmen that were so proud and bold,
> How the Flemish men bought them and sold,
> > Upon a Wednesday,
> Better them were at home in their land,
> Than for to seek Flemings by the sea strand,
> Wherethrough many a French wife wringeth her hand,
> > And singeth, Welladay!

When the English were drawn into the struggle directly, patriotism became exalted, and burst, in the first and victorious period of the reign of Edward III, into songs of triumph. A northerner, Laurence Minot,[1] came forward as official bard to

[1] J. Hall, *The Poems of Laurence Minot*, 3rd ed. revised (Oxford, 1914).

the king, to sing his victories in Scotland, Flanders, and France. Thus he celebrated, soon after the events, Halidon Hill, the naval battle of Sluys, the siege of Calais, and other royal exploits.

The heavy and pitiless irony heaped on the vanquished in these war-songs recalls the Anglo-Saxon verses. Yet with the triumph there is a certain gaiety which, although in doubtful taste, moderates that fierceness which belonged to the old poetry.

Edward and his soldiers are incomparable heroes; all their enemies are braggarts and cowards, false and perjured traitors. But justice is surely not to be expected in poetry of this kind, to which it is unessential and of which it might diminish the effect. Such religious sentiment as mingles, here and there, with the insults, has a purely conventional air, and, if it be sincere, its sincerity is superficial.

In the absence of depth, we might hope to come upon the exact or picturesque details about the various fights which would give substance to the poems without hampering their lyrical swing. But there are none such. There is hardly place for narrative in these songs: they do little more than chant the praises of the victors and cover the vanquished with insults.

All the same, they are interesting. They bear witness to the national unity and to the high self-esteem which the English nation had acquired. These trumpet-calls are a prelude to the rich literature of the next generation. We see the English avenging themselves on the Scots for Bannockburn. We see the lilies trampled underfoot, France humiliated, who had been so proud, so sure of herself, so disdainful.

It is the metrical form of Minot's songs which gives them their special value. They are written in the Northumbrian dialect and combine popular and artistic elements. Alliteration reigns everywhere, vigorously holding together verses which, none the less, are always rhymed. Sometimes the line seems to be the direct product of the old alliterative line, its rhyme being superadded. The rhyme and the very regular stanza, with its fixed form, derive from France. As often as not, moreover, the line is not purely accentual, but also as syllabic as the most correct specimens of the time. Conscious artistry is also shown in the frequency with which the most important word in the first line of a stanza echoes that in the last line of the preceding one.

All this makes of each poem a whole which owes much to deliberate arrangement, and, incontestably, the combined effect of these artifices of rhythm and structure is that Minot's poems have an impetus, a beguiling lyrical movement, not due to their thought. Nor does it proceed from their language, which is conventional, without images, and frequently prosaic, and which abounds with padding and platitudes.

The great victories of Edward III were being sung in London, and Minot's poems were current in the countryside when Chaucer was born and when his mind received its first impressions. Glory in the field of battle was followed by literary achievement as brilliant. The long period of dependence was about to end. The English language, which had hitherto conned what others said, often stammering the while, now had faith in its destiny. Nothing is more striking than the number, the originality, and the worth of the works which made the latter half of the fourteenth century a flowering season in English literature.

This brilliant efflorescence was the result of the progress made in the two previous centuries. Their arduous and obscure task was gradually to merge the so disparate elements of the new language in a harmonious whole. Whoever listens to the poetry attentively at first perceives discords and then becomes aware of the progress realized. So far, it is only by flashes that beauty is reached, but already the principles which should regulate style and verse have been discovered. The place of the old epic verse-form is not yet filled, for it has not found a fit successor either in the too slender octosyllabic line, or in the line of fourteen syllables, which is only seemingly long, since it is divided into sections $(8+6)$, but which is, for this reason, too staccato in its movement. Some poets, however, have already been able to tell their tales fluently, or to sing with some grace or warmth of feeling in short-lined verse. This English, with its popular tendencies, is still deficient in courtliness and art, but nothing remains to prevent it from acquiring these qualities as well as others, for it is on the eve of becoming the language of the court as well as that of the countryman and the burgher. As yet nothing is finished, but everything is ready.[1]

[1] *Middle English Metrical Romances*, ed. by French and Hale (New York, 1930); and G. Kane, *Middle English Literature, A Critical Study of the Romances, the Religious Lyrics, 'Piers Plowman,'* 1951; Arthur K. Moore, *The Secular Lyric in Middle English* (Lexington, Ky., 1951).

BOOK II

THE FOURTEENTH AND FIFTEENTH CENTURIES (1350-1516)—FROM CHAUCER TO THE RENASCENCE

CHAPTER I

THE FOURTEENTH CENTURY (1350–1400)—ROUND ABOUT CHAUCER [1]

1. *England in the Second Half of the Fourteenth Century. Political and Social Conditions.*—The victories of Edward III made England conscious of her strength and unity, but, with the exception of Minot's mediocre songs, they did not inspire the nascent literature. It is remarkable that almost all the works which are the glory of the second half of the fourteenth century appeared in the unhappy years between 1360 and 1400 which followed on the triumphant period.

It was in these years, after the treaty of Brétigny, that the political wisdom of Charles V won back for France almost all the English conquests, that the king, grown senile and luxurious, caused men to forget his exploits, and that his heir, the Black Prince, met with an early death. In these years also, the child Richard II began his reign, which was one of the most unfortunate England has known, whether during the period of the regency, with its miserable rivalries, or during that of the king's personal rule, capricious, arbitrary, disorderly, and spendthrift. The Black Death wasted the people; the Kentish peasants made their formidable rising under Wat Tyler; French descents insulted English land; and Wyclif incited the religious schism which divided the population into the two parties of the Lollards and the orthodox. Yet it was during these seemingly calamitous years that the poetry which is truly English had its first season of flowering. Lamentations, satire, and denunciation fill the works which treat of politics or religion. Clergy and

---

[1] Kenneth Sisam, *Fourteenth Century Verse and Prose* (Oxford, 1921).

rulers are represented as equally corrupt and incapable, immoral and undisciplined.

Nevertheless this poetry, as a whole, has such an air of energy and youth as throws doubt on the importance to daily life of the apparent realities of history.   It has to be acknowledged that, disasters and visitations notwithstanding, everyday life pursued its course confidently, eagerly, even merrily. In spite of them, the country became more and more prosperous, the burgher class grew wealthy, and the people enjoyed a measure of independence as the Norman and English races came to be almost completely fused.   In spite of everything, Merry England was born.   There were inevitable miseries, but they left ample room for joy and hope. The light of heart loved frank feasting, mirth, and holidays; the austere sighed over the world's sins, yet did not lose courage, but set themselves strenuously to reform abuses.   Social conditions were unstable, and the news of a passionate revolt could make men tremble, but the rebels were individuals who had ceased to bend beneath the yoke, and had thrown off oppression and inertia.   They were judging, blaming, criticizing, jeering, growing angry.   They had attained to free thought and free speech.

2. *Prose from 1350 to 1400.   Trevisa, Mandeville, Chaucer, Wyclif.*—The state of society is better understood after a glance at the prose literature of this time.   Its bulk is so small and its literary quality so slight that it is hardly of value except as giving information about the period.   English prose took form with a slowness which is striking in comparison with the activity of France and Italy and the value of their productions in this sphere.   Villehardouin and Joinville were writing even in the thirteenth century, and France now boasted of Froissart, Chaucer's contemporary, while Italy had Boccaccio.   Meanwhile in England, where there was no dearth of talented men, the rivals of the continental chroniclers still used Latin as their medium.   Thus the learned and intelligent Higden wrote his *Polychronicon* in Latin before 1363, and Walsingham of St. Albans, towards the end of the century, compiled in Latin chronicles which match the pages of Froissart in their spiritual descriptions of scenes.

English was still a disinherited tongue, used for translations. A Gloucestershire parish priest, John of Trevisa, undertook to translate Higden's *Polychronicon*, and completed this enterprise in 1387.[1]   He does not always understand the easy

[1] C. Babington and J. R. Lumby, *Polychronicon Ranulphi Higden*, 9 vols. (Rolls Series, 1865–86; contains the Latin text and Trevisa's translation).

Latin of his original, and his awkward prose, in the archaic dialect of the south-west, is to-day chiefly interesting because his own additions show the changes which had come to England in the quarter of a century between himself and Higden.

Higden had given a striking picture of the variety of the languages and dialects spoken in England. He had deplored that southern and northern Englishmen were hardly comprehensible to each other. He had attributed the corruption of the English language to the circumstance that French alone was taught in the schools and used in translating Latin, so that the sons of nobles were trained in French from their cradles, and men of lowlier birth turned, from snobbish motives, all their energy to learning French.

But Trevisa assures us that all this, which was true in Higden's day, had been altered in 1385. For some eight years English had replaced French in the schools:

Here avauntage is [he adds characteristically] in oon side and dis-avauntage in another side; here avauntage is that they lerneth her gramer in lasse tyme than children were i-woned to doo; disavauntage is that now children of gramer scole conneth na more French than can hir lift heele, and that is harme for hem and [if] they schulle passe the see and travaille in straunge landes and in many other places. Also gentil men haveth now moche i-left for to teche here children Frensche.

This abandonment of French, which was necessary to the growth of the language, showed its effects on prose literature only at a later time. For the moment English was used for nothing more venturesome than translations, either from French or from Latin.

The prose differs very much according to which of these two languages is that of the translator's original. As a rule, the style of the translations from French is markedly the more lucid and fluent, because of the great degree of identity which had come to exist between the syntax and construction of French and of English.

This is apparent if Trevisa's work be compared to *The Travels of Sir John Mandeville*,[1] which was believed, until recently, to be an original work, and of which the authenticity and the authorship have successively given rise to long controversies.

It is now established that this pretended narrative of

[1] *The Buke of John Mandeville*, ed. by Warner with the French text (Rox-burghe Club, 1889); *The Travels of Sir John Mandeville*, modernized version, ed. Pollard, 1900. See also p. 128.

jo.irneys to Palestine and China is a fiction of the type produced
by Defoe and Swift at the beginning of the eighteenth century.

It relates that in 1322 Sir John Mandeville, an English knight
of St. Albans, left his country to travel in the East, whence he
returned after thirty-four years, in 1356. Then, as an old,
melancholy, and gouty man, he told the tale of the extraordinary things he had seen on his road. In fact, this Sir John
had never existed, but was the creature of the imagination
of a French physician, Jean de Bourgogne, who amused himself by recounting these adventures in French, and was able,
thanks to the credulity of the age and his own apparent artlessness, to pass them off as more genuine than the matter of
Marco Polo. It is curious that this literature based on a
hoax, which was to root itself so deeply in England, first
appeared in France.

The book, with its imaginary English hero, was naturally
well received in England. Translated in 1377, it had a great
success, and the manuscripts of the translation are very
numerous. It was a work which evoked countless fantastic
scenes—countries where men were fed only on serpents and
hissed like them, countries of dog-headed men, or of men with
feet so large that they held them over their heads as sunshades.
The author himself confesses that had such things been told
him he would not have believed them. He goes on his way,
heaping together, pell-mell, true travellers' tales, bestiaries,
the scientific anecdotes of Pliny the Elder. The true and the
false are closely intermingled.

Owing to his simple, effortless, and slightly childish style,
his English translation had a happy effect on the development
of prose literature.

Chaucer's prose writings are, in point of bulk, an important
part of his work.[1] But they have little of the originality shown
in his verses. He too is no more than a translator when he
writes prose. He translated from Latin to English, about the
year 1381, the *Consolation* of Boethius, which, together with
the *Roman de la Rose*, was his habitual reading. Of the two
prose stories in his *Canterbury Tales*, one 'The Tale of Melibeus,'
which purports to be told by himself, is borrowed from Jean
de Meun, who had translated it from the *Liber Consolationis
et Consilii* of the judge Albertano of Brescia (1246), while the
other, 'The Parson's Tale,' is in part translated from the
famous French sermon of Friar Laurence, *La Somme des*

[1] *The Student's Chaucer*, ed. Skeat (Oxford).

Vices et des Vertus. Chaucer also brought together several Latin treatises in his *Astrolabe*, a work intended to teach astrology to his son Lewis, then ten years old.

On the whole, Chaucer's prose conforms to the rule already stated: it is the more English for being translated from French, the stiffer for being translated from Latin. Everywhere, however, it has the qualities which mark a good writer. It would be easy to quote pages in which it attains to loftiness, as when Philosophy appears to Boethius in his prison, or passages showing precision and swiftness, like those which enumerate the misfortunes of poor Melibeus.

Except for his Boethius, in which he happily followed Alfred, Chaucer's choice of originals is regrettable. Their scholastic character hides the beauties of form which distinguish his style from that of his contemporaries. Chaucer was not, however, so much under the influence of the schoolmen that he failed to see where they were ridiculous. He would have us read his prose tales, especially 'Melibeus,' with a smile which makes them less dry and stiff.

All these are prose-writers who were translators. We have still to speak of a man who was by turns a translator and an original writer in prose, an author of mediocre prose who gave to English prose literature an impulse and an efficacy which were decisive. This was John Wyclif, called the first Protestant, the adversary of the papacy and the assailant of Catholic dogma.[1]

He was born about 1324, was a professor at Oxford and chaplain to Edward III, and was very learned in theology and in Roman and English law. He was drawn into that struggle between the king of England and the pope which was at once political and religious, and which broke out in 1365.

The prestige of the papacy had suffered by its defeat at the hands of Philip the Fair at the beginning of the century, and by the removal to Avignon. France had set the example of revolt against the financial claims of the Church of Rome. England followed, when Urban V demanded of Edward III arrears for thirty years of the tribute which John Lackland had promised to pay to his predecessor. An anonymous pamphlet defended Urban's claim, and Wyclif was charged

---

[1] *Select English Works of John Wyclif*, 3 vols., ed. Arnold (Oxford, 1869–71); *English Works of Wyclif, hitherto unprinted*, ed. Matthew (Early English Text Society, 1880). See H. B. Workman, *John Wyclif. A Study of the English Medieval Church*, 2 vols. (Oxford, 1926).

or took upon himself to answer it. He had already the spirit of independence and the confidence in individual logic, as applied to the scriptural text, which characterize Protestantism. But he began with moderation, claiming merely to echo the national hostility to Urban's demands. Gradually the quarrel grew heated and enlarged its scope. Wyclif attacked the ecclesiastical hierarchy and the papal supremacy, and since the court supported him weakly, he appealed to the people. Hitherto, down to 1380, he had written in Latin, but he now wrote in English. With the help of others he translated the Bible, and at the same time he popularized his ideas by means of the preachers who were called 'poor priests,' and were soon to be known as Lollards. Educated but poor men, clothed in coarse woollen garments, they went from parish to parish, opposing the friars against whom Wyclif had declared war. Their severe and practical sermons were in contrast to the scholastic grandiloquence of the friars.

From 1380 onwards Wyclif's ideas, hardly different till then from those already enunciated by Langland or a little later hinted by Chaucer, had a new direction. They became an attack on dogma, for he renounced belief in the Eucharist except as a symbol, and attacked devotion to the saints and the use of indulgences.

He was forsaken by all his former friends. The Peasants' Revolt of 1381 had frightened the nobles and the burghers and brought traditional and conservative ideas back into favour, and Wyclif's doctrines were condemned by the Archbishop of Canterbury and by Oxford University. He was not, however, personally molested, and he ended his life in peace in 1384, in his cure of Lutterworth in Leicestershire.

There is no disputing his social importance in the latter half of the fourteenth century. As a writer of prose he also, in two ways, played a considerable part.

He was, to begin with, the first translator of the Bible into the vulgar tongue. He translated the New Testament, while Hereford, his coadjutor, translated the Old. Undoubtedly his translation is very faulty, for his aim was to be literal, and he had a long habit of writing Latin and found it difficult to attain, late in life, to true English prose. He abounds in Latin constructions, makes too much use of relative clauses. Nevertheless he supplied the first elements of that biblical language which was to be an integral part of English and to be used for the famous Authorized Version of 1611.

Secondly, Wyclif first appealed directly to the nation by such leaflets and pamphlets as were to swarm in the days of the real Reformation. If Wyclif in these writings shows himself destitute of every artistic quality, he yet deserves recognition for the logic and the vigour with which he posed in them certain formulas.

The agitation which his doctrine and writings stirred into being must always be kept in mind when the literature of the end of the fifteenth century is studied.

3. *The Dialects. The Reappearance in the West of Alliterative Verse.*—It is poetry and not prose which is the glory of this age. The pith of the matter was there, rich and vital. But there was an obstacle to the birth of a literary era which should be harmonious and complete. For if classes were beginning to draw closer together and races to intermingle, the language of the country could not yet be said to have reached unity. The period is perhaps that in which the diversity of the dialects of England can best be perceived. Leaving on one side the small difference of speech which distinguished almost every county from another, there were at least four dialects which were struggling for supremacy, so equally matched that it was impossible in 1380 to say which of them would have the greatest future—the northern, southern, east midland, and west midland dialects. Each had its own literature, and the awakening in the fourteenth century had at first the effect of enriching all four together, so that confusion did not lessen but was intensified. The study of the literature of this century is therefore necessarily fragmentary. The critic first perceives that progress in the north, and more especially in the west, had been far slower than in the rest of the country. It is plain, even if vocabulary and grammar be left out of account, that these districts remained attached to the forms of the past. They kept their taste for alliteration, and at least one of them retained, surprisingly, the alliterative verse-form, almost pure and still vital, able to make a final struggle for life.

Since the Norman Conquest, alliterative verse had led a subterranean existence, showing itself, here and there, even in the south, at the beginning of the thirteenth century, then lost to sight, to reappear, abundant and flourishing, in the west of England about the middle of the fourteenth century. On the Welsh border and further north, in Lancashire and Cumberland, it prospered especially, as was natural since the Welsh March was the part of England least accessible to French influence. This district was also the most backward, the last to be settled by the Saxons and by the Normans, and that in which artistic culture had been most retarded by the unceasing warfare with the Welsh.   The author of *William and the Werwolf* pleads his lack of art and genius to excuse his use of the alliterative rather than the octosyllabic line.

The provincialism of a backward district does not, however, by itself explain the return to this old verse-form.   It was due also to the failure of the new versification to fill the place of the old epic verse.   Chaucer had not yet imported from France the decasyllabic or heroic line which was to take precedence of all others.   The prevalent short and slight rhythms could not satisfy men in whose ears the last echoes of the epic verse of their ancestors were still ringing.

Moreover, the versification derived from France lacked an assured prosody.   Accent hovered, doubtfully, over the different syllables of words of French origin, and even Germanic words were infected by the uncertainty.   The relation between rhythm and tonic accent was, in consequence, not clearly perceived.   There were thus various reasons why the old verse-form should came back to life at the moment when the spirit of the nation was reborn.

The consequences of the return to the old form were that the poetry of the west regained an epic swing, resumed the use of the epithets and synonyms necessary to alliteration, revived many archaisms, and, finally, restored the Teutonic elements of the language to the first place.   This archaism, which was also provincialism, was to consign poems of this date, many of them remarkable, to a long oblivion.   As examples of the difficulty of this local poetry, verses can be quoted which are to-day as strange to read and as hard to understand as a line of *Beowulf*:

> Schon schene upon schaft schelkene blode.
> (Shone sheen upon the shaft the warriors' blood.)

Nevertheless these alliterative poets do not, like some nineteenth-century poets, submit their vocabulary to the criterion of the exclusively Germanic.   None of them makes it a rule to banish words of foreign derivation.   The new language had so penetrated the people, even of remote districts, that statisticians find almost as many French and Latin words in the alliterative poems as in Chaucer.   But these words have been more Anglicized: their spelling has grown English for the reason that the alliterative poets are generally less literate than the others, and use words not as they read them but as they hear them. Accent, in particular, gives an English character to the words of foreign root, for the initial tonic accent necessary to alliteration is imposed on them, instead of the final accent which was theirs originally and which rhyme emphasizes and preserves.

Yet it must not be thought that versification in these districts was unaffected by continental influences. If much verse was written, with even artificial correctness, on the Anglo-Saxon model, rejecting rhyme and excluding the stanza, there are also poems, like those of Laurence Minot, which are both rhymed and alliterative, and in which the lines are grouped either in irregular stanzas not unlike the *laisses* of the early French trouvères, sometimes followed by a short-line refrain, or in completely regular stanzas which observe the most minute rules of the fixed form of French poetry.

There is also a curious contrast between the form and the subject of these verses. The Cædmonian line is revived for poems of chivalry, or allegories inspired by the *Roman de la Rose*, or descriptions of customs which are plainly of a younger age. But this form, even when it is an imitation, has the advantage of giving the English poets an independence they often lack when they have recourse to a metre copied from the French. The originality is chiefly perceptible in details of style. Moreover, these alliterative poems, being really provincial, often have a roughness which is of the people, a harsh flavour of the soil, so that, for good or for evil, they are very distinct from the poetry of the court.

The earliest in date of the alliterative poems is a fragment of a romance of the Holy Grail called *Joseph of Arimathie*.[1] It is based on a French story in prose which it condenses. It acquires a certain originality from its vigour of language, particularly noticeable, as in Anglo-Saxon poems, in the narratives of war and battle. Two fragments have been preserved of a romance called *Alexander*,[2] which is connected with the romances of the ancient cycle.

The romance of *William of Palerne* or *William and the Werwolf*[3] has reached us in a complete state and its exact

[1] Ed. by Skeat for the Early English Text Society (xliv).
[2] Ed. by Skeat for the Early English Text Society (extra series, xxxi, xlvii).
[3] Ed. by Skeat for the Early English Text Society (extra series, i).   Extracts in Morris and Skeat, *Specimens*, vol. ii.

date is known. This translation of the French romance of the same name appeared in 1355. It is a real fairy-tale, its hero a prince of Spain changed into a wolf by his stepmother, but retaining, in this fierce shape, his kindly nature. The translator follows the story faithfully but not slavishly, for he makes cuts and additions, adding chiefly some pretty descriptions of nature and some artless homely details which redeem the rusticity of the language and the awkwardness of the construction. The alliterative verse is of very correct structure, and keeps its native vigour, although neither the beauty nor the harmony of the best of the old models. Here, more than elsewhere, the general defect of this verse-form in the fourteenth century is perceptible. The lack of rhyme is felt in the strongly rhythmic line. It is as though a hammer fell heavily on an anvil not of iron, but of wood, and gave out a dull and disappointing sound.

4. *'Sir Gawayn and the Grene Knyght.'* *'Pearl.'*—The four alliterative poems contained in a single manuscript and entitled *Pearl, Purity, Patience,* and *Sir Gawayn and the Grene Knyght* are much superior to those we have examined. In spite of their profound differences of subject and form, these poems have analogies of language and feeling which cause them usually to be attributed to the same poet. The dialect is that of Lancashire, the probable date round 1360–70. The author is unknown, and attempts to identify him with the Scottish poet Huchown of the Awle Ryale, who wrote a *Morte Arthur* and the *Pistil of Susan,*[1] or with the philosopher Strode, Chaucer's enigmatic friend, are no more than conjectural. If, however, it be admitted that there is question only of one poet, his works give some indications of the probable course of his life and cast of his mind. He was well versed both in the Bible and in profane poetry. He was familiar with castles, banquetings, hunts, and tournaments. He knew courtly society and he knew the country, even the wild and solitary country of the western hills. His life had periods of worldliness and periods of devout religious observance, but he was never careless of moral edification. The praise of purity and chastity is the dominant note of each of his poems. His only secular work is *Sir Gawayne and the Grene Knyght,*[2]

[1] G. Neilson, *Huchown of the Awle Ryale,* 1902.
[2] Ed. by Tolkien and Gordon (Oxford, 1936); translations into modern English by E. J. B. Kirtlan, 1912, J. L. Weston, *Romance, Vision and Satire* (Boston, 1912), Neilson and Webster, *Chief British Poets* (Boston, 1916). See G. L. Kittredge, *A Study of Gawain and the Green Knight,* 1916; G. Paris, *Histoire littéraire de la France,* vol. xxx. See p. 128.

which owes much to all the earlier Arthurian romances, and especially to the *Perceval* of Chrestien de Troyes. But its special subject, the singular adventure which is its theme, are known only through this author. There is no reason why the 'stiff and strong' work to which he alludes as his source should not have existed. Anyhow, by his choice of incidents, his pictures and descriptions, and the grouping and proportioning of the parts which make a whole, he proves himself an experienced artist.

Strange is the entry of the Green Knight, a giant on a giant horse, into the great hall of Camelot, where King Arthur is keeping Christmas among the knights of the Round Table. He has come to try Arthur's knights. He will allow his head to be stricken by the great axe he holds in his hand, if the striker will swear to come in a twelvemonth and a day and receive a like stroke from him. As they all are hesitating, and Arthur, for the honour of the Round Table, is about to take up the challenge, Gawain claims the axe and severs the head of the unknown knight from his body. Unmoved, the giant picks up his head, calls upon Gawain to keep his word, and departs at a gallop, leaving all amazed.

When the year has passed, Gawain sets out, according to his promise, to find the Green Knight. Long is his quest through rugged, mountainous country. At last, on Christmas Eve, he finds himself before the comeliest castle he has ever beheld, and is very honourably received there. For three days he is the guest of a noble old man, who is master of the house, and of his wife, who is fairer even than Guinevere. Every morning the old man goes off hunting, and every morning the lady visits Gawain's chamber to tempt him with the offer of her love. The courtly but pure Gawain resists temptation, yet accepts from the amorous lady a girdle of green silk 'with gold schaped,' which shall preserve him from being slain. And when, thereafter, Gawain comes to his ordeal, the axe, falling on his head, does no more than cut his skin, in expiation of his fault in taking the girdle. Eventually his host proves to be the Green Knight, and his temptress Morgayn la Fay, who had undertaken to humiliate Arthur and his knights. Gawain returns to Camelot, and Arthur causes a band of bright green to be worn by each of the lords and ladies of his court for Gawain's sake.

This very well-written poem is remarkable for the liveliness and variety of its scenes. There is delicate psychology in the scenes of the temptation, and the theme, the triumph of chastity, is lightened by a smile. The poet gracefully delineates the feelings of the gallant knight, mirror of courtesy, caught between his politeness and his desire to remain pure, all of whose virtue is preserved to him without a slur upon his gentleness. The story has many analogies with the tale of the second book of the *Faerie Queene*, but both in human and in dramatic interest it is superior to Spenser. Gawain is really tempted, whereas Sir Guyon is temperance incarnate, and passes, bloodless and abstract, through the voluptuousness of the Bower of Bliss. The author of *Gawayne* draws a man where Spenser draws insensate virtue.

There is also realistic vigour in the description of the three successive hunts. The details are taken from life, and nothing is left out of the stag-hunt, not even the making of the quarry and breaking of the deer. Love of the open air and a feeling for nature are perhaps the most distinctive characteristics of this poem. It has two stanzas which, before Tennyson, describe the year's cycle. The seasons succeed each other, and for Gawain their flight brings ever nearer the hour of his redoubtable tryst: the cold and gloomy winter gives place to the fructifying showers of spring; the birds sing and the flowers blow; then summer ripens the crops and hardens the grain, and finally the leaves fall and the grass is grey.

The poet is never more at his ease or more original than when he is describing rough weather and a rugged landscape. Here instinct leads him to join hands with the scops. It is the mournful scenery of *Beowulf* which rises all around Gawain as he makes his way to the green chapel. He has marvellous fights with beasts and men, but they are as nothing to the assaults of winter:

> For werre [1] wrathed [2] hym not so much, that wynter was wors,
> When the colde cler water fro the cloudes schadden,[3]
> Ner [4] slayn wyth the slete he sleped in his yrnes,[5]
> No nygtes then in-noghe [6] in naked rokkes,
> Ther as claterande fro the crest the colde borne [7] rennes,
> And henged hege [8] over his hede in hard ysse-ikkles.[9]

Elsewhere he passes through a mountain forest, with enormous oaks, whitened by the snow:

> With roge raged [10] mosse rayled ay-where,
> With mony bryddes unblythe upon bare twyges,
> That pitosly ther piped for pyne of the colde.

---

[1] War.   [2] Irked.   [3] Shed.   [4] Near.   [5] Armour.
[6] Enough.   [7] Burn.   [8] High.   [9] Icicles.   [10] Rough ragged.

He has a striking vision of a misty morning in the hills—
'each hill had a hat and a mist-cloak huge.'

Thus the Anglo-Saxon mist enwraps this poem of Celtic
origin, a poem of chivalry and courtesy which has for hero, not
the Gawain whom a tradition, followed by Tennyson, made into
the type of a quarrelsome, frivolous, and volatile knight, but
Gawain of the unstained shield, who rivalled the valour of
Lancelot and the chastity of Perceval and Galahad.

Pearl[1] is a poem entirely different in origin, structure, and
atmosphere. It is an allegory which connects not with the
Arthurian cycle, but with the *Roman de la Rose*. The author
is not unacquainted with this poem, although since he speaks
of the '*pure* rose of Clopinel,' that is of Jean de Meun, his
knowledge of its conclusion seems to be faulty. The allegorical element of his work is combined with a symbolism directly
derived from the Apocalypse, whence he borrows his concluding
vision of the New Jerusalem. This mixture constitutes the
originality of the poem, and saves it from the dry formula
of the prevailing type of allegory, with its too conventional
frame. It acquires singular greatness and religious fervour
from its biblical inspiration. There is nothing in English
poetry of this period which better recalls Dante's mystic
visions or the refinements of feeling in Petrarch's sonnets.

The poet has lost his pearl, by which he means his daughter,
a child two years old who was doubtless called Margaret, for
such plays on words, originating in the Gospels, were frequent
among medieval theologians. He has lost her in a garden;
she has passed through the grass into the ground, which means
that she lies in the churchyard in her grave. Ever since,
mourning and weeping, he has often gone to the place where
she disappeared, and his grief has thus been somewhat allayed.

On an August day he goes to this garden, and in spite of the
flowers and scents which make it delightful, he groans and
wrings his hands, then lies down on the flowery ground and
sinks into a dream which transports his soul into the realm of
the marvellous.

He is carried to a glorious country bathed in unimaginable
light, where the rocks are of crystal, the woods have leaves
which shine like burnished silver, and pearls of the Orient are
the gravel. He advances, to the sound of the joyous songs of

---

[1] Ed. by C. G. Osgood, 1906; by I Gollancz, with translation, 1907; by E. V.
Gordon, 1953. See W. H. Schofield, *Symbolism, Allegory and Autobiography
in the Pearl*, Pub. of the Modern Lang. Assoc. of America, 1909.

birds with flaming plumage, until he comes to a river with
beryl banks and a bed of pebbles which are precious stones:

> As glint through glass they glimmer'd and glow'd,
> As streaming stars, when dalesmen sleep,
> In the welkin shine, on a winter night.

It seems to him that Paradise must be on the further side,
but he seeks in vain for a bridge or ford by which he can cross.
Then he perceives, on the other bank, a child 'full debonair'
and robed in glistening white. He recognizes that he has
seen her already, and of a sudden his heart is filled with ineffable happiness. He can neither speak nor move, and fears
that his least gesture may cause the vision to fade away.
But the child herself rises and comes towards him, 'so smooth,
so small, so sweetly slight.' Her white garments are bordered
with precious stones; on her head there is a crown of white
pearls; and a marvellous and flawless stone is fastened in the
centre of her bosom. He understands that this is the pearl
he has lost for so long. The child reproaches him gently for
calling his pearl lost when she is in the beatitude of paradise.
He would rejoice, were he a 'gentle jeweller.' He must not
seek to reach her; the river between them is crossed only
through death. But she tells him of her celestial life, her
bliss as the spouse of the Lord. Is not the Kingdom of
Heaven for little children? Her innocence has ensured eternal
life to him. She is of the hundred and forty and four thousand
virgins whom Saint John saw on the mount in New Jerusalem,
clothed in their wedding garments.

The child cannot lead her father to the city of the blessed,
but the Lamb has vouchsafed her the right to give him a sight
thereof. She guides him towards the source of the river,
while they walk on opposite banks, and he sees the city as the
Apocalypse describes it, the white-robed procession of singing
virgins, clothed in pearls, the Lamb in their midst, and the
angels round about them. Then in the radiant host he perceives his little queen and would run to her, but the effort
awakens him, and he finds himself once more in the churchyard, his head upon the grave-mound, dismayed and sighing
but resigned to God's will. He cries that it is better thus,
that he cannot wish to see his Pearl again, for she is better
where she is.

The extent to which the poem borrows from the Apocalypse lessens its originality, the desire to edify overweights it,

here and there, with didactic and theological passages, and the descriptions might be called too flamboyant. None the less, there is no other allegory of the time which unites so much fervour with such beauty. When compared with *Pearl*, the most charming of the contemporary allegories, the story of the daisy, who is Chaucer's Queen Alcestis, is frivolous, for all its refinement and delicious roguery, and the most powerful of them, *Piers Plowman*, is chaotic and formless. In *Pearl* everything is harmonized to glorify purity, and at the same time a human emotion, the father's grief, in turn rebellious and resigned, gives dramatic movement to the whole poem. Through all that is imitation and through the burdensome weight of doctrine, there shines a rare refinement of feeling. Something exquisite in the poet's senses makes him susceptible to nature even in his moments of most devout mysticism.

Nothing less than this sincere pathos, this wealth of imagination, could have put life into the difficult and complicated stanza which the poet adopts. His highly alliterative line has four accents in a very marked iambic rhythm. The stanza has twelve lines, as rigorously disposed as the lines of a sonnet. It is indeed a sonnet which concludes with two couplets instead of two tercets. Further, the hundred stanzas of the poem are in groups of five, associated because the last line of the first of them recurs in the others like a refrain, so that the final rhyme of the first stanza is repeated five times. And the last word of each stanza recurs at the beginning of the next.

These rules are both strict and puerile, and the fact deserves to be noted because it throws the greater simplicity of Chaucer's versification into relief. Moreover, it is indicative of the tendency to over-refinement which afflicted the author of *Pearl*, in his remote district and with his out-of-date vocabulary.

The two other poems, which are in the same manuscript and are therefore attributed to the same unknown author, *Purity* and *Patience*,[1] are both in alliterative verse and without rhyme or stanzas. *Purity* is an epic narrative of the Fall of the Angels, the Flood, the Angels' Visit to Abraham, the Feast of Belshazzar, and the Fall of Nebuchadnezzar. *Patience* recounts the life of Jonah. In both, purity and submission to the divine will are, as in *Pearl*, the principal themes.

[1] *Purity*, ed. R. J. Menner (Yale University Press, 1920); *Cleanness*, ed. M. Day (1933); *Patience*, ed. H. Bateson (Manchester, 1918). Extracts in Morris and Skeat, *Specimens*, vol. ii.

Although didactic they give much space to pictures, and the ample rhythm and style are in harmony with the grandiose descriptions, such as that of the Flood and that of the raging sea. A suspicion of humour sometimes finds its way into these poems, as when the poet describes Jonah's sojourn in the whale's belly, but on the whole he is both serious and fervent. His epic manner recalls Cynewulf, but has less verbal exuberance and a less fluid melody, a more concrete outline and more weightiness.

5. *William Langland and his 'Piers Plowman.'*—William Langland's *Piers Plowman*, the most popular, if the least artistic, poem, of the fourteenth century, also belongs to the west. It emanates, however, not from Lancashire but from the west midlands, and certain elements of its vocabulary are taken from the dialect of the south. But although the language is more difficult than Chaucer's, it is less outlandish than that of *Gawain*. The verse is purely alliterative: it is quite uncontaminated by French versification and makes no concession to rhyme. On the other hand, the general form of the poem, a vision framing moral allegories, is borrowed from the Continent, so that this work is in the succession of the *Roman de la Rose*.

Yet how much it differs in spirit from the French poem! How national it is! How near the people! Its importance to the historian of morals and religion is such that it has called forth, even from literary critics, an admiration which is excessive in view of the lack in this work of the most elementary art.

That it appeared in three successive versions adds to the difficulty of studying it. There are three texts of very unequal length.[1] The first, the shortest and least formless, dates from 1362, so that it followed close on the treaty of Brétigny and the great plague of 1361. The date of the second text is 1377, the last year of the reign of Edward III, when the Black Prince was dead and the child Richard heir to the throne. The third and considerably enlarged version belongs to the end of the century, between 1395 and 1398, when Richard II had grown unpopular and was arousing the discontent of his

[1] They have been published in 2 vols. by W. W. Skeat (Oxford, 1886). Extracts from Text B in *The Vision of William concerning Piers the Plowman*, ed. W. W. Skeat (Oxford, 1906). Translation by H. W. Wells (New York, 1935). See J. Jusserand, *Les Anglais au moyen âge: l'épopée mystique de William Langland* (Paris, 1893); J. M. Manly, '*Piers the Plowman* and its Sequence,' in *Cambridge History of English Literature*, vol. ii, Chap. I; *The Piers Plowman Controversy* (E.E.T.S., extra issue, 1910); A. Bright, *New Light on Piers Plowman* (1928, important introd. by R. W. Chambers). See also p. 128.

subjects, particularly the London burghers, by his senseless prodigality.

Are these three texts the work of one or of three succeeding authors? Critics have posed the problem and it is still unsolved. The data given by the several texts certainly do not make it easy to construct a consistent life of the poet.

It appears that he was called William Langland, or Langley, and was born in Shropshire about 1330, that is six years after Wyclif and ten before Chaucer. He lived for some time in the Malvern Hills, then, tonsured but only in minor orders, he settled in London, in Cornhill, with his wife Kitte and his daughter Calote, and followed the craft of a public scribe. Certainly he knew the law courts and legal language. We have the picture of a tall, gaunt man with shaven crown, who passed haughtily along the streets, neither greeting the serjeants nor doing reverence to lords and ladies, and whom many took for a madman. Yet he also represents himself, not without irony, as a sort of beggar, going from door to door and pleading his tonsure to excuse himself from working with his hands, earning a livelihood by singing a *Placebo* or a *Dirige* for those who gave him alms.

Whatever his life may have been, his work is that of a man of profoundly religious mind, who is indignant at the vices of a society Christian only in name. He gives first a satirical picture of the actual world, then a vision of the world as it would be if the teaching of the Gospel were truly practised. His poem may be summed up as a work of edification, never artistic in intention and very rarely so in fact.

We have seen that from the middle of the thirteenth century England had the habit of these social satires. The novelty of *Piers Plowman* consists in its ample scale, the relief into which certain realistic scenes are thrown in the course of the allegory, and the author's fervour and energy. His rare comprehension of the political and religious necessities of his time is also new. No less than Wyclif is he convinced of the need for a reform of the secular and regular clergy, although he does not like Wyclif innovate in dogma. He recommends a parliamentary system in which the king, supported by the commons, would govern for the public weal. The boldness and novelty of his thought are, in this century, often astonishing.

The qualities of mind and heart which we feel that he

possessed could not but make his poem by turns vigorous and lofty. He had, too, such rude vital force and hearty irony that the scenes which animate his preaching are most intensely alive and full of movement.

He was, however, entirely without the art of construction or arrangement. He loses himself, and us with him, in his labyrinthine allegories and pictures. Confused even in the earliest version, his plan becomes more complicated and incoherent every time it is retouched, and to sketch the outline of the whole poem is almost impossible. Even to indicate the subject of each of its different parts is difficult.

Disguised as a shepherd, the poet falls asleep one May morning in the Malvern Hills, and has a vision of a vast field full of folk—poor and rich, workers and idlers, nobles and burghers, bad clerks and jesters. The crowd swarms as in a thronged market-place, a contrast to Chaucer's peaceful picture of his pilgrims. It seems to the dreamer that Lady Holychurch appears to him amid this disorder, and tells him that the crowd is busied with things of the earth rather than things of heaven, that man's chief duty is to seek Truth, that Faith without works is nothing worth, that only love, otherwise Charity, leads to heaven.

When the crowd of sinners, now repentant, wish to set out for the sanctuary of Truth, no one knows the road, not even the palmer who has lately visited the most famous shrines. Was there ever a pilgrim who cared about Holy Truth? Then appears the person who names the poems, Piers Plowman. For fifty years he has served Truth by working, and from Conscience and Good Sense he has learnt the road. He offers to lead the pilgrims, first describing the allegorical country through which the way lies. The difficulties cause the most corrupt and cowardly to turn back. Then Piers announces that before he starts he must plough half an acre of land, and while he does this he gives advice to the 'loveli ladies, with youre longe fyngres' to sew chasubles, and obliges every one to follow his example. Those who seek to escape their task are reduced to obedience by Hunger's rough handling. In its first form the poem ends here with the poet's awakening, closing with a peroration on the small value of papal pardons and the greater efficacy, at the Last Judgment, of an upright life.

Within this frame there are, however, two almost detached episodes which are longer than itself and unconnected with each other. They are moralities in narrative form, each possessed of independent and real dramatic merit, and they are proof of close relations with the theatre of the time. They might be called two comedies, 'The Marriage of Lady Meed' and 'The Confession of the Seven Deadly Sins.'

Lady Meed is 'wonderliche clothed,' wearing rings of precious jewellery on all her fingers, and on her head a crown richer than the king's. She is a powerful but dubious personage whose name has been perverted by the evil times to a bad sense. It once meant due retribution but now means bribery. She has a whole retinue of courtiers and flatterers who persuade her to evil. They prepare to wed her to False, and her marriage contract has been duly drawn up, when the opposition of Theology causes the business to be carried to London, to the king's court, where the righteous, by their own courage and the advice of Conscience and Reason, prevail upon the king to break off the marriage, and wreak justice upon the guilty, in spite of the devices of the wicked and their bribery of royal officers. We are given a lively description of the flight of False and his company, who take refuge with the Pardoners, the Merchants, the Minstrels, and the Friars in turn, and are gladly harboured by all of them.

'The Confession of the Seven Deadly Sins' is the sequel to a sermon by Reason, who also invites all sinners to seek 'seint Truth.' It is only the homely realism of his descriptions of the Seven Deadly Sins which is personal to Langland—for these seven are everywhere in medieval literature. Langland, however, makes them not abstractions but living beings, vitalized by the force of comedy and by many details taken from life. Of Covetousness and Gluttony he speaks with peculiar gusto. Abominable though the Sins may be, they are yet all capable of remorse. Repentance prays to God for all the kneeling sinners.

And have reuthe on thise ribaudes that repente hem here sore,
That evere thei wratthed [1] the in this worlde in worde, thouȝte or dedes.

The poem, which was already crowded, was more than doubled in length when it was rewritten for the last time. In the second text already were added a number of visions, grouped by the poet under three titles, graduated so that they hold out the hope of a clear arrangement. Having shown the ills and vices of actual life, he produces a triple vision, 'Do Well,' 'Do Bet,' and 'Do Best.' Unfortunately the benefit of the

[1] Angered.

implied classification does not go beyond the titles. Elsewhere all is disorder, incoherence, chaos. Moreover, the sequel lacks the lively scenes which form the attraction of the first part. The last version of the poem, the only one extending to the end, is a preacher's amplification of the earlier text, the work of a Langland grown old, if not of a second or third author. The thought is as vigorous as ever, the tone has loftiness, often a new nobility, but the confusion is such that the work cannot be read continuously, and only a few fine passages stand out from the rest.

As the beginning of the poem recalls the morality plays, so the sequel, which still has a dramatic turn, is often reminiscent of the mysteries. There is an imaginative effort to revivify the great scenes of the religious life. Passus XXI in the third text is a dramatic narrative of the mysteries of the Passion and the Resurrection which gives much space to dialogue, a play with magnified stage directions.

The scene is laid, as in the mysteries, betwixt heaven, earth, and hell. Jews, soldiers, thieves, the multitude who acclaimed Jesus at his entry into Jerusalem: these stand for earth.

Heaven is a dramatization of a verse of the Vulgate: 'Mercy and Truth are met together: Justice and Peace have kissed each other.' These abstractions have become angels, of whom some, severe and implacable, debate with others who are indulgent to human weaknesses, and all finally embrace, signifying thereby that Mercy will triumph over strict Justice.

Finally a loud voice is heard to cry upon hell to open its gates, and Christ, resplendent with light, enters thither in spite of Satan.

These are the loftiest and most lyrical passages of the whole work. Like gems, they would gain by extraction from their matrix.

In this conclusion of the poem, Piers Plowman is not forgotten. He reappears, from time to time, but transfigured, changed to a symbol. Sometimes he seems to be confused with Christ Himself, who also was poor and worked with His hands; sometimes he represents the mass of the faithful. From pilgrim he has become the object of the pilgrimage. Conscience, awakening from long sleep, finally sets forth in quest of him.

Such, in brief, is this powerful and formless work. Whoever

considers its ideas only, must give it high praise. Indignant at the degenerate Christianity of his century, Langland opposed to the practices of his time the essential and neglected virtues, especially work and charity. His attacks on the vices of the clergy are such as were common and current in the Middle Ages. There was a precedent for them in the *Roman de la Rose* with Jean de Meun's Faux Semblant, not to go any farther. It should, however, be noted that the vice against which Langland's satire is especially directed is not Hypocrisy. Sloth and Covetousness are rather the objects of his hatred. His satire, at its liveliest, is accompanied and directed by an intense religious fervour, unknown to Jean de Meun and hardly found in Chaucer. He does not destroy but seeks sincerely to cleanse and rebuild. He is impelled not by the need to free his reason, but by the desire to strengthen and purify the moral life of himself and those about him, and at the same time to rid political and social life of their worst iniquities. This aspiration, together with his choice of a ploughman for his hero, gives him the appearance of a rebel against the aristocratic system and social inequalities. But his real preoccupation is with the Christian life: the poor are nearer to Christ than others, less removed from Him by the vices to which idleness leads. Piers, who is a ploughman, is also the Christian; if he be not Christ Himself, he is at least one of the lowly of mankind, in whom Christ became incarnate and of whom He made His apostles.

As regards the form of his poem, Langland shows himself powerless to build up a harmonious whole, but able to create animated scenes, either comic or deeply pious. The vigorous and frank quality of his verses is striking. But partly because of his archaic versification and partly because of his real lack of art, his verses never thrill the sensibilities as poetry should. He is neither an artist nor a musician. These two deficiencies must modify his reputation, and while his work is of first-rate value to social historians, his literary merit is barely second-rate. In spite of the immense immediate popularity of his poem, he has almost no descendants. He is the last noteworthy writer of alliterative verse. A few imitations in the beginning of the fifteenth century, and, down to the sixteenth, a few sporadic essays which do not seem to derive from him: there was nothing more. English verse acquired fixed forms within his lifetime, not, however, from him but from Chaucer.

6. *Scotland. Barbour's 'Bruce.'* [1]— Meanwhile a change which had occurred in the north-east was fruitful of consequences. Northumbria had long been distinguished by the literature of the Angles, and, after a prolonged silence, had successively produced, in the first half of the fourteenth century, the *Cursor Mundi*, the *Pricke of Conscience* attributed to Richard Rolle of Hampole, and Laurence Minot's war-songs. The dialect spoken south of the Tweed was debased, but between the Tweed and the Firth of Forth it became more than a dialect, the rich and productive national language which was Scots. From the tenth century onwards Scotland constituted a nation made of mixed elements: in the north Scots who had come from Ireland and Picts, Gaelic-speaking peoples without part in literature in English; between the Clyde and the Solway Britons and Saxons whose dialect was akin to that of Lancashire; in the Lothians English-speaking Northumbrians with an infusion of Scandinavians.

It was in the Lothians and the east of Scotland that that variety of literature in English which is Scottish literature developed and flourished, the literature of a people who for long were as much England's enemy as ever the French could be. The Scottish War of Independence from 1286 to 1342 made the Scots conscious of their nationality, and united the men north of the Tweed and the Esk in a hatred of England, which, as Minot's songs prove, the English were not slow to reciprocate.

Scotland had in her recent history heroes to celebrate—Sir William Wallace, the Douglas, Robert the Bruce—and their half-historical, half-legendary exploits seemed to force poetry into existence.

About the middle of the fourteenth century the language of Scotland was hardly distinguishable from the Northumbrian dialect. Its most special characteristic was the effect of a French influence due to the alliance between Edinburgh and Paris which, from the thirteenth century onwards, drew some French courtiers to Scotland and many Scots to France. As words taken directly from France, without passage through England, were adopted into the language, so the spirit of the French versifying chroniclers penetrated the literature more than in England.

The octosyllabic line was most held in honour in Scotland,

---

[1] G. Gregory Smith, *Scottish Literature* (1919); *Specimens of Middle Scots* (1910). Extracts in Morris and Skeat, *Specimens*, vol. ii.

and the general character of the poems shows that historical and practical sense which the Normans brought into literature in English. In its tone and form, Barbour's work is in the succession of all the tribe of rhymed chronicles since Gaimar and Wace. But it was Barbour's fortune to find a national subject of powerful interest. His frank simplicity and ardent patriotism lead us to overlook the almost consistently prosaic character of the thirteen thousand lines of his *Bruce*.

John Barbour, archdeacon of Aberdeen, of whom nothing is known save that he made two journeys to England and two to France, composed a *Siege of Troy* and some lives of the saints, but it is by his *Bruce*,[1] written between 1375 and 1378, that he has earned his place in literature. This poem is to Scotland what the *Chanson de Roland* is to France, the supreme national poem. The difference of the two in date is, however, such that the *Bruce* lacks the epical character of *Roland* and its element of the marvellous, and is a chronicle in verse, very nearly a history, its facts no more transformed than they would be by a patriot historian. It is not an epic but history, and recent history, hardly three-quarters of a century old when it was written, so that the author could get information from living witnesses. It is the work of a man who has investigated happenings and wishes to tell the truth. It was, as he states at the opening of his poem, his opinion that:

> Storys to rede are delitabill,
> Suppos that thai be nocht but fabill;
> Than suld storys that suthfast wer,
> Hawe doubill plesance in herying.
> The fyrst plesance is the carpyng,[2]
> And the tothir the suthfastnes
> That schawys the thing rycht as it wes;
> And suth thyngis that ar likand
> Tyll[3] mannis heryng are plesand.
> Tharfor I wald fayne set my will,
> Giff[4] my wyt mycht suffice thartill,
> To put in wryt a suthfast story,
> That it lest ay and with in memory,
> Swa that na lenth of time it let,
> Na ger[5] it haly be ferget.

---

[1] Ed. by W. W. Skeat for the Early English Text Society. Extracts in Morris and Skeat, *Specimens*, vol. ii.
[2] Telling.   [3] To.   [4] If.   [5] Make.

And Barbour's verses have indeed, by a singular and merited good fortune, become a source for all historians.

At the same time, Barbour is a moralist, and also an artist in so far that he is careful of the general unity of his work. Numerous as are the events about which he rhymes, he has only one hero, Robert the Bruce, the centre of the whole poem, and he intends that one moral idea shall reign over his whole work. The Bruce began his glorious career by a criminal act, by slaying a traitor at the foot of the altar in a place of sanctuary. This is Barbour's opening. The Bruce's heart will therefore not rest in the Holy Land according to his desire: this is the conclusion of the poem.

There is a greater amplitude in the ideas of freedom, patriotism, and independence which animate all these verses.

For the work is one of those in which matter is infinitely more important than manner. The subject in its naked simplicity is more arresting and wonderful than the most romantic imaginings of the Middle Ages. Nothing is more moving than this story of a struggle for independence maintained by a people fewer in number than their oppressors, whose yoke they had already felt, and who had seized their strong places and overrun their country with soldiers.

Deliverance sprang from the lowest depth of misery, when the Bruce took to the open country and for years led the life of a hunted beast, hidden in the mountains and perpetually in danger of capture, escaping by killing his assailants with his own hands, by climbing barefoot over sharp cliffs, by the cunning with which he divined and forestalled the traps laid for him. At last, he fled to the small island of Rathlin, and thence returned at the head of a growing company, which finally, in 1314, won the great victory of Bannockburn over Edward II and secured the independence of Scotland.

Step by step, Barbour follows his hero through the struggle. He does not obtrude himself but leaves facts, which he knows to be more moving than all the rhetoric of poets, to speak for themselves. If he interrupts his narrative, it is to draw from the past lessons useful to the present. He wrote at a time when the glory of Bannockburn had been tarnished by sanguinary defeats. The misfortunes of his country in the first years of the Bruce's career had come of dissensions and of a foolish appeal to the king of England to decide the disputed succession to the Scottish throne, and Barbour would have his countrymen remember this:

> And wys men sayis he is happy,
> That be othir will him chasty,[1]
> For unfayr thingis may fall, perfay,
> Als weill tomorn as yhisterday.

He would have Scotland keep for ever the freedom that is of greater worth 'than all the gold in world that is':

> A! fredome is a noble thing!
> Fredome mays man to haiff liking;
> Fredome all solace to man giffis:
> He levys at es [2] that frely levys.

7. *The Dialect of the East Midlands or King's English. John Gower.*—However important literary production, in the dialects we have reviewed, may have been, no one of them triumphed over the others. Victory fell to the speech of the east midlands, the district of London and the two universities of Oxford and Cambridge, and that in which the king had his residence. For this reason this language has been called the King's English. Its pre-eminence was established once for all in the end of the fourteenth century.

Although to-day this victory seems quite natural, since social forces were already making London the political and social centre, the universities the intellectual centre of the nation, the dialect of the east midlands was perhaps, when it was on the very eve of becoming English like none other, the poorest, the most completely disinherited of literature. Since Anglo-Saxon times, almost all English poetry had been produced apart from it. It could boast of hardly a poem besides the romance of *Havelock* and Robert Manning's *Handlyng Sinne*. Reflection shows that the fact is not astonishing, for it was in the neighbourhood of the court and the universities that the English language was most degraded and existed most precariously, that it was always subordinate either to Latin or to French or rather Anglo-Norman. King, nobles, and clerks despised it. French, long the only tongue of those outside the vulgar herd, had its natural stronghold in this district, and was more tenacious of life here than elsewhere. Men better endowed than their fellows avoided the common language or had recourse to it only for practical ends. Their literary ambitions did not find scope in a tongue which was so meanly prized.

[1] That will chasten himself by (the example) of others.   [2] Ease.

The case of John Gower [1] is very representative of prevalent conditions. He used Latin and French in turn, and reached the point of writing in English only late, probably under the influence of Chaucer's success. The date of his birth is unknown. Was he, as was long believed, some ten years older than Chaucer, or was he his junior? He died eight years after him, in 1408, and was probably his exact contemporary. The work of the two poets grew side by side, and, although Gower is not without merit of his own, he is chiefly valuable because he serves to measure the greatness of his rival.

He was a Kentish man, but this origin had only a slight effect on his language, which is hardly at all different from that of London and the court. He was a gentleman, possibly a clerk who did not take major orders. He was well read, and his library, if the word may be used, seems to have contained much the same French and Latin books as Chaucer's.

Undoubtedly he was once young, for he wrote love ballades in English-French, ballades which lack fire but are not without a certain grace. This was a lover on the courtly model, seeking in vain to touch an unfeeling heart:

> En le douls temps ma fortune est amière,
> Le mois de Maij sest en yverne mué;
> Lurtie truis si jeo la Rose quière,
> Vous êtes franche et jeo suis fort lié. [2]

(*Ballade XXXVII.*)

The third line at least needs translation—

> I find the nettle when I look for the rose—

for its language is not Parisian. He is aware of the fact and excuses himself for it:

> Et si je n'ai du français la faconde,
> Pardonnez-moi que je de ce fors voie, [3]
> Je suis Anglais; si quiers par telle voie [4]
> Être excusé. . . .

The very rhythm of his French verse tends to be Anglicized, to beat time to the iambic measure. In spite of his effort after

[1] Complete works, ed. by G. C. Macaulay (Oxford, 1899–1902); selections from *Vox Clamantis*, ed. by G. C. Macaulay (Oxford, 1903). See C. S. Lewis, *The Allegory of Love*, Chap. V (1936).

[2] In the sweet season my fate is bitter,
The month of May has changed into winter;
I find the nettle when I look for the rose;
You are free whereas I am fast bound.

[3] I go astray.   [4] And therefore I beg.

correctness, Gower proves better than any one else how artificial was this uprooted language, at once learned and corrupt. He reminds us of Chaucer's Prioress:

> And Frensch sche spak ful faire and fetysly,
> After the scole of Stratford attë Bowe,
> For Frensch of Paris was to hire unknowe.

Gower is the last in date of the Anglo-Norman poets. He deserves to rank among them less by a few little love-pieces than by his long poem, or rather his long sermon in verse, which is called *Speculum Meditantis*, or *Miroir de l'Homme*, and has recently been rediscovered. It is a sermon against the immorality of the age, and it justifies Chaucer's epithet of 'moral Gower' which was to cling to his friend's name for ever. This clerk, concerned especially to note and display the vices of his generation, was indeed much more a moralist than a poet. He is without a trace of that joy in life and pleasure in observing it which are so vivid in Chaucer. He compares what he sees with his ideal, that of a pious clerk and a student, finds all abominable, and condemns unreservedly.

Thus it was with his most remarkable work, *Vox Clamantis*, which was inspired by the Peasants' Rising of 1381 and which he elected to write in Latin. It is a very substantial poem which has real historic value, a pendant to *Piers Plowman* written by a member of the wealthy class, by a frightened landlord whose misfortune it was to live in Kent, the county in which the formidable rebellion broke out. Gower's terror gives these verses a strength and emphasis which are lacking in his other work.

This rising under Wat Tyler and Jack Straw began near Gower's land, and more than one of his tenants was doubtless among the rebels. It was during the first years of the minority of Richard II. The impoverishment of the Treasury, the levy of new subsidies for an unfortunate war, and the insolence of the farmers of the taxes had provoked popular anger and rebellion. Several tax-collectors were put to death, and after them lawyers, courtiers, and partisans of the real regent, John of Gaunt, Duke of Lancaster. The number of the rebels increased. One hundred thousand men marched on London, demanding the abolition of serfdom and the reduction of rents. A true social revolution had been let loose in the country, and for a moment the insurgents were masters of London, where they sacked the palaces of the Archbishop of

Canterbury and John of Gaunt. They destroyed but they did not steal: they even hanged a man in their own ranks for theft. Then the king rode out to meet them, and Wat Tyler, while in parley with him, was slain by the mayor. The king procured the dispersal of the rebels by promising redress of their grievances, then revoked his promise, and the rising was ended by cruel repressive measures.

Gower, now in his fifties, was haunted by this rebellion as by a nightmare. His interests were all on the side of the land-lords. He had no sympathy with the popular cause, yet considered the ills of society to be the outcome of social vices which were ruining the state. His alarms and his grievances are voiced in the Latin distichs of *Vox Clamantis*.

The poet first has a vision of a crowd of members of the populace changed into wild beasts and uncurbed by reason— asses, fierce as lions, who will bear no more burdens, oxen who refuse to draw the plough, dogs who bark at huntsmen, cats who have reverted to wildness. A jay, who stands for Wat Tyler, harangues them, to the sound of shouts of 'Down with honour! Perish the law!' and at the tail of their company John Ball, an excommunicate priest, preaches on the text:

> When Adam delved and Eve span,
> Who was then the gentleman?

The swarming mass of people lays Troynovant, or London, waste. Its strength is broken by the death of the jay, but the ship of the state is still adrift and puts in at the island of Disorder. Then a voice from heaven advises Gower to write down what he has seen in his nightmare.

The rest of his poem contains his waking thoughts and is entirely didactic. The misfortunes of the age spring from the general corruption. There are three classes of society, the clerks, the warriors, otherwise knights and nobles, and the third estate, namely the villeins and labourers, the traders and the lawyers. All are riddled with vice. The court is a meeting-place for everything abominable.

The poem ends with a prayer to the young king, Richard II, to bring virtue back to the court, and with an appeal to all men to mend their ways, remembering how short is earthly life. Gower declares his love for his country: he has wished, he says, that men should hear not only what he himself feels to be true, but also the voice of the people, which is often the voice of God.

It is a great pity that this work, into which Gower has put the best of himself, his utmost sincerity of thought, vehemence of satire, and depths of narrow but coherent morality, should have received the dress of a dead language, while on the one occasion when he used the speech of his country he worked against the brain of his temperament and talent, and wrote an entirely artificial poem.

For he did finally make up his mind to write in English, perhaps incited by the growing reputation of Chaucer, who had already produced most of his works and was soon to begin *The Canterbury Tales*. It was about 1383 or 1384 that Gower composed his single English poem, his *Confessio Amantis*, an immense compilation of stories extending to forty thousand octosyllabic lines. He tells us he did it at the bidding of King Richard, who charged him that 'some newë thing I shuldë boke,' and thus he excuses his use of the vulgar tongue:

> And for that fewë men endite
> In oure Englisshe, I thenkë make
> A bok for King Richardës sake.

He has the credit of having sought, a little before Chaucer, a thread on which to string some hundred stories. The idea was not quite new: it had been exemplified in the *Speculum Historiale* of Vincent de Beauvais, the *Gesta Romanorum*, and the *Sept Sages*, to which the *Decameron* would have to be added, were it not clearly unknown to Gower as to Chaucer. The idea was a happy one, but how awkwardly Gower executed it!

He tells us with a sigh that he is going to sing of love, rather than follow his own taste and write a moral book. Love is the last subject he would choose for himself, but something must be conceded to the reader who prefers amusement to wisdom:

> For thilkë cause, if that ye rede,
> I woldë go the middel wey
> And write a boke betwene the twey,
> Somwhat of lust, somwhat of lore.

It happens that Venus, who has little fondness for him, advises him one day in May to make his confession to her priest Genius. The obedient poet goes to the confessional and asks Genius to question him, point by point, thus sounding his conscience in the article of love. Genius consents, but declares that, in order that the confession may be complete, he will be obliged, in the course of the examination, to speak of the different vices.   He will explain each of them by means of a story, so that the lover may know whether or no he have the same guilt on his conscience.   When the confession has ended, Venus mocks this superannuated lover, who decides to withdraw.

The device allows the seven deadly sins, subdivided into many secondary sins, to defile through seven books.   Genius has received a complete scholastic education, but he ceases to excel when he endeavours to adapt his examples to his precepts. To illustrate hypocrisy he tells the tale of the deceiving Trojan Horse.   To show that murder, an effect of anger, is to be condemned, he relates the story of Pyramus and Thisbe: Pyramus kills himself out of despair, which is anger, when he believes that Thisbe has been the lion's victim, and the moral is that nothing should be done in a hurry.   The proof that carelessness is injurious to love is found in the story of Phaeton, who drove his father's chariot carelessly, freezing and burning the earth by turns, so that Phoebus caused him, as a punishment, to fall from the chariot and be drowned.

The connection of these stories with the morality of love is so absurd that, after praising Gower for attempting a unified plan, we are tempted to regret that he did not write his little stories haphazard, without trying to give them a frame.   For as a narrator he is abundant and clear, and since he has read much, he has had no difficulty in finding curious and sometimes attractive stories among his books.   Several of his tales recur in Chaucer, who sometimes preceded and sometimes followed him in selecting them.   Once or twice Gower was inspired by a better original than Chaucer, as when he took the story of the Knight Florent which corresponds to the tale of the Wife of Bath.

This is as much as can be claimed for Gower.   An almost immeasurable distance separates him from Chaucer.   He is doing penance when he obliges himself to treat of love, undertaking a task so ungrateful and so contrary to his nature that he could have discharged it well only with the help of the sense of humour he lacked deplorably.   Like him, Chaucer posed as despised by Venus and ill-used by Cupid, but—not to speak of his unrivalled and unfailing power to awaken sympathy for lovers—his confession of impotence is delightful because it is wrapped in humour.   In Gower, there are, or seem to be, velleities of humour, but they are invariably abortive.   There is too much reality in the awkwardness with which this poet resigns himself to his distasteful subject.   Once and again, a sigh escapes him because he cannot return to the moral teaching natural to him, and these regrets are the sincerest part of his poem.   He is indeed, as Chaucer said, 'moral Gower,' and it is unfortunate that he ever forsook his role.   Venus was right when she told him:

> And tarie thou mi court nomore
> But go ther vertu moral dwelleth,
> Where ben thi bokes, as men telleth,
> Whiche of long time thou hast write.

And we are grateful to Gower for having made the goddess own Chaucer for her true disciple and poet:

> Of dités and songës glad
> The whiche he for my sakë made
> The land fulfilled is over al.

Gower, learned, industrious, and copious, is the typical average poet of his century.   His writings are what Chaucer's might have been without Chaucer's genius.

Additional material on Mandeville (see *ante*, p. 100, n. 1): *Mandeville's Travels*, texts and translations by M. Letts, 1953.   See M. Letts, *Sir John Mandeville, The Man and his Book*, 1949, and J. W. Bennett, *The Rediscovery of Sir John Mandeville* (New York, 1954).

Additional material on *Sir Gawayn and the Grene Knyght* (see *ante*, p. 107): E. Pons, *Sire Gauvain et le Chevalier Vert.* (Translation, with introduction and notes), 1946; and J. Speirs in *Scrutiny*, vol. xvi, 1949.

Additional material on Langland (see *ante*, p. 113): Text A has been edited by Knott and Fowler (Baltimore, 1952).   See E. T. Donaldson, *Piers Plowman, The C Text and its Poet* (New Haven, 1949); D. W. Robertson and B. F. Huppe, *Piers Plowman and Scriptural Tradition* (Princeton, 1951).   Modern rendering by N. Coghill, *Visions from Piers Plowman*, 1949, and by J. F. Goodridge (B text), 1949.

CHAPTER II

GEOFFREY CHAUCER (1340?–1400)[1]

1. *Chaucer best expresses his Century.*—All the writers of this time reveal some aspect of contemporary life and of prevailing feeling and thought. The author of *Pearl* shows us the mysticism of refined minds, Langland the anger which was threatening the abuses of governments and the vices of the clergy, Wyclif the ardour for religious reform which already might amount to Protestantism, Gower the fear aroused in the wealthier class by the Peasant Rising, Barbour the break between the literature of Scotland and of England and the advent of patriotic Scottish poetry. Each had his own plan, his dominant and, on the whole, narrow passion, a character which was local and of his time. Each was enclosed within the limits of a restricted experience, if not within those of a dialect incapable of expansion and without a future.

It is Chaucer's distinction that he turned impartial, eager, and clear-sighted eyes not only on the past, which his books discovered to him, but also on all the society of his time, on foreign countries, and on every class in his own country. His work reflects his century not in fragments, but completely. More than this, he is often able to discern permanent features beneath the garments of a day, to penetrate to the everlasting springs of human action. His truthful pictures of his age and country contain a truth which is of all time and all countries.

[1] Bibliographies: by E. P. Hammond (*Chaucer, a Bibliographical Manual*), New York, 1908; and by D. D. Griffith, Seattle, 1926. Complete editions: *The Oxford Chaucer*, ed. by W. W. Skeat (6 vols. and supplement, Oxford, 1894–7), and *The Student's Chaucer*, ed. by Skeat (1 vol., Oxford, 1895); *The Globe Chaucer*, ed. by A. W. Pollard and others, 1898; *Student's Cambridge Edition*, ed. by F. N. Robinson (Boston and Oxford, 1 vol., 1933). Separate works: *Troilus and Criseyde*, ed. by R. K. Root, 1926; *The Canterbury Tales*, ed. by J. M. Manly, E. Rickert, and others, 8 vols., 1940. See publications of the Chaucer Society from 1868; R. K. Root, *The Poetry of Chaucer* (1906; revised 1922); É. Legouis, *Chaucer* (1910, trans. 1913, revised 1922); G. L. Kittredge, *Chaucer and his Poetry* (Harvard, 1915); L. Cazamian in *The Development of English Humour* (New York, 1930); A. Brusendorff, *The Chaucer Tradition*, 1924; J. L. Lowes, *Geoffrey Chaucer*, 1934; C. S. Lewis, *The Allegory of Love*, 1936; E. Rickert, *Chaucer's World* (a selection of contemporary texts) (New York, 1948); C. Muscatine, *Chaucer and the French Tradition*, 1957; K. Malone, *Chapters on Chaucer* (Baltimore, 1951); J. Speirs, *Chaucer the Maker*, 1951; H. S. Bennett, *Chaucer and the Fifteenth Century*, 1947. For Chaucer's sources, a good introduction is in T. R. Lounsbury, *Studies in Chaucer*, 3 vols. (New York, 1892). For Chaucer's influence, see C. Spurgeon, *Five Hundred Years of Chaucer Criticism* (2 vols., 1914–21; 3 vols., 1925).

He was born in London about 1340, the son of a city wine-merchant, and therefore by birth a member of the burgher class.   At seventeen, however, he was a court page, for whom a pair of red and black breeches was provided.   Two years later he became a soldier, took part in the campaigns of Artois and Picardy, was captured by the enemy, and remained a prisoner until the king paid his ransom.   After his return to England he was attached to the king's person, first as valet and then as squire, but his great patron was John of Gaunt, Duke of Lancaster and son of Edward III.   From the age of about thirty he was charged with diplomatic missions to France, Flanders, and Italy, in succession.   He was granted a pension and also, in 1374, the office of comptroller of the duties and aids on wools, hides, and wine in the port of London.   In this way, as a courtier, he was again brought into touch with the London burghers among whom he had been born.   In 1385 he was released from his office of comptroller, and in the next year he was returned to Parliament as a knight of the shire of Kent.

Lancaster's disgrace supervened, and Chaucer fell on evil days.   He lost his place and part of his pension, but was accorded other favours when the duke returned to power. For a time he was clerk of the king's works at Windsor, and by Edmund Mortimer, Earl of March, he was made forester. He relapsed into poverty, but his fortunes recovered just before his death in 1400, when the son of John of Gaunt usurped the throne as Henry IV.

Thus his life was active and his employments diverse.   He was page, squire, diplomat, and official in turns.   He mingled with courtiers, soldiers, and city burghers and merchants. He had dealings with foreigners in Flanders, France, and Italy. And throughout he remained, for such part of his days as his official duties left free, an impassioned student and untiring reader.

What is most striking in Chaucer is the interest he took in every one of the different worlds through which he passed and all his heterogeneous occupations.   He was at his ease at court, among traders, among clerks, with the people.   To observe was as much his joy as to read.   It is inconceivable that there was an hour of his life whence he did not extract pleasure.   He could bear a heavy burden of work, easily, with the air of an idler whose life is all pleasure.   The literary work he accomplished is considerable in extent, but far more remarkable for the radiance of his sympathy and the length and breadth of his clear vision.

2. *His Part in the Formation of English Poetry.*—We know nothing of the work of artistic preparation which is to be presumed from Chaucer's success in poetry, but it was indubitably intense and long. Genius doubtless accounts for the lengths by which his poetry outdistanced Gower's, but something is due to the persevering will of an artist who gave himself unstintingly to the acquisition of necessary technique. Alone among his contemporaries, Chaucer put art first. He did not seek to direct men, to judge events, to reform morals, or to present a philosophy. Poetry was his only object. Up to the very end, the task he set himself was to write verses which should have charm and life. To realize the immense effort which this involved it is only necessary to remember the state in which he found the versification and the poetic language of his dialect.

It is hardly possible to exaggerate the part he played as creator of English versification. Save the frail octosyllabic line already in use, he had himself to forge all his instruments. He imported the decasyllabic line from France and, under Italian influence, made it pliable. It became the heroic line which was the surpassing vehicle of the great poetry of England. We have seen that the progress of this poetry was barred by the lack of a verse-form at once ample, ductile, noble, and sonorous. Chaucer used the new line alternatively in stanzas and in couplets, the stanza for songs and the couplet for narratives. He cast it in moulds unknown to his country— the roundel, the virelay, the ballade. Out of all his essays two came to dominate: the seven-lined stanza (*ababbcc*), to which his name has since attached, and the couplet. But what fashioning and refashioning, what experiments and doubts, this presupposes! All his youth and part of his maturity must have been mainly dedicated to this labour which, since nearly all his earliest works are lost, cannot be traced.

His immediate choice of his own dialect as the vehicle of his poetry is proof of his decision and of his sure judgment. He did not, like Gower, allow himself to be tempted either by Latin or by French. He risked his whole literary fortune on London English, the King's English, of which it has been said how poor it was. He found it a thing of naught and left it so rich that English poetry had but to add blank verse to it in order to be fully equipped.

Chaucer's first act of faith in the only tongue which was to him a living language, notwithstanding he clearly saw its defects, was to inculcate in it all the delicacy and refinement he perceived in the poetry of France. He disregarded the debased, artificial, and prosaic Anglo-Norman, and went straight to the Continent to seek masters and models.

To wed the vocabulary of his native land to the courtliness of France was his first essential task. He recast English words —that is, surviving words of Teutonic origin and acclimatized words of French origin—in the moulds of the French poets. He expressed in English all the graces and refinements he found in the poetry of France.

Unlike the authors of *The Grene Knyght* and *Piers Plowman*, he definitely broke with the Anglo-Saxon literary tradition. His face was turned to the south, and he took the whole of his ideal from the Continent.

He might be thought unlucky in his time. There never was a period in which French poetry was apparently more frail and destitute than that which intervenes between Rutebeuf and Villon or between the *Roman de la Rose* and Charles d'Orléans. In this poor, meagre, and pretentious garden there was little but artificial flowers to cull. And, because of the accident of date, it was from one of the most debilitated of the French poets, Guillaume de Machaut, that Chaucer took his first lessons. He could learn from him neither animation nor vigour, nor frankness of style, nor strength of feeling and thought. But Machaut was refined, as much a musician as a poet. Although not a great artist he was yet pure artist, and well fitted to give the young Englishman the teaching he needed in the rules of his craft. In France, it was Machaut who chiefly propagated the poems made in fixed forms, the ballades, roundels, *chansons royales*, and it was from him that Chaucer learned to use these forms for his lyrical verses. For his narratives and descriptions he is no less in debt to Machaut's lays. He often also emulates those French pupils of Machaut who were his contemporaries, Eustache Deschamps, Froissart, Otto de Granson. His work is full of details borrowed here and there. He followed with slightly ironic curiosity a tenson on the comparative merits of the Leaf and the Flower. He took part in the symbolic cult of the Marguerite or daisy, which in the second half of this century, out of deference to some great ladies named after that flower, superseded that of the Rose.

Nevertheless, it was above all to the *Roman de la Rose* that he owed his initiation as a poet. At some unknown moment of his life, probably as his youth was ending, he translated the famous *Roman* into English verse. It is not unlikely that he produced the version of which we possess a part, and which is most faithfully and exactly translated. This was excellent practice, calculated to bring discipline into the versification and style of a young poet. If he did not always attain to such fresh colours and sonorous rhymes as Guillaume de Lorris, it is that he was hindered by his interpreter's task and by a language as yet unformed. He was conscious of the fact. He complained that 'ryme in Englisch hath such skarsetë,' and meanwhile he practised to such good purpose that he brought nearer the day when this difficulty disappeared.

The *Roman de la Rose* did more for him than discipline his style. It was the work which had the most comprehensive and constant hold on him. Its double character, due to the difference, amounting to contrast, between the two poets who composed it, did not shock Chaucer as an interruption of unity, but made this work—this Bible of poetry—double attractive to him. According to his mood, he was inspired by Guillaume de Lorris or by Jean de Meun. Guillaume, with his delicate grace and the clarity of his atmosphere of love, caught him first, in his youth. Later it came to pass that the flood of ideas, satire, and classical reminiscences, which rolls through the work of Jean de Meun, was better suited to his need of more solid and humorous nourishment, and this poet began and continued to charm him more than any other, so that he borrowed from him again and again, even for his final masterpiece.

The first effect of the *Roman* was, however, in one sense to pervert his genius while it helped to fashion his style. It led him into the sphere of the allegorical and kept him there for many years. Chaucer's reverence for this poem was such that it delayed the flowering of his dramatic genius, which he neglected until after his journey to Italy. Such prolonged restraint would be more regrettable had he not produced some entirely charming works in the form of allegories, and had his art not gained by the slow process of cultivation and ripening to which it was subject when, as it were, he put himself to school. Only after these trials did he risk the hard enterprise, often so dangerous to formal beauty, of representing life directly.

His debt to France goes beyond the many imitations which can be discovered in his work, the reminiscences of the trouvères in lines, reflections, descriptive touches, opinions, or quips. He owes another debt to France which is vaster, more diffused through his poetry, less easy to apprehend but not less certain. He is no mere recipient of her largess. She has bequeathed to him a whole heritage, not isolated possessions but his very nature. His mind is as French as his name, which is a form of *chaussier*. He is the lineal descendant of the French trouvères, one of them in all but language.

It was not that he gallicized his grammar or vocabulary more than his contemporaries. But this first great literary artist of his country attempted to express in his own language the poetic beauty which he felt in the best French verses and which answered to his urgent instinctive need. This ideal, to which he attained, was the very inverse of that of the scops.

As the reader passes from their works to his, he has again, in striking degree, the impression of dawning clarity which he received when he left Anglo-Saxon for old French poetry. The rarefied, white light shed over Chaucer's work, hardly ever touching the violent colours of more southern poetry, is exactly the same in tone as that which shone for the poets of the Île-de-France. A Frenchman may enter Chaucer's country and be conscious of no change of sky or climate.

Like the French trouvères, Chaucer has a lightness of heart which is not tumultuous but diffused. It is born of his pleasure in life and is revealed by his taste for the well-lit pictures which call up spring, the month of May, flowers, birds, and music. One line, in which he resumes the youth of his Squire, might be the device of all his poetry:

He was as fressh as is the moneth of May.

This line is entirely French, the essence of the earliest French poetry.

The same may be said of his pitch, neither too high nor too low. His voice, too, has a pure, slightly frail quality. He never forces his tone; rather, he sometimes uses a mute. It is an even voice, made to tell a long story without weariness or jar, perhaps not rich or full enough for the highest lyricism, but wont to keep to the middle tones in which meaning is conveyed to the mind most clearly and exactly.

There is the charm of fluent simplicity, complete correspondence of words and thoughts. Chaucer's best verses merely note facts, external details, or characteristics of feeling.

There is constant restraint, alike in expressing emotion and satire. When he touches the pathetic, he stops short of cries and weeping; he tempers his irony with wit, and he provokes smiles rather than unchecked laughter. Everywhere there are undefinable sobriety and good manners which imply that the poet is ruled by intelligence, rather than carried away by passion. In other words, his temperamental and intellectual powers are perfectly balanced.

All these qualities belong, in the same measure, to the old French poets and to Chaucer. His French extraction is proved by his possession of all of them, and by the fact that he goes beyond them only at those rare moments when, under an Italian influence, he rises above both his own nature and French nature. When Chaucer forsakes France he is a little denaturalized.

It should be added that with the virtues of the French trouvères he has the faults from which the best of them are not exempt. Like them, he too often does not condense, is garrulous, often charmingly but yet indisputably. There are times when he lacks the sinew and the pace which an occasion demands, when he dawdles instead of hastening his steps, walks instead of flying. His discreet poetry is near the border-line of prose; it has its awkward, slow, and platitudinous moments. There is padding at which we smile, but which we must recognize for what it is. Again like the old French poets, Chaucer has, however, a good-humoured, artless way with him, which makes all these manifest defects into an additional attraction. Sometimes he even uses them to point his sharpest quip.

These characteristics do not belong only to his youth, but are permanent in him. Chaucer cannot be said to have had a French period. He is always French, although he sometimes gathered riches abroad, as he marvelled at antiquity or at Italy. Fundamentally unchanged, he acquired from the Italians and Latins a certain adventitious diversity, and ended by using his French manner to paint the society of England.

3. *His Lyrical and Allegorical Poems.*—Chaucer seems to have begun his work by composing love lyrics, but nothing remains of his earliest poetry. There are, however, enough of his roundels and ballades, written at a later date in moments

spared from his more ambitious poems, to prove the virtuosity of which he was capable in this field. He was certainly
the equal of the most skilled of his fellows in France, and often
he imported a characteristic of his own into these conventional
forms—his pity, always moved by the sufferings of a woman,
in the *Compleynt of Anelida*, the savour of his homeliness, or
his humour which makes jests against himself. In his *Ballade
of Griselidis*, which is his triumph in the field of lyricism, he
mingles the extreme artifice of a learned craftsman with the
most comic sportiveness. But in these works he merely gives,
as in play, some proofs of his mastery of their style. He turns
from them to that domain of narrative in verse which is
properly his and in which he did almost all his work.

It took him a long time to decide on direct narrative. He
could not at first rid himself of the poetic artifices of the age.
From the time of the *Roman de la Rose* every poem begins with
a dream which leads to an allegory, and for many years Chaucer
let himself be carried along by this current. He accepted the
received formula almost as though it were a necessity, submitted to such restraint without apparent effort, merely
inserting, from time to time, an episode or a detail which
expressed his nature or is the medium of his comments.

The first of his poems which can be dated is *The Boke of the
Duchesse*, written on the death, in 1369, of Blanche of Lancaster, the wife of John of Gaunt, in order to sing her praises
and depict the grief of her husband. This voluminous and
composite funeral monument, astonishing to-day by the
artificial rather than ingenious complexity of its plan, yet
reveals, here and there, the poet's nature. Flowers which are
fair, fresh, and delicate grow abundantly between the stones of
this flamboyant architecture. In the poem Chaucer represents
himself as a lover racked by sleeplessness, reading from the
Metamorphoses the touching story of Ceyx and Alcyone.
When finally he does fall asleep, he dreams that he is present
at a hunt of the Emperor Octavian, and that while endeavour-
ing to follow it he discovers in a wood a handsome knight,
all clothed in black, who is mourning and who describes to
him the charms of his lost and well-beloved wife, and the
ineffable joy he knew during his too brief union with her.

As though to assert its origin, the poem abounds with imitations of the *Roman de la Rose* and Machaut's *Dits*. It is, moreover, an occasional poem, inspired by the desire to please the
Duke of Lancaster by transfiguring his grief. It suffers from

prolixity and makes, at a first reading, an impression of some confusion. Nevertheless, whoever reads it, remembering its date, and compares it with the existing English verse, is struck by the progress it marks. It is the first poem in this language to contain fully artistic passages. The lines which are the farewell of the phantom Ceyx and relate the death of Alcyone are the perfection of simple pathos. Nothing could surpass their harmonious tenderness, their exquisite restraint, and the grace and aptness of their divisions and their rhymes:

> 'And farewel, swete, my worldës blissë!
> I prayë God your sorwë lissë:
> To litel whyl our blissë lasteth.'
> With that hir eyen up she casteth
> And saw nought: 'Ah,' quod she for sorwë,
> And deyd within the thriddë morwë.

Over and over again the allegory gives place to realism. A conversation, on the whole both probable and lively, is held between the poet and the unknown knight, and if this partly dramatic character of the poem be given full value, it will be seen to modify its defects, and even to excuse them by giving them probability. The mourner's prolixity and repetitions and his confused enumeration of his lady's virtues are in place in this sudden outpouring of his feelings. They make the picture appear less circumscribed and didactic. There is a pathetic element in the very exuberance and incoherence of this overflowing sorrow. Already, too, there is a hint of humour in the appearance of the questioner, the poet himself, who figures, on this his first coming into his own poetry, as a man 'of little wit,' slow of understanding, amazed by the spectacle of a strong passion of which the lyricism is beyond him.

Chaucer was again to have recourse to allegory in 1382, when he wished to celebrate the betrothal of Richard II and Anne of Bohemia, this being the probable subject of his *Parlement of Foules*. The frame is even more heavily laden than is that of *The Boke of the Duchesse*, for Chaucer had read much between the dates of the two poems, and had added Latin and Italian models to those he found in France; for instance, Cicero's *Somnium Scipionis* and Boccaccio's *Teseide*. He again represents himself as falling asleep after reading. This time his book is the *Somnium Scipionis*, and it is Scipio in person who appears to him in his dream to lead him to marvellous gardens where Venus has her temple, but where Nature is 'the vicaire of thalmightye lorde.' It is the fourteenth of February, St. Valentine's Day, and Nature enjoins the male birds to choose their mates. She holds in her own hand a female eagle of great beauty who shall, with her own consent, go to the worthiest.

The interest of the poem lies in its variety of moods, its transitions from the lofty to the homely. Nature holds a full parliament: there are the lords, namely, the eagles and other birds of prey, who express the most delicate sentiments ever heard in courts of love, and there are the commons of winged society, the water-fowl, the eaters of worms or grain, who are deaf to chivalrous eloquence and voice coarse and selfish good sense. This diversity of tone gives unexpected dramatic liveliness to the narrative. The comic is allied with the purely romantic, so that in *The Parlement of Foules* there is the germ of that antithesis between the ideal and the real which is the special glory of *The Canterbury Tales*. We are already confronted with a scene in the human comedy, and with the impartiality of this narrator, who has, doubtless, a preference for noble sentiments, but makes it his duty to leave room for other feelings beside them. Even while he chides the material-ists, he is plainly aware of their good sense, and uses them to denounce the slightly forced element in the refinements of courtly love.

The same quality saves and redeems Chaucer's most ambitious effort in the field of allegorical poetry, his *Hous of Fame*, in which he seems to have wished to compete with the *Roman de la Rose*, raising as ample a symbolical structure. His avowed object is to tell of the capricious nature of glory, and the strange fashion in which rumour and news are fabri-cated and spread in the world. To shed light on this theme, he has recourse to all the customary machinery. The action of the poem is introduced with extreme slowness. There is a discussion on the origin and truth of dreams. The god of sleep is duly invoked. At last comes the dream itself; the poet finds himself in the temple of Venus, where he sees the whole story of Aeneas painted on the walls. A golden eagle carries him aloft in a giddy flight to the House of Fame, which is reared in the heavens and accessible to all the sounds of the earth. He meets there all the authors he has read and admired. He sees the goddess herself and is witness of the strange way in which she distributes her favours. Thence he passes to the House of Rumour in order to discover how news is manufactured.

From every side he sees bearers of false and true messages arriving, and his ears are deafened by the din. At this point the poem breaks off suddenly.

Chaucer did not care to finish it, a sure proof that the fiction was not entirely to his taste. He found, as he wrote, that he was incapable of sustaining his part, of persevering in artifice as a good allegory requires. The real made too frequent an appeal to him. He could not maintain his own illusion uninterruptedly. The best passages of the poem are those in which his sense of humour bursts, with a quip, the bubble he has blown in the air. When *The Hous of Fame* arrests our attention to-day, it is that Chaucer is speaking familiarly of himself, of his life 'as an hermyte,' absorbed in reading, who goes home from his work to abstract himself from the world and lose himself in his beloved books, 'tyl fully dasewyd ys [his] looke.'

The passage in which the golden eagle bears him through the air is very characteristic. It is possible that this bird was born of that by which Dante was rapt to the fiery sphere, and that Chaucer had read the *Divina Commedia* immediately before he wrote his poem. He wishes to make it clear that he is not of the race of Dante. The way in which the London burgher follows the great Florentine on his voyage through space is curious. The justice of his self-characterization is delicious: he is, he says, not apt for sublime flights, but he consoles himself with the light scepticism which is of his nature, stating his preference for walking with his feet on the solid earth. He is much afraid that Jupiter intends to 'stellifye' him. For a moment he admires his near view of the Signs of the Zodiac and of the Galaxy or Milky Way, but soon he declares that he is too old to learn the secret of these marvels, and fears to burn his eyes by looking at the stars from so near. Flying is not for him: give him feet, not wings. From the height of the empyrean he is thinking regretfully of the good muddy tracks which plough the road from London to Canterbury.

In this imperfect and characteristic poem, Chaucer, with his intelligent, bantering spirit, strolls through the 'highest heaven of invention.' He refuses, once for all, to give himself wholly to the sublime or to believe profoundly in purely spiritual conceptions.

For analogous reasons, Chaucer did not finish his *Legende of Goode Women* which he wrote about 1385. This, indeed, has nothing of the allegorical except the prologue, and the prologue is charming. It is Chaucer, the conventional poet, at his most graceful and most personal. He has an unstudied expansiveness, tells us again how much he loves the books which hold all the stories, which he leaves only in the month of May to go to the meadows and pay duty to Nature personified in the daisy. It is when he has spent a whole fine day admiring the little flower he so loves, that he dreams at night in his arbour where he 'bad men sholdë me my couchë make.' He sees:

> The God of Love, and in his hande a quene,
> And she was clad in reäl habit grene.

Her head is crowned with a garland of daisies,

> For al the world ryght as a dayësye
> Ycorouned ys with whitë levës lyte,
> So were the flourons of hire coroune white.

Behind the royal couple walk nineteen most noble ladies,

> And trewe of love thise wemen were echoon.

The god finally perceives the poet on his knees before a daisy, and chides him for daring, all unworthy, to approach love's flower. Is he not love's heretic, since he has translated *The Romaunt of the Rose*? Has he not, by depicting Criseyde's unfaithfulness, thrown suspicion on all women? The good queen intercedes for the poet, who has also, she says, written books of pure love and devotion. She asks leave to choose his penance, and decrees that he shall compose a glorious legend of virtuous women, virgins and wives, who were loyal in their lives, and tell also of the knaves who betrayed them. It appears during the course of the prologue that the good queen is Alcestis, that incomparable wife who sacrificed herself in order to give back life to Admetus. We are thus led to see a glorified Anne of Bohemia in this Alcestis, and her young husband, Richard II, in the handsome and irritable god of love. As for the nineteen fair ladies in the train of Alcestis, they are those whose virtue the poet is commanded to celebrate.

Chaucer begins by throwing himself into his task. He always excels at depicting the self-denial and suffering of women in love, and he makes use of ancient sources, especially Ovid's *Heroides*, to write several most pure and touching legends, those of Thisbe, Lucretia, Philomela, and Ariadne, among others. But the same mocking good sense, which prevented him from finishing *The Hous of Fame*, came to whisper irreverently in his ear as he was writing out his legends, to grumble that he should have to enhance the beauty of the deserted women and vilify their seducers. It seemed to him that this was not reality, and even his books revealed to him certain faults in some of the heroines who were the set objects of his praises — Cleopatra, for instance, and Medea. The outcome was that this poem also was not finished. The task imposed by the queen became an intolerable penance, and there is not a doubt that Chaucer was right to leave it for *The Canterbury Tales*. Yet the legends, incomplete as they are, contain exquisite passages, and moreover they did Chaucer the service of taking him away from allegory—only the prologue of this poem is allegorical—and inducing him to tell, after the ancient masters, some imperishable tales of love and grief. Now translating and now adapting, Chaucer was able to give a personal turn to these famous themes. He has not Ovid's brilliant rhetoric, but there is an advantage in the artlessness of his style. He is both less witty and more feeling than his model. This poem is the last he wrote before the *Tales* and it leads to them directly. It is, further, in this poem that Chaucer first used the ten-syllabled rhyming couplet to which he returned in his masterpiece.

4. *Chaucer under Italian Influence. 'The Knight's Tale.' 'Troylus and Criseyde.'*—Taken as a whole, all the poems which have been mentioned are in the French succession. But the three last, written after Chaucer's first journey to Italy in 1372, show numerous traces of the influence of Italian poetry. He was immediately sensitive to the genius of the great Italians whose works he knew at least in part—Dante, Petrarch, and Boccaccio. From them, better than from the too distant poets of antiquity, he learnt to enrich his line which was still a little slight, to find more glowing images and more impassioned themes. The influence which these three poets had on him was, however, very unequal. He was, without doubt, fully conscious of the greatness of Dante, whom he calls the 'gret poet of Itaile,' but he was no less aware of the difference between his own genius and that of the sublime visionary. As we have seen, he banteringly refuses to follow Dante to the regions of the air, and he borrows from him only very sparingly. It is when, in 'The Monk's Tale,' he tells the story of Ugolino, that he comes nearest to emulating him, and then he transforms the terror of the scene so that it becomes touching. Fear does not render Chaucer's Ugolino speechless or leave him dry-eyed when he knows himself condemned to

die by starvation, but the poet compensates by the moving, homely complaints he puts into the mouth of the youngest child who weeps for a little bread. Chaucer was not made, like Dante, to plunge into hell or rise to paradise.

He probably knew Petrarch personally, saw him at Padua, and heard him read his story of Griselda in Latin. He retained high respect for this poet:

> Fraunces Petrark, the laureat poete,
> Hightë this clerk, whose rethoriquë swete
> Enlumynd al Ytail of poetrie.

But Chaucer could not follow in the footsteps of the great humanist, so near to the ancients, so cognizant of philology, so much ahead of his contemporaries on the road of the Renascence. As for Petrarch the sonneteer, his excessive subtlety and his idealism refined to a quintessence could not appeal to a nature as normal as Chaucer's, whose tenderness was never far removed from joviality.

It is significant that Chaucer's only important borrowing from Petrarch is the story of Griselda, a Latin translation of the last of Boccaccio's tales. Boccaccio was assuredly the Italian to have most influence on Chaucer, who, none the less, never mentions his name. Boccaccio provided him with some of his most remarkable stories, and also, almost invariably, with a model for the most splendidly decorated and warmly passionate of his verses. It was, however, only Boccaccio the poet and the compiler of *De Casibus Virorum Illustrium* and *De Claris Mulieribus* whom Chaucer knew. He does not seem ever to have read the *Decameron*, for all that he was to figure to posterity principally as the storyteller who rivalled Boccaccio.

Chaucer's debt to the poems of Boccaccio's youth is especially considerable. He condensed and abridged the *Teseide* to make his 'Knight's Tale,' retelling the story of the rivalry of Palamon and Arcite, two youths who were as brothers, their affection heightened by a shared captivity, until the day when love for the same maiden brought them to face each other as enemies, armed for a fight. Chaucer, adapting freely, was able to extract from the exuberant *Teseide* the romance of sentiment which is buried in those pseudo-epical ten thousand lines. He kept the best of Boccaccio's descriptions, yet introduced homely scenes of his own, and made Theseus into a humorous personage after his own mind.

The most memorable result of his contact with Boccaccio's poetry was, however, *Troylus and Criseyde*,[1] a poem half translated and half adapted from *Il Filostrato*. In this Boccaccio uses a frame borrowed from the *Roman de Troie* of Benoît de Sainte-More to express all his feelings as a lover 'laid low by love' (*filostrato*). In the person of the knight Troilo, he is loved and then betrayed by Cressida, and his love is served by his mistress's young cousin, the sceptical yet disinterested Pandaro, who abounds with worldly wisdom and considers that to aid a passion is a fine and virtuous action.

This burning, harmonious, and swiftly moving poem was retold by Chaucer, who took as many liberties with it as he had done with the story of Palamon and Arcite, but this time enlarged and lengthened his original instead of condensing it. The changes involved are due to a different conception of characters and sentiments. Boccaccio's first object had been to depict passion and voluptuousness, but Chaucer was drawn especially to the study of character. In his poem, the ardent, breathless tale of love is accompanied by a comedy of which Pandarus is the central character, and a very different Pandarus from Boccaccio's Pandaro. Pandarus is not the cousin but the uncle of Criseyde, a man in middle life, familiar in his ways, fond of chaff and inclined to gossip, such a great quoter of proverbs and maxims that he sometimes reminds us of Polonius and sometimes of Sancho Panza, playing, the while, the part of Macette. It is his interminable chatter which constitutes Chaucer's addition of two or three thousand lines to the Italian poem. In consequence, the action of Chaucer's poem is markedly slower than Boccaccio's, but its added element of comedy relaxes that strain of the pathetic which is felt in *Il Filostrato*. Instead of expressing the sentimental, like Boccaccio, Chaucer's aspiration is to reflect life. He lets a livelier air, as from an open window, into the heavy and perfumed atmosphere of the boudoir in which Boccaccio confines us. The most poetic passages of the poem are literal translations from the Italian, for instance the description of the despair of Troylus after the departure of his mistress (Book V, st. 29–98), but all the drollery has been invented by Chaucer. It is strange that Chaucer, faced with a Latin author, deals with him exactly as an English dramatist of the Renascence would have done. He does what Shakespeare was to do again and again. He accepts and preserves, almost

[1] Ed. R. K. Root (Princeton University Press, 1926). See also p. 154.

intact, the tragic elements of his theme and the sentimental beauty of the youthful leading characters, but everywhere he rearranges, transforms or creates anew, the character-studies. Even thus Shakespeare faithfully retells the love of Romeo and Juliet, but develops the characters of the nurse and old Capulet on original lines and creates Mercutio. Whatever force the tragic and sentimental scenes of the English dramatist may have, they are rarely the element in their plays which is most personal to them. It is with the comic that they are especially concerned. Chaucer, by instinct, made a precedent for the great national dramatist who wrote more than two hundred years after him.

Although his *Troylus and Criseyde* does not quite conceal his efforts to reconcile originality and imitation, although it has lost the just and certain proportions of its model, and makes exotic Neapolitan flowers bloom beneath unquiet Kentish skies, it is yet an admirable work, astonishing if its date be remembered, far superior in point of style and versification to anything in contemporary English literature. And from the fact that he felt himself hampered while he wrote it, Chaucer learnt a fruitful lesson. Instead of pursuing further these imitative exercises which left him only half his freedom, he sought a subject which should be truly his own. In his *Troylus* he was half Italian and half English. In his masterpiece he was to be all English.

5. '*The Canterbury Tales*.'—Up to this time Chaucer's work, although he sought inspiration in France and Italy, or rather because he was the too docile pupil of foreign masters, is interesting mainly to the English. He deserves admiration for having civilized his country poetically, but he had spent his strength almost entirely on translating and adapting. He was still no more than the 'great translator' praised by Eustache Deschamps, the word being taken in its wide sense. His part was that of interpreter between the Continent and his country. Who could have hoped that, as he neared his fiftieth year, he would suddenly be revealed as himself a master, the painter of English society, and the creator of a work which in this fourteenth century would leave the contemporary poetry of France far behind it, and even, in some respects, that of Italy also?

The genius which was to flower had been his from the beginning. He did not suddenly become an observer. He had already seen and retained much, although hitherto he had not found among his models a mould in which to cast his observations. Without doubt, there was already that rich diversity in his nature which made him curious of the beautiful and the ugly alike, which was compounded of poetry and prose, piety and scepticism, grace and humour. When, however, he wished to house this complexity, he found only literary forms apt to isolate one or other of its aspects. He had been held by allegory or lyrical narrative when his genius was impelling him, irresistibly, towards dramatic and realistic storytelling, the weaving of a web in which the threads would be both comic and sentimental.

So far, he had brought only two considerable poems to completion, the one a mere translation of the *Roman de la Rose*, the other his adaptation of *Il Filostrato*, a poem whose original harmony he disturbed by his efforts to introduce into it matter of his own. He had begun two other important poems, but had been unable or unwilling to finish them. *The Hous of Fame* discouraged him by the factitiousness of its allegorical machinery and the use, or rather abuse, of personified abstractions which its plan entailed; he wearied of *The Legende of Goode Women*, because it imposed on him a partisanship, obliged him, by its preliminary conditions, to be unfailingly sentimental and partial, and therefore necessarily monotonous. Did he wonder whether he would ever find a more pliable and wider frame, in which he could fit stories as varied as life and mobile as his changing moods, stories in which he could be lyrical and epical by turns, which he could tell tenderly, swiftly, poetically, feelingly, humorously, or merrily?

It was at this moment that he bethought him of the collections of stories of which several had been made in the Middle Ages, on the plan so awkwardly reproduced by his friend Gower in the *Confessio Amantis*. The *Decameron* would undoubtedly have stimulated him further had he not been, to the best of our knowledge, unaware of it. Yet even Boccaccio's example was not such as to fulfil his aim of variety. That society of elegant young gentlemen and ladies, hardly distinct from each other, telling tales while the plague raged in Florence, was not the band of storytellers he wanted. It was strongly individualized narrators, taken from the most diverse classes, whom he wished to interpose between himself and his readers. And at last he had the very simple and yet quite novel idea of a pilgrimage which would unite people of every condition. Since the spring of 1385 he had been living at

Greenwich, on the road of pilgrims from every county in England who were constantly drawn to the shrine of Saint Thomas à Becket at Canterbury. Often and often he had watched the progress of their variegated cavalcades, men and women, knights and burghers, handicraftsmen and clerks, mingled in momentary fellowship. One fine day, moved by devoutness or mere curiosity, he may himself have joined one of these troops. No sooner had he got his idea than the work went of itself. He had but to describe his pilgrims, give each of them his individual characteristics as well as the marks of his rank, then put an appropriate tale into his mouth.

Thus the first requisite was to present a band of storytellers clearly. No enterprise could be more difficult at any time, difficult to-day and more difficult at a date when nothing of the sort had yet been attempted. The simplicity of Chaucer's method, its complete lack of any artifice, the sure hand with which he traced portraits to form the prologue of his *Tales*, are surprising. He made his group of pilgrims into a picture of the society of his time of which the like is not to be found elsewhere. Except for royalty and the nobles on the one hand, and the dregs of the people on the other, two classes whom probability excluded from sharing a pilgrimage, he painted, in brief, almost the whole English nation.

There are thirty of the pilgrims, following the most diverse trades. The Knight with his son, the Squire, and the Yeoman who bore the Squire's arms, represent the fighting class. A Doctor of Physic, a Man of Law, a Clerk of Oxford, and the poet himself, give a glimpse of the liberal professions. The land is represented by a Ploughman, a Miller, a Reeve, and a Franklin; trade by a Merchant and a Shipman; the crafts by a Wife of Bath, a Haberdasher, a Carpenter, a Webbe or Weaver, a Dyer, and a Tapicer; the victuallers by a Maunciple, a Cook, and the Host of the Tabard. The secular clergy provide the good Parson, and the odious Sompnour or summoner of an ecclesiastical court, who are joined on the road by a Canon addicted to alchemy. The monastic orders supply a full contingent—a rich Benedictine Monk, a Prioress with her chaplain Nun, a mendicant Friar; and not far from these religious lurks a doubtfully accredited Pardoner.

Chaucer, desiring distinct outlines, first used the easiest and clearest method of differentiation, which is to contrast various callings. This results—especially in those days did it result—in a whimsical medley of colours and costumes which at once catches the eye, and it allows a whole series of habits and tendencies to be suggested by half a word. Only the generic features, the average characteristics of each calling, have to be marked, in order to give a sufficiently definite picture which has its own identity. Thereafter all that is left to do is to make each person talk as befits his station and nature.

The idea looks so simple that all the noise it has made in the world might be thought exaggerated. It was, however, a novelty. It had no precedent outside obscure corners of a rudimentary drama, and it was to mark a turning-point in European thought. It was more than a literary innovation. It was a change of mental attitude. Poetry turned, with tolerant curiosity, to the study of man and manners. For the first time, the relation between individuals and ideas was clearly realized. Ideas ceased to be an end in themselves, and became interesting as revealing him who expressed them, who believed in them, or who was pleased by them. And they acquired therewith an unforeseen value. The ideas which Chaucer had hitherto given to the world could not be called very original. They were less novel and perhaps less powerful than those, for instance, of Jean de Meun. It would be easier to extract some sort of philosophy from Jean de Meun's works than from Chaucer's. When, however, Chaucer's ideas emanate from a man of a given temperament, represent the prejudices of a class or the routine of a trade, they immediately take on youth or fun, become penetrating and sometimes profound, although they themselves are unchanged. It is that dramatic use is made of them. Their value in isolation or abstraction matters as little as ever, but they are richly significant, because they fall from the lips of a definite person who reveals or betrays himself by their means.

For such an end it is necessary that the author should efface himself voluntarily. Chaucer is fully conscious of the realism to which he obliges himself. He assumes the part of mere interpreter, a chronicler and no more, who relates without altering a word or a tone stories he has heard told. By his grouping of representatives of the different callings, and by his impartiality which allows individuals to speak and never dictates their thoughts or words, he has painted, with minute exactness, the body and soul of the society of his time. He is as truly the social chronicler of England in the late fourteenth century as Froissart is the political and military chronicler of the same period.

Chaucer has collected the descriptions of the pilgrims in his general prologue, which is a true picture-gallery. His twenty-nine travelling companions make almost as many portraits, hung from its walls. They face us, in equidistant frames, on the same plane, all hanging on the line. Chaucer is a primitive, aiming at exactness of feature and correctness of emblem. He is a primitive also by a certain honest awkwardness, the unskilled stiffness of some of his outlines, and such an insistence on minute points as at first provokes a smile. He seems to amass details haphazard, alternates the particulars of a costume with the points of a character, drops the one for the other, picks either up again. Sometimes he interrupts the painting of a pilgrim's character to put colour on his face or his tunic. It is an endearing carelessness, which hides his art and heightens the impression he makes of veracity:

> Ses nonchalances sont ses plus grands artifices.

Who ever enters this gallery is first struck by some patches of brilliant colour, dominating one or other of the portraits, the Squire's gown:

> Embrowded was he, as it were a mede,
> Al ful of fresshë floures, white and reede,

and near him the Yeoman who serves him 'in coote and hood of grene.' How the Prioress's rosary 'of smal coral,' with its decades, 'gauded al with grene,' and its hanging brooch 'of gold ful schene,' stands out against her dress! There are faces as strongly coloured as any of the fabrics or accessories—the pustulous countenance of the Sompnour, 'a fyr-reed cherubynës face,'

> With skallëd browës blak, and pilëd berd,

and the Miller, whose beard 'as any sowe or fox was reed,' with his wart whence sprouts a tuft of red hairs, his wide and black nostrils, and his mouth 'as wyde as was a gret forneys.' There are also duller colours to rest the sight, and to make the cruder hues more brilliant by contrast. The pious and modest Knight was 'nought gay':

> Of fustyan he werede a gepoun,
> Al bysmotered with his habergeoun.

The poor Clerk was 'ful threadbare,' the Man of Law 'rood but hoomly in a medled coote,' the Reeve wore a 'long surcote of pers,' or blue, and the good Parson is drawn without line or colour, so that we are free to imagine him lit only by the light of the Gospel shining from his eyes.

Essential moral characteristics are thrown into relief with the same apparent simplicity and the same real command of means as the colours and the significant articles of clothing. Mere statements of fact, suggestive anecdotes, particulars relating to calling and individual traits, lines of summing up a character—all these make up a whole which stands out upon its canvas. The outline is strong and clear, although sometimes a little stiff, in the steady light which is shed on it, and it is unforgettable.

Chaucer was not content to make his pilgrims typical only of their several callings. Sometimes a classification of another kind crosses with that by trades and enriches it. Thus the Squire stands for youth and the Ploughman for the perfect charity of the humble, while in the Wife of Bath there is the essence of satire against women. Nor is this all. Chaucer, by details he has observed for himself, puts life into conventional descriptions and generalizations made by others. He adds individual to generic features; even when he paints a type he gives the impression that he is painting some one person whom he happens to have met. He mixes these two elements in varying proportions and with great although imperceptible skill. His figures, a little more generalized, would be frozen into symbolism, mere cold abstractions, while a few more purely individual features would cause confusion, destroying landmarks and leading attention astray.

Thus English society, which to the visionary Langland seemed a swarming and confused mass, a mob of men stumbling against each other in the semi-darkness of a nightmare, was distributed by Chaucer among a group which is clearly seen, restricted in size, and representative. Its members pause before us long enough for us to identify each one. Each has his own life and an identity which is for all time, yet together they sum up a society.

Chaucer does not only draw frank or delicately traced portraits which give to his characters the immobility of permanence. He also makes each pilgrim step out of the frame in which he first placed him. The artist does not pass straight from portrait to tale. He does not let us forget, on the road to Canterbury, that each storyteller is a living being who has his own gestures and tones. As the cavalcade pursues its course, the pilgrims talk among themselves. The poet shows them calling to each other, approving each other, above all squabbling. They criticize each other's stories, and so betray their preoccupations, feelings, and interests. In this way a comedy of action goes through the whole poem, connects its different parts, a comedy which is no more than sketched, yet is adequate, in its incompleteness, to reveal the author's intentions and his dramatic vigour. The persons he has painted are again discovered by their own acts and words. As always happens when an analytical portrait gives place to a direct presentment, some of the pilgrims are found to be more complex, their limitations less discernible, their characteristics more numerous, and their outline less definite than had appeared. This is certainly true of the famous Wife of Bath, indubitably the most vigorous of Chaucer's creations, who lives less by her tale than by the immense monologue in which she gives outlet to her feelings as she rides along the road. As she speaks, she seems to be magnified before our eyes, to overflow the exact boundaries which the portraitist set to her personality, and to acquire pantagruelian dimensions. Not until Panurge and Falstaff arrived was there her like in literature. The same is true of the Host of the Tabard, the pilgrims' jovial guide, who is barely sketched in the prologue, but who, little by little and by successive touches, by his various remarks as they journey, is made to tell us much of his temper, his tastes, his dislikes, and his private life. He is all the more real and living for never being analysed.

The tales gave Chaucer one means of finishing the portraits of his pilgrims. He found them in every corner of medieval literature, as diverse and unequal as he could wish. The poet used their lack of originality to impart an added probability to his poem, for his pilgrims are supposed not to invent but to retell stories. Above all, he used the tales to characterize the tellers. He choose for each of them a story suited to his class and character, or, at least, he did this admirably where he had time. His first plan was immense, each of the thirty pilgrims undertaking to tell two tales on the way to Canterbury and two on the way back, so that there would have been one hundred and twenty tales altogether. In fact, Chaucer was not able to allot even one story to each of his travellers, nor, still more regrettably, had he time in every case to adjust story to teller. He was still hesitating about the assignment of certain tales when death surprised him. Enough was, however, accomplished to allow us to appreciate his design and his executive talent.

In a certain number of cases, the tale is so subordinate to

the vast comedy in which it has place that its original form has a little suffered. More often, it is its meaning which is changed. It is possible to consider a story by itself to judge whether the writer has succeeded in his aim of producing the strongest possible impression by his distribution of the parts, his manipulation and unravelling of the plot, and his arrangement of details in view of the surprise of the conclusion. The excellence of a tale then depends simply on the skill with which its thread is followed, and on the grace or liveliness of its writing. But the same story may be told to reveal an alleged narrator. It then behoves the author to conceal himself, to sacrifice his own literary talent and sense of proportion, and give place to another, who may be ignorant, garrulous, clumsy, foolish, or coarse, or moved by enthusiasms and prejudices unshared by his creator. Chaucer follows this principle to most of its consequences in that part of his work to which he was able to put the finishing touches. He very carefully allows more than one of his pilgrims to reveal themselves by introducing into their stories irrelevances, digressions which break the even course of a tale but which give an opening for the information, the discursiveness, or the fads of the speaker. We notice this as we read the tales of the Wife of Bath, the Pardoner, and the Yeoman of the alchemist Canon.

Elsewhere, the very fact that a story is assigned to a particular person is enough without any digressions, as when the tale of Griselda, fount of abnegation, is told by the good idealist Clerk, or when the graceful and mincing Prioress tells the story of the little cleric, devotee of Mary, who was slain by the Jews, or the Nun relates the tale of the miracle of Saint Cecilia, with its conventual atmosphere.

Chaucer goes so far as to give us stories which he invites us to think repellent or ridiculous. The Monk recites a litany of lugubrious and monotonous 'tragedies,' which sadden the Knight's good heart and make the Innkeeper yawn. He is not allowed to tell his funereal beads to the end, and when interrupted relapses into silence. The poet is prevented from finishing the tale of Sir Thopas which he allots to himself. The Host of the Tabard chides him for singing a chivalrous ballad, with rhyme but without reason. In such instances as these, the reader is expected to find his pleasure not in the excellence, but in the very extravagance or tediousness of the stories.

Such tales are deliberately exceptional. In general, the poet's gift of life is revealed within the stories as in the frame of the poem. Chaucer's own contribution is of varying importance. In the serious, strictly poetic part of *The Canterbury Tales*, his original work is very slight: he makes only insignificant additions, restrained in detail, to his borrowed material, and his merit is mainly in his style, which is often admirable for simple pathos and gentle humanity. The comic and realistic stories, which have analogies with the French *fabliaux*, are in very different case. These he has so much enriched that he might be called their creator. He deserves this title, at least in part, even when he is compared to the author of the *Decameron*, who put so much heat and red blood into a literary form usually of the driest. While, however, Boccaccio observed the conciseness proper to this form and did no more than paint manners, Chaucer, less condensed and less passionate, addressed himself more and more to the study of character. He repeats within several of his stories that effort to capture individuality which is the glory of his prologue. Boccaccio is on the road to picaresque fiction, but Chaucer is pointing the way for Molière and Fielding. As we read the *Tales*, especially those of them which are humorous, we have constantly the impression that a birth is in progress. A leaven of observation and truth is fermenting within these established literary forms, which once had a perfection of their own, but which are narrow and about to be discarded. In this travail, modern drama and the modern novel are showing their first signs of life.

6. *Conclusion.*—If all this poet's work be regarded together, he is clearly seen constantly to have advanced nearer truth. He found poetry remote from nature, its essence being fiction in the accepted belief, while its task was the ingenious transposition of reality in accordance with artificial rules. In the beginning Chaucer submitted to the received code, dreamt with his contemporaries, like them had visions of allegorical figures and combined imaginary incidents. Or he sought the matter of his poems in books, borrowing his subjects and characters. Then, by degrees, he reached the point of deeming nothing as interesting and as diverse as Nature herself. Relegating his books to a secondary plane, ridding himself entirely of the allegory and the dream, he looked face to face at the spectacle of men and set himself to reproduce it directly. He made himself the painter of life.

It is well known how dry, morose, and bitter such reproduction of reality can be. It may breed disgust with life and men.

Chaucer, without flattering his model, placed it in an atmosphere which is good to breathe. No one can read him and not be glad to be in the world. Whoever enters through the door he opens feels a healthy air blow on him from all sides. This is partly because Chaucer writes in a dialect still new, uses words which he was the first to put to real literary use. The language breathes a freshness, as when earth is turned in April, such vernal youth as it could never have at another time. Usually this novelty of language coincides with crudity of thought and puerility of art. But Chaucer, who begins English poetry, ends the Middle Ages. It happened that he inherited all the literature of France, rich by three centuries of generous effort, free of speech and fertile of thought, already a little weary because it had produced too much. For Chaucer, a literature in its autumn and a language in its spring combined as they have rarely, if ever, done before or since. He is at once very young and very mature; he unites the charm of a beginning to the experience of long life. When he repeats a description or an idea which has become a little jaded in its native language, he often gives back to it the grace of novelty by the artlessness of his expression. In his highly skilled verses, English words, frozen by a long winter of waiting, first gave forth their fragrance.

To this advantage, due to exceptional circumstances, Chaucer added natural gifts, the first of them the wide sympathy which is otherwise called indulgence. To this especially his poetry owes the soft, lovable, and smiling light which is shed on it. For some of his fellow-men he feels affection or respect; about all the others he has so much curiosity that they interest him. No one is excluded. He is not easily repelled. He loves the world's variety, is grateful to defects for their difference from virtues. He looks at himself without illusions, judges himself without bitterness, is carried away by no desire to excel. He places himself on the average level, and finds all the multitude of men beside him. It is the consciousness of shared failings which makes fellowship among men. Of all writers of genius, Chaucer is the one with whom it is easiest to have a sense of comradeship.

Sympathy of this kind, founded on clear self-knowledge, is a form of intelligence. If it were absolutely necessary to define in a word the novelty of Chaucer's masterpiece, it might be said to show, most of all, the progress of intelligence. It evinces a weakening of the passion which leads to lyricism or satire and is supported by self-confidence and by the energy of desires, hopes, loves, and hates; a weakening also of the imagination which transforms and magnifies reality, projecting it on to another more or less arbitrarily chosen plane, and which produces epical, romantic, or allegorical poems. In *The Canterbury Tales* the element of the poet's personality has been subdued, superseded by pleasure in observing and understanding. Hitherto this degree of peaceful, impartial spectatorship had never been reached by poets. More noble and more essentially poetic works had indeed been written: we have but to name two with different claims to greatness, the *Chanson de Roland* and the *Divina Commedia*. Some of the line of French song-makers, stretching from the twelfth-century romancers to Rutebeuf, and past him to reach its apotheosis, a hundred years after Chaucer, in Villon, were more exquisite than the English poet and sounded more thrilling notes than he, nor did he ever attain to the refinements of feeling and language which Petrarch put into his sonnets. But where, before *The Canterbury Tales*, can we find a poem of which the first object is to show men, neither exalted nor demeaned, to display the truthful spectacle of life at its average? Chaucer sees what is and paints it as he sees it. He effaces himself in order to look at it better.

He is the pioneer of that group of spectators who regard with amused indulgence, without seeking to redip it in dye of one colour, the warp and woof of variously coloured threads which is the chequered stuff of a society. Doubtless he has judged certain colours to be more beautiful than the others, but it is on the contrasts they afford that he has founded both his philosophy of life and the laws of his art.

Additional material: H. G. Wright, *Boccaccio in England from Chaucer to Tennyson* (The Athlone Press, 1957).

CHAPTER III

1. *Chaucer's Imitators and Disciples in England.*—England took two centuries to produce a poet worthy to rank with Chaucer. Nothing better proves his genius than the powerlessness of the succeeding generations to equal or even to understand him, a fact the more striking because all the poets knew him and rendered him homage. When, however, they believe themselves to be imitating him they do no more than follow his inferior work, in which he does not surpass the average level of his time. They leave on one side the poems in which he rose above his contemporaries. Most of them barely reach the plane of Gower. Criticism in the fifteenth and even in the sixteenth century was so incompetent that it constantly placed Chaucer and Gower together, and Lydgate, that retrograde and prolix disciple of Chaucer, beside the two of them.

The years from 1400 to the Renascence were a period disinherited of literature. Several causes of this destitution may be discovered, but none which is satisfying save the fact that no writer of genius was born during these long years. The only excuse for the poverty applies to poetry alone. It is that, in the transition to the analytical modern English which was in course, the last inflections were disappearing. The result was that Chaucer's accurate and sure versification ceased to be understood soon after his death. When the final *e* had become entirely mute, Chaucer's line, badly read and transcribed, and later badly printed, seemed to be variable and irregular, to contain a differing number of syllables and irregularly distributed accents. His successors, whose ear was imperfect, were not offended by this lack of rhythm, but felt that it authorized them to licence in their own verse-making. The English verse-form was thrown off its balance and definitely recovered a sure rhythm only with Spenser.

This cause of decline was one which a harmonious poet would have charmed away, as indeed the poets of Scotland did exorcise it. Other causes of decadence, drawn from history, might be revealed by diligent search. The fatal effects on art

---

[1] See H. S. Bennett, *Chaucer and the XVth Century* (Oxford, 1947). Anthology: *English Verse between Chaucer and Surrey*, ed. by E. P. Hammond, 1927.

of the Wars of the Roses (1454–83) might, for instance, be exaggerated, although this terrible civil conflict covered only a fourth of the vast desert space of time.   Before this war, England under Henry V experienced a time of military glory which recalled and exceeded the victories of Edward III, and the finest works of the fourteenth century had appeared during the deplorable and humiliating reign of Richard II.   But it came to pass that neither triumphs nor disasters could inspire literature.   Miserly Nature created only imitators and reiterators of outworn themes.   The sense of the beautiful seems to have died with the sense of life and of reality.   Contact with the Continent, once so fruitful, could not revive the flagging literary impulse.   Contact hardly existed except with France, herself disabled.   Italy, which Chaucer had revealed, remained forgotten for a whole century.

England suffered not only checked progress, but also retrogression.   Literature resumed its course as though *The Canterbury Tales* had never been written.   The decline was immediate. Its signs appeared even in those who knew Chaucer, were near him and called him master, in Occleve and Lydgate.

Both were aware of his superiority.   It is touching to see how Occleve represents himself as the stupid scholar of an excellent master:

> My derë maister—God his soulë quyte—
> And fader, Chaucer, fayne wold have me taught,
> But I was dulle, and lerned lyte or naught.

Occleve, dull indeed, saw in Chaucer only an all-wise philosopher, a pious poet, almost a saint.   Chaucer's humour escaped him.   Lydgate is more discriminating, for while he agrees with Occleve that no poet was left 'that worthy was his ynkehorne for to holde,' he was conscious of Chaucer's wit, and shows his indulgence, not unmixed with scepticism, for verses submitted to him by his youthful disciples.   But neither Lydgate nor Occleve was capable of continuing Chaucer's work.

Thomas Occleve [1] (1370?–1454?) is the author of a *Letter of Cupid* long ascribed to Chaucer.   It is a translation of the *Épistre du Dieu d'amours* of Christine de Pisan, which was a reply to Jean de Meun's sarcasms against women.   It recalls *The Legende of Goode Women* in theme, but it substitutes reasonings for imagination, humour, and life.

In his *La Male Règle de T. Occleve*, which is a sort of confession, the poet informs us that he led a debauched youth, and

---

[1] *Regement of Princes*, ed. Furnivall (E.E.T.S. extra series, lxxii); *Minor Poems*, ed. Furnivall and Gollancz (ibid., lxi and lxxiii).   Now spelt Hoccleve.

that none was better known than he to the keepers of taverns and cook-shops in Westminster. The story of his irregularities entails some descriptions of London which are historically interesting, although they have no value as poetry.

His principal work is the *De Regimine Principum*, written in 1411–12 to win the favour of the Prince of Wales, afterwards Henry V. It is a series of lessons on conduct, imitated from the Latin work of the same name which the Roman Aegidius wrote for Philip the Fair. Dissertations, historical samples, and tales are used to inculcate the lessons. The whole is clear, fluent, and sufficiently correctly versified, but the intellectual and artistic weakness is reminiscent rather of the didactic Gower than of Chaucer.

John Lydgate [1] (1373?–1450?) has the distinction of being the most voluminous poet of the fourteenth century and even of all the Middle Ages in England. About 140,000 lines of verse, authentically his, are extant. This Benedictine monk of Bury St. Edmunds was principally an indefatigable translator and compiler. His longest poems are *The Storie of Thebes* and *Troye-Book*, which retell the famous romances, *The Falls of Princes*, adapted from the Latin of Boccaccio, *The Temple of Glas*, a heavy allegory of love, *The Pilgrimage of the Life of Man*, translated from Guillaume de Deguileville, and some lives of saints, those of Saint Edmund, Saint Margaret, Our Lady, and others.

Lydgate's retrograde tendency is striking. He reverts in his *Troye-Book* to the original story, whence Boccaccio and Chaucer, in *Il Filostrato* and *Troylus and Criseyde*, had extracted the dramatic essence. He has forgotten that Chaucer took the best of his *Falls of Princes* for his 'Monk's Tale,' and ironically ignored the rest, that Chaucer caused a nun to relate the life of a saint with all its marvels, and thus disclaimed responsibility for it, and that he wearied of the allegory of his *Hous of Fame*, much as it exceeded *The Temple of Glas* in animation and picturesqueness. But no example could stay Lydgate's flow of words.

With Lydgate decomposition overtook English verse. He admits that he 'toke none hede nouther of shorte nor longe,' that is, of accentuated and unaccentuated syllables, a candid confession which excludes the possibility of blaming copyists for the irregularities of his verse.

---

[1] Works published in E.E.T.S. extra series: A. Erdmann, *The Siege of Thebes*, cviii and cxxv; H. Bergen, *The Troy Book*, xcvii, ciii, cvi; idem, *The Fall of Princes*, cxxi–cxxiv; J. Schick, *The Temple of Glass*, lx; Furnivall and Locock, *The Pilgrimage of the Life of Man*, lxxvii, lxxviii, xcii; MacCracken and Sherwood, *Minor Poems*, cvii. See W. F. Schirmer, *John Lydgate* (Tübingen, 1952).

Much read and much admired by his contemporaries, who were grateful to him for telling so many stories, and telling them with a certain briskness, Lydgate has been a long time undisturbed except by courageous specialists. The small number of his verses which are still read are those extracted, as in an anthology, by Warton from his *Lyf of Our Lady*, or a few short pieces, religious and secular, a few fables, and, especially, *London Lickpenny*, which hymns with some liveliness the griefs of a countryman suing for justice in London. Unfortunately, Lydgate's authorship of this, the most popular of the poems ascribed to him, is uncertain.

Here and there, especially in the most Chaucerian of his poems, *The Complaint of the Black Knight*, there are pleasant descriptions, but in spite of them we ask whether this Benedictine ever had time to lift his eyes from his books and papers and look at nature. It is certainly from books that he seems to have taken most of his verses which speak of nature.

Much more attractive than the works of Occleve and Lydgate are certain short poems of which the authors are unknown or uncertainly known, and which were long attributed to Chaucer, so that they are included in many editions of his works.[1] A study of their versification and language has, however, proved that they belong to the fifteenth, a few of them even to the sixteenth, century.

A translation of Alain Chartier's *Belle Dame sans Merci*, made by Sir Richard Ros about 1450, is negligible. It dilutes the French octosyllabic lines into the heroic metre, filling them out with expletives and padding, and the result has no merit but correctness of rhythm. *The Cuckoo and the Nightingale* (1403), now restored to Sir Thomas Clanvowe, who knew Chaucer, is, however, an agreeable poem, gracefully relating an argument between the two birds. Its rhythm is light and rapid, and its well-turned and pure language recalls both the *Parlement of Foules* and the prologue to *The Legende of Goode Women*. It is true that the charm of these three hundred lines is in the detail, for the conception—the debate between love and chastened experience—is not new. It goes back to the thirteenth-century debate between the Owl and the Nightingale.

The prologue of *The Legende of Goode Women* also inspired a charming allegory, *The Flower and the Leaf*, which was modernized by Dryden, who took it for Chaucer's. But

[1] In the seventh volume of Skeat's edition of Chaucer (Oxford, 1897).

Chaucer certainly did not write these disjointed verses, and they are now admitted to be the probable work of an unknown lady of the middle fifteenth century. The author reproduces the debate between the flower and the leaf to which Chaucer made only passing allusion.

The Leaf symbolizes work and the serious and useful life, the Flower frivolous leisure. It is, however, possible to disregard the moral of this poem, and be charmed by the delicious opening descriptions of spring and nature, richer and less restrained than those of Chaucer. There are pretty effects of light and shade in the oak-wood to which the lady who cannot sleep resorts one spring day. There she sees appear, first the ladies and knights of the Leaf, dazzling in their pearls and ornaments or clad in gilded armour, and all crowned with laurel chaplets, who seat themselves beneath an oak. From another side there enter an equally sumptuous company of knights and ladies wearing flowery chaplets, who engage in a merry dance. It is all artificial, but the colour and brilliancy are delightful. A storm supervenes, and the followers of the Flower are drenched, their adornments spoilt. The queen gives them shelter and restores their beauty, and then all disappear.

This poem, like the one noticed before it, marks if not an advance on Chaucer's work, yet a difference from it. It is less substantial, real, and humorous, but it has some added lightness, agility, and airiness, and a new dewy quality. Although the fiction of a dream has been abandoned, the poem is more purely dreamy than its predecessors. This is, assuredly, the most exquisite product of the fifteenth century.

The Court of Love is a less freshly coloured poem, but one which is more mischievously witty, shows greater power of characterization, and has a surer rhythm. It is the one of these poems which might best be claimed for Chaucer, had it not the 'gilded' style which hints at *rhétoriqueurs*. It is, in point of fact, the furthest removed from him in date, recent criticism having ascribed it to the first half of the sixteenth century. The author, who calls himself 'Philogenet, of Cambridge Clerk,' loses his way in the palace of Cytherea, where Admetus and Alcestis are vice-regents. Philabone, a lady of the court, informs him of the rules of the place, and shows him the persons who have obeyed or broken the laws of love. Among the latter are such as have deliberately refused to love and are now tormented by regrets. The poet enters the service of the fair Lady Rosial, who at first treats him harshly, but becomes gracious at the entreaty of Pity. The poem is concluded by a choir of birds, of whom each one intones a beautiful hymn of the Church.

Were this poem not too imitative, and did not 'Philogenet' rather preserve acquired qualities than add to them or transform them, the fifteen hundred lines of this *Court of Love* would redeem the sterility of this impoverished time.

To imitate was then the rule. Langland's imitators matched Chaucer's. As early as the extreme end of the fourteenth century, an unknown author wrote *The Crede of Piers Plowman*,[1] a vigorous satire against friars of all orders. At an unknown date 'The Ploughman's Tale,'[2] which Chaucer had not time to write, was annexed to *The Canterbury Tales*, serving as a vehicle for the grievances of some Lollard. There is a whole series of fairly mediocre poems, alliterative or other, which are evidence of the continued popularity, well into the sixteenth century, of the great fourteenth-century satire.

They occur both before and after the Wars of the Roses. When, after this long period of sanguinary civil conflict which suspended all literary activity, poetry reappears in the reign of the first Tudor sovereign, Henry VII, its languor and weariness and its unrhythmic verse are strangely reminiscent of Occleve and Langland. Yet, when the nausea produced by the repetition of so many old characteristics and old faults has been overcome, it is possible to discern in it vague signs of the coming Renascence.

The mediocre poet Stephen Hawes[3] (1475–1523) illustrates this point. He is yet another of the allegorists, but, while he is too much an echo of the past, he also feebly heralds Spenser. When the Wars of the Roses destroyed almost the whole of English chivalry, they relegated the old chivalrous poetry to a dreamlike past. The attempts to revive it which were made at court did no more than reconstruct an empty show, for the soul of this poetry had gone. It had become imaginative material, almost as unreal as allegorical scenes and personages. In compensation, however, chivalry had acquired the prestige which belongs to the remote, and the melancholy which attaches to regret, both elements of romanticism. It is only this vaguely romantic atmosphere which gives some interest

---

[1] Inserted in W. Skeat's edition of *Piers Plowman* (Oxford, 1906).
[2] In vol. vii of W. Skeat's edition of Chaucer (Oxford, 1897).
[3] *The Example of Vertue*, 1509.   *The Pastime of Pleasure*, ed. Mead (E.E.T.S., 1928).   See V. L. Rubel, *Poetic Diction in the English Renaissance*, 1941.

to the languishing platitudes and uncadenced verses of Hawes. He complains that no one but himself in his generation culti-vated true English poetry. So neglected was it that his king, Henry VII, reverted to an old precedent, and made a French-man, Bernard André of Toulouse, his poet laureate. Hawes, who acknowledged as his masters the trinity Gower, Chaucer, and Lydgate, and especially Lydgate, is like a ghost from the past. He writes allegories according to the formula of the *Roman de la Rose*, and, like Spenser, complicates it by the addition of chivalrous elements. Learned and didactic, he rejects all poetry which does not enclose a lesson.

He anticipates Spenser in that the subject of his principal works is the fashioning of man, by discipline, to an ideal of virtue. In his *Example of Vertue* (1503-4), he relates the allegory of a youth led by Discretion or Reason who finally marries fair Purity, the daughter of the King of Love. So long is the road he travels, so many his obstacles, and so fearful the monsters he must slay, that he is sixty years old when he reaches his goal, and there is nothing better left for him to do than to ascend straight to heaven with his beloved.

Hawes's chief work, *The Pastime of Pleasure*, or *Historie of Graunde Amoure and La Belle Pucel* (1505-6), has a like plan. His aim in it is to exemplify a transcendent education, to show by what degrees of study and prowess perfection can be reached.

Graunde Amoure, the hero of the poem who tells his own story, relates that after falling asleep in a flowery valley he sees the Lady Fame appear to him. She tells that La Belle Pucel dwells in the magic tower of Music, but that giants bar the way thither. After serving a long apprenticeship to Ladies Gram-mar, Logic, and Rhetoric, who constitute the Trivium, and Arithmetic, Music, Geometry, and Astronomy, who are the Quadrivium, and after having slain the giants with his sword Clara Prudence, Graunde Amoure finally attains to La Belle Pucel, marries her, grows old, and dies. Time writes his epitaph in the only lines of Hawes which still live in men's memory:

> For though the daye be never so long,
> At last the belle ringeth to evensong.

In general Hawes's style, sometimes aggrandized by Latinized words, sometimes entangled by awkward constructions, is among the worst known to English poetry. Never did poetry in English sink to lower depths of the prosaic than when Lady Grammar explained the nature of a noun to her pupil. The verses on the garden of Greek roots and on cooking recipes are much better than these.

Barclay and Skelton, the last two writers of verse who are in the medieval tradition, at least show some novelty of subject or manner.

Alexander Barclay [1] (1474–1552), a Dominican, careful of doctrine, morals, and orthodoxy, and a good Latinist, is hardly more than a translator, yet a free translator who adds matter of his own to his original.   He is also the first of his nation to have come across a subject of German origin.   His *Ship of Fools* is a translation made in 1509 from the Strasbourg poet Sebastian Brant, not directly but through the medium of a Latin and a French translation.   This fiction of a ship in which all fools are invited to embark, so that the author is able to review every kind of folly and insanity provided by mankind, had a great success in England, as on the Continent. Barclay did not miss his opportunity of adding some peculiarly English types to the crew.

He was also the first to introduce the eclogue to his fellow-countrymen.   In his youth he had written five eclogues, which he published in 1514, two of them imitations of Mantuanus, who was to be one of the classic Latin authors of the Renascence.   They have nothing of the idyll, but are moral satires, discussions between a townsman and a countryman, between a poor poet and a rich miser, an exposition of the miseries of a courtier's life.

Barclay chose his models well, and he has the merits of sincerity of speech and a realism sometimes racy, but his style lacks ductility, his language is rude, and his verse suffers from the general lack of rhythm.

John Skelton (1460?–1529) [2] is a fantastic personage, hard to classify or define.   As a learned humanist who won praise from Erasmus, an Oxford laureate famous for his Latin verses and known as a grammarian, he belongs to the Renascence. He is very well acquainted with ancient poets and mindful of the mythology of antiquity.   His occupations were serious, for he was tutor to the future Henry VIII and rector of Diss in Norfolk.   But he writes verses like a buffoon, in many

[1] *The Ship of Fools*, ed. T. H. Jamieson, 2 vols., 1874; *Certain Eclogues of Alexander Barclay* (E.E.T.S., 1928), and *The Mirror of Good Manners* (Spenser Society, 1885); C. H. Herford, *Studies in the Literary Relations of England and Germany in the Sixteenth Century*, 1886; *The English Versions of The Ship of Fools*, by A. Pompen (New York, 1925).
[2] *The Poetical Works of John Skelton*, ed. Dyce, 2 vols., 1843.   See also p. 198.

respects like a man behind his times. He is faithful to satirical allegory, and sets fine order and classic nobility and elegance at naught. He found heroic verse debased, and, instead of attempting to reform it, most often abandoned it in favour of a short irregular line and rhymes multiplied until a dozen of them sometimes follow each other. His verses might have been improvised by some untiring tavern poet. He deliberately turns his back on beauty, is fully aware of what he is about, and acknowledges that his only aim is to strike hard and straight:

> Though my rime be ragged,
> Tatter'd and jagged,
> Rudely raine-beaten,
> Rusty and moth-eaten:
> If ye take wel therewith,
> It hath in it some pith.

The pith is mostly satire. In this age of dull repetitions, Skelton pleases because he is brutal and coarse. No one has handled prelates more roughly, not even the Protestants among whom he is not numbered. Of his numerous poems, many of which are lost, the most interesting are *The Bowge of Court*, *The Boke of Colin Clout*, and *Why come ye not to Court?*

The first of these (1509?) is an allegory which recalls *The Ship of Fools*. The poet is on board a magnificent ship which is to take him to the land of Favour, and his voyage is troubled by the intolerable company of Fortune's friends, Favell or Flattery, Suspecte or Suspicion, Disdain, and Dissimulation. They conspire against him, and he is about to throw himself into the sea in order to escape them, when he awakes—all has been a dream. How familiar is every one of these allegorical figures! Yet never, perhaps, have they been as living and as busy as in this poem. Exceptionally it is written in the stanza of seven heroic lines called Chaucerian.

Colin Clout (1519) is a peasant, another Piers Plowman, who like him chastises the vices of the clergy. With disorderly energy Skelton poses as the mouthpiece of popular wrath.

The last of these three poems, written in 1522, is a violent indictment of Cardinal Wolsey, the all-powerful minister of Henry VIII. It includes a stinging description of the terror in which he was held by the noblest of the kingdom.

Although Skelton's habitual tone is satirical, and he uses complacently the coarsest insults and worst indecencies, he yet showed himself capable, on occasion, of feeling and even of a certain grace, as in his *Boke of Philipp Sparowe* (1503–7), an elegy on the death of a sparrow who belonged to fair Jane Scroupe. It echoes the little poem of Catullus, with the difference that the Latin poet's eighteen lines have become 1,382 lines of Skeltonic verse. It is a hotch-potch of reminiscences and buffoonery, alternating with passages full of freshness and charm. There is something of everything in John Skelton, that first rough sketch for Rabelais. Taken all together, however, his poetry represents rather the last stirrings of the dying Middle Ages than the first signs of life of the Renascence.

2. *Scottish Poetry from 1400 to 1516.*—There is pleasure in passing from the English to the Scottish poetry of the fifteenth century. It is not that the matter of poetry had been renewed in Scotland. North as south of the Tweed, the allegorical school was dominant and Chaucer's personal influence reigned. The Scots had, however, kept the artistic sense and a line which had an assured rhythm, and they had a vitality which contrasted happily with English languor. This is the most glorious period of all their old poetry.

The patriotic impulse which had caused Barbour to write his *Bruce* in the previous century had almost ceased to be felt. The only poem which matches *Bruce* is *Wallace*,[1] written about 1461 by the minstrel called Blind Harry. He differed from Barbour, who related the comparatively recent exploits of the Bruce, for he went back to an earlier hero whose date was a hundred and fifty years before his own. The fabulous element looms much larger in *Wallace* than in *Bruce*. Wallace's exploits are magnified and multiplied. But the two poems tell their tale with the same naked simplicity. Barbour's prosaic quality is even intensified in Blind Harry, who is platitudinous. He is devoid of poetry, merely amasses detail, and his substitution of decasyllabic couplets for Barbour's eight-syllable verses only protracts the line awkwardly and increases its monotony.

This poem is isolated, and it heightens, by contrast, the ornate, even exaggeratedly brilliant, character of other Scottish verse in this century.

The first in date of the poets of Scotland who were influenced by Chaucer is King James I (1394–1436). Doubts have been thrown on his literary claims, but they have not seriously shaken the beautiful and touching tradition that *The*

[1] Ed. by J. Moir for the Scottish Text Society, 1884–9.
[2] *See* F. Brie, *Die National Literatur Schottland*, 1954.

Kingis Quair [1] expresses in verse a romantic incident of his life which he himself commemorated.

At eleven years of age he was taken captive by the English, together with the ship which was carrying him to France, and, in spite of the truce between Scotland and England, was kept a prisoner for nineteen years, but honourably treated and carefully educated.

During this captivity he fell in love with Lady Jane Beaufort, niece to Henry IV, whom he married in 1424.

His poem describes his love, and is a graceful medley of allegory and reality. Chaucer's work must have been much read by the young prisoner, for *The Kingis Quair* is full of Chaucerian reminiscences. Especially James remembers the charming passage of 'The Knight's Tale' in which Palamon and Arcite see, from the window of their dungeon, the fair Emely walking in the garden, and at once fall in love with her. He had read and re-read Chaucer's translation of the *Roman de la Rose* and the love-scenes in *Troylus and Criseyde*, particularly that in which the lovers first meet, and his head was filled with the poems in which a dream leads to a marvellous allegorical vision. His poem is inspired from all these known sources, but because he himself had partly lived through the traditional fictions, there is a freshness in his imitations which is quite personal, and more than once his stanzas surpass their models in emotion.

His complaint on his long captivity, his contemplation of the 'gardyn faire' 'fast by the touris wall' of his prison, the birds' song, 'so loud and clere,' which stirs him to love—all this is the most natural prelude to the appearance of the girl:

> For quhich sodayn abate,[2] anone astert
> The blude of all my body to my hert.

The sight of her is such that

> My hert, my will, my nature and my mind,
> Was changit clene ryght in another kind.

He recovers enough to gaze at the fair vision, to note her features and ornaments, and especially the heart-shaped ruby:

> That, as a spark of lowe,[3] so wantonly
> Semyt burnyng upon her quhytë throte.

---

[1] Ed. by Skeat for the Scottish Text Society, 1911; by W. M. Mackenzie, 1939. Extracts in Skeat, *Specimens*, vol. iii. See J. J. Jusserand, *Le Roman d'un roi d'Écosse'* (Paris, 1895, trans. 1896); E. W. M. Balfour-Melville, *James I, King of Scots*, 1936.

[2] Shock.   [3] Flame.

There was in her

> Beautee eneuch to mak a world to dote.

This prelude has so much charm and emotion that we
willingly follow the poet through the dream which leads him
from the palace of Venus to those of Minerva and of Fortune.
Others have taken us thither before, but James can often point
out a graceful or brilliant detail. And throughout the fantastic journey suspense reigns as to the outcome of a passion
we know to be sincere:

> O besy goste![1] ay flikering to and fro,
> That never art in quiet nor in rest.

It is easy for us to share his joy when he wins to the
'presence suete and delitable' of his mistress:

> And thankit be the fair castell wall,
>   Quhare as I quhilom lukit forth and lent,
> Thankit mot be the sanctis marcial,[2]
>   That me first causit hath this accident.
>   Thankit mot be the grenë bewis[3] bent,
> Throu quom, and under, first fortunyt me
> By hertis hele,[4] and my comfort to be.

This royal pupil, who commends his book to Gower and
Chaucer, his 'maistris dere,' is a correct and harmonious ver-
sifier. His dialect is tempered by his assiduous reading of
English models, and exempt from the difficulty increasingly
felt in the poetry of his successors.

These, on the other hand, have more raciness, for they had
not spent their youth in the English court. One of the most
interesting of them is the Dunfermline schoolmaster, Robert
Henryson (1425–1500),[5] who evinces a real independence even
when he is imitating Chaucer.

He had read and admired *Troylus and Criseyde*, but his
moral sense was shocked by the conclusion of the story.
How could the faithful Troylus be killed and the fickle Criseyde
be happy with Diomede thereafter?

> Quha wait[6] gif all that Chaucer wrait was trew?

Henryson, one cold day in Lent, set himself to recast the conclusion of the story and write *The Testament of Cresseid*.

---

[1] Restless spirit.   [2] Saints of March.   [3] Boughs.   [4] Healing.
[5] Complete works edited by G. Gregory Smith (Scottish Text Society, 3 vols.,
1906–14); *Poems and Fables*, ed. H. H. Wood (Edinburgh, 1933); *The Testament
of Cresseid*, ed. Bruce Dickins (Edinburgh, 1925). See Tillyard, *Five Poems*,
1948.   [6] Knows.

His Diomede soon deserts Cresseid, who becomes a light-of-love among the Greeks, and in punishment is afflicted by Heaven with leprosy. Then 'with cop and clapper' she goes begging from door to door. One day Troylus, who is not dead, is returning from a glorious expedition and passes near the place where she sits. Not recognizing her, yet reminded by her 'of fair Cresseid, sumtyme his awin darling,' he gives her a generous alms:

> For knichtlie pietie and memoriale
> Of fair Cresseid.

When he has gone, and she learns from the other leper folk who he is, she falls to the ground. Before dying she writes her testament, bequeathing her body to the worms and toads, and all her goods to the lepers, save a ring, set with a ruby, which is to be carried to Troylus after her death. When he receives it and hears her story,

> For greit sorrow his hart to birst was bown.

He causes 'ane tomb of merbell gray' to be raised above her grave.

Henryson seems to have been guided by his sense of reality at least as much as by a moral aim. He thinks this miserable end the most probable for the Cresseids of this world. Chaucer, in pity, had drawn a veil over the life of his heroine after her fall. Henryson is no less pitiful: his heart aches for Cresseid even while he is describing her horrible chastisement. His morality is penetrated with sympathy and humanity. His *Testament of Cresseid* has been accepted as the natural sequel to the romance. It is written in the same stanza as Chaucer's poem and is as correct and harmonious.

Henryson was no mere sentimental moralist. His moral fables show him in more homely guise, capable of mischievous energy. He tells us that he has had a vision of an old man,

> The fairest man that ever befoir I saw,

who declares that he is a Roman and named Aesop. This Roman Aesop without a hump—how remote we still are from the Renascence!—can tell a good story, with a mischievous smile, and the thirteen fables he dictates to Henryson—*The Cock and the Jasp, The Uplandis Mous and the Burges Mous, Schir Chantecleir and the Fox, The Lyoun and the Mous, The Wolf and the Lamb*, and the others—are among the best fables ever told. The matter is commonplace and everything is in the manner. They are not epical fables, such as Chaucer wrote when jestingly and in heroic tones he sang the adventures of the fox, but they are copious, crowded with detail and with notes of customs or characteristics, abundantly picturesque, much more extensive than those of La Fontaine.   What life and go there is in the most celebrated of them, which is imitated from Horace, *The Uplandis Mous and the Burges Mous*! How amusing the contrast between the rural mouse in her 'sillie scheill' (poor hut),

Withouten fyre or candill birnand bricht,

and her sister, the burgess mouse, whose dwelling is a larder in a rich man's house, and who says to the other:

My Gude Fryday is better nor your Pace! [1]

All this is told with a swing and with fine humour, in the seven-lined Chaucerian stanza, and with sympathy for the animals brought on the scene.   Happily the moral is placed by itself, so that nothing spoils or hinders the pleasure of the story.

Other qualities are revealed in Henryson's other short poems.   *Orpheus and Eurydice*, founded on Boethius, has a pathetic lyricism, and *Robene and Makyne*, which is half-way between a *pastourelle* and a pastoral, is ingeniously constructed.   Makyne has vainly sighed for Robene for 'yeris two or thre,' but he cares nothing for her, thinks only of his sheep, and repels her harshly.   Hardly has she left him when he regrets her, and it is then his turn to beg and implore. But she reminds him of his hardness, laughs at his sighs, and bids him adieu:

Makyne went hame blythe anewche [2]
    Attour the holtis hair. [3]
Robene murnit, and Makyne lewche; [4]
    Scho sang, he sichit sair: [5]
And so left him bayth wo and wreuch,
    In dolour and in cair,
Kepand his hird under a huche [6]
    Among the holtis hair.

The *estrif* or *disputoison* is recalled, save for the fresh country air that blows through the poem.   Of all the Scottish poets of this time, Henryson has most rustic realism and savours most of the soil.

The one of this remarkable group who is justly reputed the

---

greatest is, however, William Dunbar (1460?–1520?).[1] This churchman, first in Franciscan habit, then unfrocked, at one time a wandering preacher, at others sent by James IV on embassies to London and Paris, became in some sort the poet laureate of Scotland. Some hundred of his poems are extant. Nearly all of them are short, but their variety of subject and versification is surprising. Dunbar's prolificity has nothing in common with the flat long-windedness of a Lydgate. He is an artist, even, in some respects, a great artist. It is true that there is nothing new in his thought or feeling. He does not abandon the medieval frames; both his allegories and his satires keep to the traditional grooves. Nor does he ever, like Villon whose verses he knew, thrill with a personal and vibratingly emotional note. He is without Chaucer's and Henryson's fine gifts of observation. But he has to a rare degree—one never reached before him and seldom since—virtuosity of style and versification. No one hitherto had put so much colour in pictures; no one, above all, had given such a swing to lines and stanza. It matters little that Dunbar has not much to say which touches the heart or the mind. He dazzles the eyes and ravishes the ears.

It is brilliancy which is especially remarkable in his official allegories, for instance *The Thrissil and the Rois*[2] in which he symbolizes the marriage in 1503 of James IV to Margaret Tudor, daughter of Henry VII, that union of Scotland and England. Dunbar has recourse to the convention of a vision during sleep, but what a wealth of coloured words he uses, how rapidly the allegories, usually so slow, unfold themselves in his hands! His flamboyant style can doubtless be criticized, yet artifice is in place in such occasional verse. Poetry of this kind, in which conventionalized and highly coloured heraldic figures are substituted for real beings—the lion, the eagle, the thistle, the rose—is surely suited to the celebration of a marriage between two countries. The very violences of the style are those of an artist whose effects are new, as when he speaks of birds singing

> Amang the tendir odouris reid and quhyt.

He goes farther in his *Golden Targe*, in which he uses unremittingly a nine-line stanza having two rhymes. Nothing in this allegory shows an advance on the *Roman de la Rose*.

[1] Works ed. W. M. Mackenzie, 1932. See R. A. Taylor, *Dunbar, the Poet and his Period*, 1931; C. Steinberger, *Étude sur William Dunbar*, 1908; J. W. Baxter, *William Dunbar; a Biographical Study*, 1952. [2] See Skeat, *Specimens*, vol. iii.

There is yet another dream and description of a day in May; the white sail appears of a ship from which seven ladies 'in kirtillis grene' are landed. The poet is accused by Dame Beauty and defended by Reason, who shields him with a golden targe or shield, so that his enemies are powerless against him until Presence blinds Reason by casting a powder in his eyes. The poet is then held prisoner until he awakes.

Certainly Dunbar does not wish to be taken seriously, but he gives the reader the pleasure of dazzling decoration and of a freedom of movement which, for once, keeps at bay the tedium which threatens all allegories. Can this rainbow-hued country, in which all the colours of precious stones—rubies, beryls, emeralds, sapphires—radiate together, be grey Scotland? It would be easier to believe ourselves transported to the kingdom of a Haroun al Raschid. The oriental imagination of this northerner is astonishing.

The natural must not be expected of this great decorator, nor mystical and fervent piety of this Franciscan. It occurred to him, one day, to bring the seven deadly sins on to his stage, but for no graver purpose than to set them spinning in a wild, macabre dance. We have enough edifying pictures of these sins to allow us to thank Dunbar for treating them as no more than the pretext for a mad whirligig. His *Dance of the Sevin Deidly Synnis*, written in lyrical twelve-lined stanzas, is perhaps the most characteristic of his poems. We do not seek in it either propriety of detail or religious horror of vice. It has instead the marks of a strange coarseness, and is fuller of buffoonery than of edification. It ends with a rough jest against the Highlanders whom Dunbar held in derision. But the verbal swing and the giddy liveliness of these ten stanzas are marvellous.

Dunbar was a master of satire, especially of the jovial invective and repeated and unbridled insults which Scots call 'flyting.' Rabelais himself could hardly have held his own with him in this field, in which his vocabulary positively seems to be drunk, so dizzy is the play of rhymes and alliterations.

It should be added that Dunbar was ingenious in his choice of themes for his satires and framework for his mocking invective. Now he sees in a dream a demon in the guise of Saint Francis, who brings him the habit of his order, and to whom he explains why it does not please him to resume it

(*How Dunbar wes desired to be ane freir*).   Now he makes a
pretended apology to the corporation of tailors who have
complained of his ridicule, which he is thus enabled to repeat
with more sting than ever (*The Tournament*).   Or again, in
order to mock a charlatan who has tried to fly on wings of
his own making and has fallen and broken his leg, Dunbar
pictures him attacked by all the fowls of the air when he
takes his flight (*The Fenyeit Freir of Tungland*).

In every verse-form he excels.   He uses Langland's alliterar-
tive line with as much success as the Chaucerian metre.   He
unites the metres of both masters when, with extraordinary
cynicism, he relates the fable of *The Two Mariit Wemen and
the Wedo*, whose scabrous conversation he overhears as they
sit in their garden after some hearty drinking.   The remarks
on the obligations of matrimony which, in alliterative verse,
he puts in their mouths would have brought blushes to the
cheek even of the Wife of Bath.

On occasion, however, he is capable of a higher lyricism.
There is a note of melancholy in his *Lament for the Makaris*,
in which he names the poets of his country and of England
who have died.   It recalls Villon's enumeration of the
illustrious ones whom death has ravished.   The Latin refrain: 'Timor mortis conturbat me,' sounds in these short
stanzas the knell of the departed.   But they have not Villon's
sober exactness nor his intimate thrill.   The effect produced
is more external, and is due, above all, as it always is in
Dunbar, to astonishingly skilful rhythm.

The fact that Dunbar's merits may, in the last analysis, be
summed up as mastery of form, does not impugn his right to a
place of honour.   For with him there is no question of inert
perfection, but of intense life such as belonged to none of the
rhétoriqueurs whose contemporary he was.   Far from bending
beneath the load of his rich vocabulary, he carries it easily.
He has dash, and this is to say that he is half-way to
lyricism.

Very different from this frequently coarse Bohemian was the
high-born Gavin Douglas (1475?-1522?),[1] a churchman who
became a bishop, and whose personal history mingled with that
of Scotland when, after the disaster of Flodden in 1513, he
was drawn into politics.   While he hardly corresponds to the
usual idea of a prelate, he was yet a man of heart and of honour,
and also a man of letters who first gained distinction in the

[1] *Works* (4 vols.) by John Small, 1874; L. M. Watt, *Douglas's Aeneid*, 1920.

field of traditional poetry, and ended by showing himself almost a precursor of the humanism of the Renascence.

In his youth he began with allegory. At twenty-six he wrote *The Palice of Honour* (1501) in which he imitates Chaucer's *Hous of Fame*. The difference between the subjects of the two poems is reflected in their titles. It is the House of Honour which this poet enters in his dream, where dwell illustrious men who in their lives have followed the laws of truth and loyalty. Douglas modestly declares that he can find no place there for himself. In the course of the dream he mixes the sacred and the profane, moral allegory and mythology. The nymph Calliope explains the redemption of man to him, at his desire. There is a scholar as well as a moralist behind these puppets.

Later, Douglas wrote *King Hart*,[1] in which he shows much maturer psychological power. His great model is still the *Roman de la Rose*, but he also knows the *Séjour d'Honneur* of Octavien de Gelais whom he has already imitated in his earlier poems, and he has felt the influence of the morality plays which were then supreme in the theatre.

There is a constant mingling of humour and melancholy in this allegory. King Hart, or Heart, is made captive by Dame Pleasance, and delivered by Dame Pietie, then marries the charming enemy who has overcome him. But, after seven years, Age knocks at the gate of the palace of Pleasance, and all the young and flighty courtiers, who once had surrounded her, flee, and are at last followed by the dame herself. Reason and Wit then warn the king to return to his own castle, where he is ere long assailed by the hideous army of Decrepitude. Before he dies he makes an ironic testament.

The scene of the arrival of Age, most unwelcome of visitors, is full of life, and there is much graceful melancholy in the king's farewell to Youth:

> Sen thou man pas, fair Youth heid, wa is me!

In spite of their merits, these poems have too little novelty to have ensured Douglas's renown by themselves. He has another claim to fame in that, first in Great Britain, he translated Virgil into verse (1512–13). Before him, only Chaucer had rendered a few fragments of the Latin poet, and in such reedlike tones that he seemed to be writing a parody. Caxton, the first printer, had published a prose version made from a

---

[1] Extracts in Gregory Smith, *Specimens of Middle Scots*.

pretended French translation which was really a medieval
romance, and of which Douglas says that, although Caxton
had called it 'Virgil in Eneados,'

> It has na thing ado tharwith, God wait,
> Ne na mair lyke than the devill and Sanct Austyne.

Douglas aimed at translating exactly, word for word, but need
for comprehension and the imperfection of his language often
led him to render one word or one line by several.   He retains
something of the Middle Ages and travesties characters, as
when he makes a nun of the Sibyl or a gentle lord of Aeneas.

He translates into heroic couplets in which he uses more
licence than in his other poems.   Altogether this is an
interesting work, energetic and sometimes brilliant.

Its most curious part is the prologues which precede the
books.   These contain the most original and most Scottish
verses of the poet.   In them Douglas writes as his fancy bids
him, of himself or of the season.   In a description of winter
which begins the seventh book, and one of spring which opens
the twelfth, he may be said to have anticipated by two centuries his fellow-countrymen Thomson, of *The Seasons*, for he
is as faithful to nature and prodigal of detail.   His exuberance
is especially striking, his abundant colours, scents, and sounds.
He is like a Dunbar striving for realism.   But in the long run
his scene is felt to be crowded: mind wearies and eyes ache.
His language is, moreover, the most difficult of the period, because of the number of the learned and popular sources whence
it derives.   An Englishman is unable and a Scot hardly able
to read Douglas without a glossary.

In his prologues he allows himself full rein, for he writes
them only for his own pleasure.   In that to Book XII[1] he
would merely have us know how the singing of the birds woke
him at four in the morning and he resumed his translating.
Sometimes his readers share the diversions of a humanist, as
when he adds to Virgil a thirteenth book translated from the
Italian Maffeo Vegio.   Its prologue informs us that in a dream
the writer is charged by Vegio to make this translation.   He
at first refuses, pleading unfitness, but Vegio insists that he
who has translated the poem of a pagan is far more bound to
do this service to a Christian, and finally the Italian poet
prevails by the argument of twenty blows with a cudgel.

These particularities of his Virgil show, almost as much as

---

[1] Printed in Skeat, *Specimens*, vol. iii.

his earlier allegories, that Douglas was not in the full stream of the Renascence. He stood on its brink, marking the transition from one age to another.

We have still to speak of his countryman Sir David Lyndsay, who poetically was even more attached than he to the past. Lyndsay's life was, however, a long battle which coincided with the Reformation, and he definitely belongs to the sixteenth century.

3. *The Old Ballads.*[1]—The works we have reviewed constitute, in Scotland as in England, the official poetry of the fifteenth century. This is far from being all the poetry of the period. There were also anonymous popular verses, both ruder and more truly alive, which often cannot be localized or dated with any precision. They cannot all be claimed for the fifteenth century, for poems of the sort must have had an earlier beginning and certainly were produced until a later time; but the impulse to make them seems to have been particularly active in this century, to which, moreover, the oldest extant specimens belong.

The word 'ballad,' vague as it is, denotes them best. But they must be in no way identified with the courtly ballade, which was fixed in form and peculiarly learned and artificial. The two words doubtless share a derivation from *baller*, to dance, and the ballad and ballade both originated in the poetry which accompanied dancing and implied musical declamation with a collective refrain. But hardly more than the traces of this prototype remain. When the popular ballad of Great Britain emerges from the shadows it retains no more of its primary form than warrants a presumption, more complete than for other kinds of poetry, of co-operation between the poet and his audience. It has even been supposed that a ballad is the spontaneous and joint composition of a group of people. Reflection shows, however, that this theory has little plausibility. There could be agreement for the purposes of poetry among a number of people only in the sharing of a passion, and the work of an artist or several successive artists has to be recognized in a ballad of any length. It was artists, however primitive, who interpreted the multitude. Once a ballad existed, the public did in some sort collaborate in its

[1] F. J. Child, *The English and Scottish Popular Ballads*, 5 vols., 1882–98, critical edition; edition in 1 vol. with introduction by G. L. Kittredge (Boston, 1904); F. G. Gummere, *Old English Ballads* (Boston, 1894); *The Popular Ballad* (Boston, 1907); Louise Pound, *Poetic Origins and the Ballad* (New York, 1921); M. Hodgart, *The Ballads*, 1950; G. H. Gerould, *The Ballad of Tradition*, 1932.

making, for memory altered, modified, or suppressed, and new
circumstances suggested opportune additions. Oral tradition
changed the form of the poem. Like money in circulation,
it lost, little by little, its imprint; its salient curves were
blunted; and long use gave it a polish it did not have originally.
The exact fact to which it owed its birth grew misty in retro-
spect, and form being, in a humble way, historical, the ballad
became romantic and acquired the prestige of the remote.

Perhaps, therefore, it is time rather than the mode of their
making which gives ballads their special character. They
differ from other poems because we never, or hardly ever,
hear them as they were originally. At some moment of its
life, already, it may be, a long one, a ballad becomes public
knowledge, and the subtle effect of the human emotions
excited while it has been endlessly repeated may indeed
have given it the value of a collective work.

It may be said that this is equally true of the old songs
which were not written down for many years. But a ballad
is not a song. Usually it holds a story: it is the fragment of
an epic; sometimes it is plainly the summary of old chivalrous
poems of which only the essence has been kept for the purposes of a short recitation and to make a rapid impression on
simple minds. Or else the ballad relates for a district a
glorious or ill-omened incident which is known to all and has
familiar heroes, so that, however allusively the poet expresses
himself, he is sure of being understood even by the most
ignorant.

The ballad exists everywhere in Europe, but is most copious
and lively in the outlying regions, in Spain in the south and in
Scandinavia in the north.   Great Britain, insular and isolated,
produced many ballads, especially on the Border, the scene in
old days of so many sanguinary encounters of Scots and English.

We have spoken of the popular rhymes, dating from the
fourteenth century, on Robin Hood, bowman and outlaw,
but the ballads, a whole cycle of them, which are consecrated
to his exploits do not go back further than the sixteenth
century. While the existence of numerous ballads in the
fourteenth and fifteenth centuries may be conjectured, there
are only two which can certainly be placed before the
Renascence: *Chevy Chase* and *The Nut-brown Maid*.

Chevy Chase[1] is the oldest and the finest of the epical
ballads. In theme and sentiment it is akin to *Roland* or

[1] Text in Skeat, *Specimens*, vol. iii.

Byrhtnoth. It is at least half-historical, its subject the struggle between Percy of Northumberland and the Douglas of Scotland at the beginning of the fifteenth century. The manners it reveals are at once violent and chivalrous, a love of battle combining with generosity to enemies. But that which in *Byrhtnoth* has an epic swing is here lyrical. This ballad is a sung recitation, a sort of melopoeia. Already it has the metre which was to be pre-eminently that of the ballads, the seven-accented line in two divisions (4 +3) and the rhymes in couples. The division is so fixed that the couplet can be considered as a quatrain:

> The Persé owt off Northombarlonde
> An avowe to God mayd he
> That he wold hunt in the mountayns
> Off Chyviat within days three.

The division often leads to the rhyming of the first and third sections, giving quatrains with cross-rhymes (*abab*). The tendency to regularize rhythm also has the effect in the later ballads of making the lines syllabic, that is to say alternately of eight and six syllables. In *Chevy Chase* the verse is primitive in its rudeness and has the minimum of ornament.

There is in this ballad a manifest basis of realism. It tells an incident all too truly characteristic of life on the Border, where there was little distinction between warfare and brigandage. Percy wishes to hunt in enemy country, less for love of the deer than to provoke his adversary. He rejoices greatly when, after the hunt, the Douglas arrives and the battle begins. Yet these wild opponents have the spirit of chivalry: the Douglas, in order to spare 'guiltless men,' proposes to Percy to meet him in single combat. But the ardour of Percy's followers, who would think it shame to leave all the danger to their chief, cannot be restrained, and the fight is general. When the Douglas is slain, Percy, who a minute before had been drunk with battle, gives rein, before the body of his enemy, to artless grief and sincere admiration:

> The Persé leanyde on his brande, and sawe the Duglas de;
> He tooke the dede man be the hande, and sayd, Wo ys me for the!
> To have savyde thy lyffe I would have partyd with my landes for years thre,
> For a better man of hart, nare of hande, was not in all the north countrè.

The minstrel who so vigorously sings the fine sword-play is mindful of the evils to which such violence will give rise:

> The chyld may rue that ys un-borne, it was the more pittè.

Sincere emotion is betrayed by these very contradictions. The poem wins us by the truthfulness of its feeling as of its restrained decoration and its details. Whether or not the details be strictly historical, we follow the vicissitudes of the conflict, the part played by the English bowmen, the tactics of the Douglas when he caused his men to advance in scattered formation, the hand-to-hand struggle.

There is a sort of Homeric impartiality in this war ballad. The Percy and the Douglas show equal heroism, although their virtues are opposed like those of an Achilles and a Hector. The poet's English patriotism is clearly discovered only at the end. When he hears that the Douglas is slain, the king of Scotland is in despair, but Henry IV, learning Percy's death, is undismayed in his pride:

God have merci on his soll, sayd kyng Harry, Good Lord, yf thy will it be!
I have a hondrith captayns in Ynglonde, he sayd, as good as ever was hee:
But Persé, and I brook my lyffe, thy deth well quyte [1] shall be.

He then dispatches an army which wins the victory of Humbledon.

It is almost impossible to exaggerate the importance of this short literary epic. Its success was not confined to the people, but extended to men of letters and poets. Sir Philip Sidney wrote of it about 1581:

I never heard the old song of Piercy and Douglas, that I found not my heart more moved than with a trumpet; and yet it is sung but by some blind crowder with no rougher voice than rude stile; which being so evil apparelled in the dust and cobweb of that uncivil age, what would it work trimmed in the gorgeous eloquence of Pindar?

As though to obey Sidney's wish, a poet of the first years of the seventeenth century gave to the ballad, without deforming it overmuch, a correct form, modernized language, and regular rhythm. Addison, in the full stream of the classical period, read it in this version, which yet seemed to him ancient, and praised it discriminately in the *Spectator*. He realized the ballad's Homeric qualities, and used it as a text to preach that the beautiful is the simple. He loved it as Molière loved the old song of Henry IV of France and for the same qualities—just style and natural feeling. Finally Bishop Percy (1765) inserted the oldest text in his *Reliques*,

[1] Requited.

and *Chevy Chase* was one of the medieval poems which induced Romanticism. Soon the very irregularity of its verses was found to have a special charm, and this rudeness inspired Coleridge to give a new harmony to his *Ancient Mariner* and, above all, to his *Christabel*. It is sincerity of tone, like that of *Chevy Chase*, which, down the ages and among extravagances and artifices, brings back to natural truth the poetry which has left nature too far behind.

Such fine romantic ballads as *Sir Patrick Spens*, *Clerk Saunders* and *Child Waters* cannot be certainly ascribed to the fifteenth century, for the versions of them which have reached us are all of later date. But a poem of a special kind, which encloses the elements of a simple ballad in the frame-work of a courtly *disputoison*, may be claimed for this century.

A lady is represented as using the story of *The Nut-brown Maid*[1] to free women of the reproach of inconstancy con-stantly levelled at them by men. The dark maid, who is a baron's daughter, is visited by her lover whom she believes to be a squire of low degree, and who comes to bid her farewell because he has killed a man and must hide in the woods as an outlaw. But neither his picture of a life of pains and peril, nor even his avowal that he has another mistress, can bend her from her will to follow him for love's sake. He has but proved her, as Griselda was proved, and, sure of her heart, he reveals himself as an earl's son who will make her lady of his heritage in Westmorland.

There cannot here be question of a popular composition. Nothing could be more artistic than these thirty six-lined stanzas with their alternating refrains. Each stanza has lines of seven accents, divided in $2+2+3$, and a system of multiplied rhymes puts very severe constraint upon the poet. Yet the simplicity of style and sincerity of tone do not at all suffer. While the lady, who may be supposed to be the author, plays the part of the Nut-brown Maid, the other speaker takes that of the outlaw. There is a dialogue, each of them in turn speaking a stanza with its refrain. The dramatic interest and liveliness thus given to the little poem cause its thesis to be forgotten in its story. The unadorned stylistic fabric, which admirably renders emotion, does not lack broad images, such as those in the first answer of the enamoured lady

[1] Text in Skeat, *Specimens*, vol. iii.

when her beloved announces his crime and banishment
to her:

O lord, what is this worldys blysse that changeth as the mone!
My somers day in lusty may is derked before the none.
I here you say, farewell: Nay, nay, we dèpart nat so sone.
Why say ye so? wheder wyll ye go? Alas! what have ye done?
All my welfàre to sorrowe and care sholde chaunge, yf ye were gone;
For in my mynde, of all mankynde I love but you alone.

If this poem be not a popular ballad but the work of a
courtly poet, it does but show the degree to which even the
learned poetry of the time could absorb popular songs and be
inspired by them. In this echo of some humble love-ballad
there is not one false note. Whoever can bring himself to
read the lamentable imitation of it which Matthew Prior made
in the beginning of the eighteenth century, and in which everything is falsified, both style and sentiment, will recognize that
the essence of poetry existed in this disinherited fifteenth
century as it did not in the classical period. *The Nut-brown
Maid*, which was printed in 1502, belongs incontestably to the
reign of Henry VII.

4. *The Drama of the Middle Ages.*[1]—It is with the drama as
with the ballad. It cannot be said to have been either created
or fully developed in the fifteenth century. But this was the
period in which most of the cycles of the Christian theatre
were compiled and in which the miracle plays, not yet subject
to competition from dramatic performances of a more modern
kind, reached their climax. It is therefore fitting to determine the characteristics of the medieval dramatic art of
England in this rather than in another century.

Such characteristics are, in point of fact, few in number.

The religious theatre is an institution of Christianity which
had the same origin and a like evolution in all the Christian
countries of Europe, so much so that it is seen wrongly or out

[1] For the history of the English theatre in the Middle Ages, see E. K.
Chambers, *The Mediaeval Stage*, 2 vols. (Oxford, 1903), and *The English Folk-
Play*, 1933; J. J. Jusserand, *Le Théâtre en Angleterre jusqu'aux prédécesseurs
immédiats de Shakespeare*, 2nd ed. (Paris, 1881); A. W. Ward, *History of English
Dramatic Literature to the Death of Queen Anne*, 2nd ed., 3 vols., 1899; C. M.
Gayley, *Plays of our Forefathers, and some of the Traditions upon which they
were founded* (New York, 1909); E. N. S. Thompson, *The English Moral Plays*,
(New Haven (Conn.)), 1910; A. P. Rossiter, *English Drama from Early Times to
the Elizabethans*, 1950. For texts, see A. W. Pollard, *English Miracle Plays,
Moralities and Interludes*, 8th ed. (Oxford, 1927), *Everyman and Mediæval
Mystery Plays* (Everyman's Library). Pieces excellently selected as repre-
sentative of the development of the drama are given by J. M. Manly in vol. i
of his *Specimens of the Pre-Shakespearian Drama*, 2 vols. (Boston, 1900–3).
K. Young, *The Drama of the Mediaeval Church*, 1933.

of perspective if it be studied in one country alone. In that great common fatherland which was Christendom in the Middle Ages, nations were, from the spiritual point of view, hardly more than are to-day the provinces of a centralized state. Therefore to relate the history of the Christian drama of England is, in many respects, little more than to repeat what is known of that of France. It is thus possible to deal with the subject allusively and rapidly.

Every one knows that this drama, was an offshoot of the liturgy, which, with its solemn staging, lent itself well to dramatic development. The germs of the drama were in the offices of the Church, in the chants alternating between the priest and the congregation or the choir which represented it, the recitative passages, the plastic decoration, the processions, the ritual of movement and gesture. It was in the form of 'tropes,' or declamation in dialogues, that drama made its first appearance. Two tropes of the Easter office, which were declaimed in England in the tenth and eleventh centuries, before as well as after the Norman Conquest, have been preserved, and made it almost certain that, with or without the Conquest, religious drama would have evolved in England as in every Christian country.

First given within the church and declaimed in Latin, these dialogues developed into small dramas when they left the church and were played in the porch and when they exchanged Latin for the vernacular, two conditions essential to the needed liberty. The best-known example of a transitional play of this kind is *Adam*, which was written in French, but by a Norman or Anglo-Norman of the twelfth century, and which seems to have been performed not in France, but in England. Very interesting because of its place at the origin of two great dramatic literatures, it is so also intrinsically. Restrained, even a little bare, but grave in thought, its sentiment just, decided, and precise, and its language vigorous, it has a real value. It comprises three parts—the fall of Adam and Eve, the death of Abel, and a procession of the prophets who announce the coming of the Redeemer. The scene of Eve's temptation by the devil shows a certain refinement and some poetic grace. Almost all and the best characters of the religious drama are to be found in this old Anglo-Norman play.

But is was necessary for this drama to emancipate itself completely from the Church. It had to leave the church precincts for the highways, to take up its station in the market-place or the streets. Moreover, before the plays could be popular, they had to abandon not only Latin, as in France, but French also. It was essential that their language should be English.

Dramatic progress is connected with the development of the fairs, the increase of wealth, the rise of the burgher class, the prosperity of corporations, and finally the emancipation of the vulgar tongue. Little by little drama severed its connection not only with the Church, but also with the clergy, who at first provided all the actors. Not without resistance from the clerks, the mendicant friars, and the Franciscans, who lost their monopoly, the actors came to be laymen. As a rule, henceforth, the clergy were no more than the play-wrights. This change became marked and was accelerated from the second half of the thirteenth century onwards. The first plays in English were performed under Henry III, and at the same time a certain realism was introduced upon the stage.

In this reign also the great cyclical representations had their beginning, those in which the sacred history relating to an annual feast was depicted in successive scenes on the holiday. The Easter and Christmas cycles were the first in date, but the institution in 1264 of the feast of Corpus Christi and its generalization early in the next century gave this day pre-eminence. The Easter and Nativity cycles, hitherto distinct, were united and were performed together on Corpus Christi Day, which was less crowded with other events than Christmas and Easter Day and which fell in the summer. All Holy Writ was thus staged at the same time and place, all the great facts of religious history reproduced in sight of the people. In some places, as in Chester, the performance was on Whitsunday rather than on Corpus Christi Day.

Some towns, because of the fame of their fairs or the power-ful organization of their gilds, became celebrated for these representations, and the English miracle-plays we now possess are named after the places in which they were given. The cycle, embracing the whole of sacred history, is always the same, but differs locally in detail, mood, language, and versi-fication, its tone being more dignified or homelier in one place than in another. The plays of Chester and Coventry—Shake-speare may as a child have seen these last, those of Woodkirk Abbey, near Wakefield, called the Towneley Plays, and those of York have been preserved, as well as fragments of the Digby,

Newcastle, and Dublin plays.   Other towns had cycles which have been lost,

The cycles were first compiled in the fourteenth century, but we possess them only as they were rearranged in the fifteenth, or even sixteenth, for some were played until the theatre of the Renascence was nearing its apotheosis.

The popularity of the miracle plays in the fourteenth century is attested by Chaucer, who relates in his 'Miller's Tale' of Absolon, the merry clerk, that

> Sometyme to shewe his lightnesse and maistrye
> He playeth Heródes on a scaffold hye;

and who shows the Miller himself to be well informed about Noah's quarrels with his wife in the play of the Flood.   Langland gives a yet more significant proof of the influence of the theatre, for he has cast more than one scene of *Piers Plowman* in the mould of the miracle plays.

We can picture one of these immense representations, for instance that at York on Corpus Christi Day.[1]   Every gild in the town contributed to it, and the festivities included forty-eight plays which comprised the whole of Scripture. We know not only the order of the plays, but also the gild responsible for each of them, appropriately chosen as far as possible.   To the Armourers fell the expulsion from paradise (the flaming sword), to the Shipwrights the building of the Ark, to the Fishermen and Mariners the Flood, to the Chandlers the shepherds following the star, to the Goldsmiths the adoration of the Magi, to the Bakers the Last Supper, to the Pinners and Painters the Crucifixion, to the Butchers the Mortification of Christ, to the Scriveners Doubting Thomas, and so forth.

An idea of the staging can be had if the meaning of pageant, a word of uncertain etymology, be understood.   It sometimes referred to the platform on which a play was given, sometimes to the representation itself.   Some platforms were fixed in a particular place, and the audience went from one to another of them, following the series of the plays.   But elsewhere the pageant was mounted on wheels and movable, and the spectators stayed in one spot while these stages on wheels successively paused before them, gave their performance, and passed on to another point where the performance was repeated.   Most of the gilds had their own pageants.   Sometimes the action made several pageants necessary for one

---

[1] See H. Morley, *English Writers*, vol. iv.

play; for instance one for paradise, one for the earth, and one for hell. Each included, beneath the stage, a room in which actors spent the intervals between their appearances and properties were kept.

The duration of the performances varied with the number of the plays, but was always several days. In Chester, where the series included only twenty-four plays, it took three days. The first nine were given on Whit-Monday, nine more on Whit-Tuesday, and the last six on the Wednesday.

What we know of the English theatre in the fifteenth century shows that it was very powerfully organized, that the gilds took an important part in its development, and that there was long local resistance to the engrossing of the plays by professional actors. In fact, its vitality and popularity were such as were surpassed nowhere. The number and diversity of the provincial centres, particularly in the north and the west, prove how widespread was the passion for the theatre.

Two points in which the English drama differed from the French must be noted. In England, although all the plays of the period are generally called miracle plays, there are hardly any traces of what the French call *miracles*, that is, plays concerned especially with the Virgin and the saints, as distinguished from the *mysteries* which were founded on Holy Writ. All the cycles preserved in England are of scenes from the Bible. Secondly, the growth of the religious theatre was less disturbed in England than in France, and its development checked less early. It continued to flourish when the Renascence was in full swing, so firmly was it established in local custom and popular favour.

The extant English cycles offer another advantage to modern students. While the French mysteries in the collection compiled by the Brothers Greban are, on the whole, mediocre and monotonous, there is in the very various English plays a dignified emotion or a homely swing which sometimes makes itself felt through the awkwardness and rudeness of the style. It may be said that these plays, in the form in which they have reached us, prove that great artistic effort, no less real where it was mistaken, went to their making. They are almost all written in complicated and difficult stanzas, which have the fault that they are apt to sacrifice dramatic quality to lyricism. There are stanzas which multiply their rhymes and unite lines different in measure—

as *aaabab* or *aaabaaab* or *aaaabcccb*, *b* standing for a short two-accented line among others usually of four accents. But while the stanza is learned, the rhythm is, as a rule, unformed and metrical padding abounds. The principal defect is due to the unfitness of such stanzas to render dramatic movement or easy-going dialogue. The difficulty of finding a metre appropriate to drama was the great obstacle to dramatic progress until nearly the end of the sixteenth century. The unknown authors of the miracle plays are not poets enough to animate their awkward stanzas. Yet they are, at moments, capable of pathos, and more frequently there is full-flavoured comedy in their scenes.

As elsewhere, the religious drama had a value due to the simple grandeur of the total conception, and the artlessness of the means used to call up the whole of Scripture before the people is disarming. The poets effaced themselves before their subjects. They had no freedom of invention, hardly of composition, and were debarred from discovering motives for action except within strict limits. Since the stories were known to every one, the principal interest was in the spectacles. Only here and there and accidentally does the author himself intervene, analysing passions or sentiments.

This happens in the play *Abraham and Isaac*,[1] which was written in the fifteenth century and belongs to an unknown cycle. It has one scene of two hundred lines, than which nothing could be more pathetic. It is that which depicts the conflicting sentiments of the father who has the will to obey God, but is stayed by love for his child, and of the son divided between submission to his father and fear of death. Little Isaac trembles before the gleaming sword, thinks of his mother in grief, asks for the fatal stroke yet would avert it. The *Iphigenia* of Euripides has not more feeling, nor Shakespeare's *King John* when little Prince Arthur implores his executioner. We are irresistibly moved to tears; moral emotion and physical suffering are mingled. The only defect of this touching scene is its slowness, which has a slightly monotonous effect. The succeeding scene, in which Isaac, saved from death, expresses his childish joy and tenderly thanks the ram sacrificed in his stead, is very charmingly artless.

It is, however, in comic passages that the English playwrights show most go and originality. Comedy in the Middle

---

[1] There are two texts: one, ed. L. Toulmin Smith, is printed in *Anglia*, vol. vii (1884), the other, ed. R. Brotanek, in *Anglia*, vol. xxi (1899).

Ages often mingled, in varying proportions, with solemn themes, in concession to a public condemned to listen to many an edifying declamation. Comedy of this sort has never been more developed than in certain English cycles. We have spoken of the fortunes of the fabliau in Great Britain, its progress in the hands of Chaucer, and the part it assigned to nature and observation. It has also an important place in some of the English plays, especially the Towneley Plays, which are more rustic than the others. In these, the fabliau is not in the unfinished state of a rough sketch, but has been retouched, again and again, and betrays a long experience of scenic effects. The complicated stanza which contains it, to which we have already alluded, is proof of real artistic labour.

It was only in the comic parts of the plays that their authors were fully independent; in the passages which owed nothing to Holy Writ saving the scenes in which they could safely be introduced. Sometimes the playwright enlivened secondary biblical characters; sometimes he entirely invented characters in order to provide comic relief where the gloom was heaviest. Thus a dramatist cheered the first human tragedy by the gift of a servant named Garcio to Cain, while others gave a realistic vigour to the detractors of the Blessed Virgin, to the soldiers sent to kill the Innocents, to the Pharisees who brought before Christ the woman taken in adultery, to the beadle of Pontius Pilate, to the workmen who set up the Cross, to the soldiers who watched by Christ's sepulchre. There was nothing to prevent them from lending the manners and speech of the common people they knew to these supernumeraries. Shakespeare and his rivals did exactly the same thing, kept the tragic central pattern of their source often intact, and added to it a comic border of their own.

Of the English comic scenes, two took up more space than others in the Towneley Plays,[1] those concerned respectively with Noah's wife and with the shepherds who followed the star.

Noah's quarrels with his wife, when he has to make her enter the ark, are very lively. He is most respectful of the divine injunction, but cowed by his mate, who is the typical scold of the fabliaux, shrewish, contradictious, stormy, giving blow for blow. Frightened as she is of the Flood, the arrangements of the Ark do not please her, and she has barely entered it when

[1] *Towneley Plays* (E.E.T.S., 1897). See J. Speirs in *Scrutiny*, xviii, 1951–2.

she takes herself off to spin alone in a corner. Her husband and her sons and daughters implore her vainly: she will not budge. But no sooner does Noah tell her to do just as she likes than she changes her mind and comes on board. She is still, however, in a bad temper, and Noah has to beat her soundly before things are in train. From the moment of her beating Mrs. Noah is appeased and becomes a charming travelling-companion, helping to navigate the ark and send forth birds, all her talk good sense and kindliness.

The broad comedy of this character in no way lessens the piety of the play, and occurs amid such artless simplicity that it is hardly discordant. Goodman Noah conversing with the Lord, monologuing as he builds the Ark, describing what he does as he goes along and complaining of his stiff back, and the concluding ingenuous dialogue which suggests the various incidents of the voyage: all this makes a homely, cheerful whole, in which the buffoonery is not out of place.

The same mingling of simple piety and farce goes to make the nativity play, but here the farce is more developed and almost constitutes an independent comedy in rustic northern dialect.

With the honest shepherds, who appear telling the troubles of their life—hard winters, the oppression of gentlemen—or who complain of the cantankerousness of their wives, there mingles a certain Mak, a cunning scamp, almost a precursor of the Shakespearian Autolycus. The action of the farce is that he steals a sheep from the others and conceals it, and that his theft is discovered. The sheep is put in a cradle, and Mak's wife, on her bed, groans as though she were just delivered of a child. When one of the good shepherds wants to give the baby a sixpence, the trick is exposed. And no sooner has Mak been tossed in punishment than the angel begins to sing 'Gloria in Excelsis,' and the good shepherds, led by the star, set out for the Crib, discoursing on the angel's beautiful song and on the prophecies. Before the Crib their demeanour is the same as before the cradle of the sham baby. They are touched by the infant's charm; they bring him simple presents, one a bird, another cherries—at Christmas time!—the third a ball to play at tennis. Their words of adoration alternate with their pity for the frailty and tininess and the poverty of the Divine Child.

It is very remarkable that in these two plays, *Noah* and *The Nativity*, the very brisk and copious comic element does not

clash with the religious sentiment. This is due to the hearti-
ness of the comedy, which has neither reservations nor irony.
It does not imperil the dignity of the play to which it belongs.
It is not destructive. It can be reconciled with faith and
tender emotion. It is at once bold and artless. We shall
see that, for like reasons, the comic blends easily with romantic
or tragic elements in the best of the Renascence dramas. On
the other hand, the cynical realism of *Maître Patelin*, also a
fifteenth-century work, would be hard to imagine in a religious
frame. *Maître Patelin*, with a theme somewhat analogous to
the Mak episode, is markedly superior to the artless Towneley
Play in refinement of analysis and pointed wit, but has a
fundamental harshness, a certain dryness and cruelty. Nor
is the French play in any sense rustic: it does not breathe
the healthy country air which surrounds the shepherds of
the *Nativity* and good-for-nothing, sheep-stealing Mak. In
differences of this kind, rather than in a diversity of theory, the
profound causes are to be discerned for the eventual triumph
in English drama and rejection by French drama of the
mingling of the tragic and the comic.

The earliest moralities preserved in England also belong to
the fifteenth century. Later born than the mysteries, which
are linked up with the epical period of the Middle Ages, the
moralities are a product of the allegorical period. To the
plays taken from the Bible, they are as is the *Roman de la
Rose* to the old epics. For the characters of sacred history
they substitute abstractions, vices or virtues. They are at
their origin as much penetrated as the miracle plays with
Christian teaching, but they have a more intellectual character.
While a miracle play is essentially a spectacle, appealing
primarily to the sight, a morality demands greater attention
to the spoken word. Its text is more important than its
scenery.

Although generally, as we pass from the miracle plays to
the moralities, we seem to go from the greater to the less
great, to what is less alive and more coldly and artificially
constructed, the morality must none the less be recognized
to mark a necessary stage and, in a sense, a considerable
advance in the progress towards the modern drama. The
author of a morality can arrange his subject freely, attempt
construction and unity. He is led to analyse human qualities and defects, to emphasize psychological characteristics.
Miserliness, for instance, cannot be presented without study

of the character of a miser. In this way the morality, even the religious morality, prepared drama for emancipation from religion. Its theme is the struggle of the forces of good and evil which contest for the human soul. This problem continued to confront the poet who was no longer inspired by the Christian faith. The permanent basis of every dramatic work had been discovered.

The material conditions of the theatre were transformed. Instead of multiplied, often movable pageants, the morality used a single, unchanging stage. In the earliest extant English morality, *The Castell of Perseverance* [1] (early fifteenth century), the unchanging scene showed a castle in its centre, and in its corners scaffolds for the World, the Flesh, the Devil, and God. As the miracle plays led to the numerous and changing scenes of historical drama, so the moralities prepared the way for tragedies restricted to one plot.

The exact date at which the morality had its rise is unknown. It was doubtless not later than the middle of the fourteenth century, not far removed in time from Langland's great religious satire which was so filled with animated, almost scenic moral allegories. Allegories were early introduced into the miracle plays. In the Coventry cycle there are such characters as Contemplation, Calumny, Detraction, Truth, Justice, Peace, Death; and, in the Digby Mysteries, especially in the play on Mary Magdalene, the World, Luxury, and Curiosity figure, as well as the Seven Deadly Sins.

In *The Castell of Perseverance*, the oldest and longest of the moralities, the reign of allegory is undisputed. 'Humanum genus,' placed between his good and his bad angel and long the slave of Pleasure and Folly, takes refuge in the Castle of Perseverance with the Christian virtues. He is seduced by Covetousness, who makes his way into the castle and prevails on him to leave it. But before his death, as his soul is about to be carried to hell, he is saved by the intervention of Peace and Mercy.

An analogous conception recurs in the shorter moralities, *Mankind*, approximately of the same date, and *Mundus et Infans* and *Hyckescorner*,[2] which belong to the early sixteenth century. These plays are, however, less tensely grave and have comic passages. In *Mankind* it is the demon Tityvillus

[1] See A. W. Pollard, *English Miracle Plays*, and Early English Text Society extra series, xci; abridged, by J. Quincy Adams (*Chief Pre-Shakespearian Dramas*, 1924).

[2] These three moralities are printed in J. M. Manly's *Specimens*.

whose jokes give the comic relief, while in *Hyckescorner* the scamp who names the piece plays malicious tricks with his companions in debauchery, Free Will and Imagination.

These moralities, by turns cold and scholastic or comic in a very mediocre degree, have little merit. But another of the same period is really impressive and might well be called the masterpiece of its kind, the play of *Everyman*.[1] For long it was believed to have originated in Holland, having been printed in Dutch as early as 1495 and before any edition of the English text. To-day, however, the dominant opinion is that the play was born in England, where certainly it seems to have been very popular down to the Reformation.

The tragedy is that of Christian death, and it is staged with poignant restraint and force. God sends Death to summon Everyman, and he, in anguish, implores a respite, and obtains only a few hours to gather together the friends who shall go with him on his supreme journey. Everyman appeals vainly to Fellowship, his boon companion, to Kindred, and to Goods. None of them will hearken to him. Then he remembers Good Deeds, whom he has long abandoned, who is lying on the ground, weak and miserable, but who hears his prayer, helps him, and recommends him to her sister, Knowledge. Knowledge sends him to Confession, and Everyman, shriven of sin, is ready to meet God. At the moment at which he reaches the grave, Beauty, Strength, Discretion, and Five-Wits depart, in spite of their promise to follow him. Knowledge would go with him but cannot. Only Good Deeds is left; she alone is not vain and will plead for him. Everyman dies pure of sin and forgiven.

The conception is simple and enthralling. There is here no classical influence, and yet nothing could be more classically constructed. The beauty of the work is its sincerity. There is an inevitability in the subject. In a sense, every dramatic work, whether ancient or modern, seems frivolous by the side of this essential tragedy. It has recently been revived in Great Britain and the United States and has made a profound impression on its audiences. All the moralities, controversial in character, which followed *Everyman*, have something small and ephemeral as compared with it. It would be a complete masterpiece were its form less naked, less dull, less devoid of brilliancy. The artistic impulse seems wholly to

---

[1] Printed by F. Sidgwick (1902), by Farmer, Early English Drama Publications (1906), by J. S. Tatlock and R. G. Martin, in *Representative English Plays* (1916–23). See also p. 198.

have exhausted itself on the construction, which is itself no
more than a severe staging of the transcendent message of
Christianity.

After the fifteenth century the miracle plays were still
performed, but their form had been fixed and was not changed
henceforth.   The morality, on the other hand, had an active
life, and was used by the dramatists of the Renascence and
the Reformation as a means to their ends.

5. *Prose in the Fifteenth Century*.[1]—English prose of the
fifteenth century amounts to little if the name be reserved
for writings which have originality and some artistic value.
There was the same reason for inferiority as in the preceding
period; Latin still attracted writers whose purpose was not
strictly utilitarian or who were more than mere translators.
The bold movement of Wyclif and his partisans had, moreover, been checked.   The first half of the fifteenth century
was a period of narrow orthodoxy in which the cruelly persecuted Lollards were reduced to silence.   Only in the second
half of this century did a few rare works which deserve notice
appear in English prose.   It would, however, be wrong to
conclude from this dearth that the spread of reading and
learning had been arrested.   Education made its way in spite
of foreign and civil wars and was diffused.   The number of
persons able to read and write increased and the first epistolary
collections were made.   The lateness of English as compared
to continental prose is principally due to the fact that it
was still imitative and contented itself with translations of
numerous foreign and especially French books which continued completely to satisfy the reading public.   In this
century men had not yet abandoned the paths of the Middle
Ages.   Literary sentiment was still not national, which is to
say that there was as yet no artistic ideal.

It was the desire to bring the last Lollards back to orthodoxy
which decided the learned Reginald Pecock (1395–1460?) to
write in English.   This Welshman, who had taken orders and
become bishop, first of St. Asaph and then of Chichester, was,
as early as 1447, disquieting the clergy by the arguments he
used to defend them, and he put the finishing touch to their
indignation in 1455 by his *Repression of Overmuch Blaming
the Clergy*,[2] in which he defends images, pilgrimages, the

---

[1] For extracts from prose writers of the fifteenth century see A. W. Pollard,
Fifteenth Century Prose and Verse (1903), and Skeat, *Specimens*, vol. iii.
[2] Ed. C. Babington for Rolls Series, 2 vols. (1860).

temporal goods of the Church, the hierarchy, the papacy, the friars and the monks, but founds his argument only on reason. He puts natural law above Scripture and the sacraments. He has recourse only to logic and does not defer to the principle of authority.

To Wyclif and his disciples, who founded all their faith on Holy Writ, he retorted by invoking, as superior to the Scriptures, 'the boke of lawe of kinde writen in mennis soulis with the finger of God.' The words of Scripture ought, he says, to be 'interpretid and brought forto accorde with the doom of resoun in thilk mater; and the doom of resoun oughte not forto be expowned, glosid, interpretid and broughte forto accorde with the seid outward writing in Holi Scripture.'

To establish these principles in the vulgar tongue was in those days to create a scandal among the orthodox, the very class whom Pecock professed to champion. It was criminal to reason about religion with so much independence, to argue with heretics, to bring the people into these disputes by speaking to them in their own language.

Summoned to disown his book or go to the stake, Pecock chose disavowal, and not he, but his book, was burnt.

This logician, as intrepid as indiscreet, stands in isolation, and was afterwards mistaken by the Protestants for an adherent. He was understood neither by his own nor by the following century.

His prose shows a marked advance on that of his predecessors. He had clarity, the gift of choosing homely examples, and a wealth of words. His vocabulary was even excessive: drawing on its double source, English and French, he is tautological and redundant.

Sir John Fortescue [1] (1394?–1476?) was a lawyer who wrote mainly in Latin. Like Pecock, he based his arguments on the law of nature, for instance in his *De Natura Legis Naturae*, but his object is to establish the right to the throne of Henry VI, the grandson of the Lancastrian usurper. He premises that there are three kinds of government—absolute and monarchical, republican, constitutional and monarchical. The Lancastrians are legitimate kings because of the English constitution. Fortescue was the first to admire the constitution of his country, which he praises in his *De Laudibus Legum Angliae* (1468–70).

---

[1] *Sir John Fortescue, his Life and Works*, ed. Lord Clermont, 2 vols., 1869; *On the Governance of England*, ed. S. B. Chrimes (Cambridge, 1942).

When the Lancastrian cause was lost, Fortescue went over to the Yorkists and wrote, this time in English, his little treatise of forty pages on *The Governance of England*. He had stayed in France with Henry VI when that king was a fugitive, and he takes France as the type of an absolute, England as that of a limited, monarchy. This writer affords the first example of national political pride. He admires his own country, as compared with France, for its greater liberty and more abundant riches, his patriotism leading him so far that he celebrates the outstanding valour of his compatriot highwaymen. The French, he says, are, like the Scots, too cowardly to steal. 'Ther is no man hanged in Scotland in vii yere to gedur ffor robbery. . . . But the Englysh man is off another corage. Ffor yff he be pouere, and see another man havynge rychesse, wich mey be taken ffrom hym be myghte, he will not spare to do so.'

The Paston Letters,[1] the correspondence of the Paston family, are interesting rather to the historian than to the student of literature. While scholars, clerks, and nobles still wrote in Latin, the middle class was taking to English. The letters have been preserved of three generations of the Pastons, a well-to-do Norfolk family, and they give much intimate and curious information about English life from 1422 to 1509. Passages are not lacking which suggest the barbarism of the period, but the picture as a whole is of a very modern middle-class society, much engrossed by money matters, leases and the letting of land, the management of property, lawsuits, home comforts, domestic cleanliness. We learn what men read in those days and how severely they brought up their children. Dame Agnes inquires if her son Clement be working well at the Inns of Court, and begs his tutor that otherwise 'he wyll trewly belassch hym, tyl he wyll amend, and so ded the last maystr, and the best that ever he had, att Caumbrege.' There is a sure and serious affection between husband and wife, and they work together to establish the family fortunes. The wife shows great courage when the house is attacked by a band of enemies during her husband's absence.

There is nothing literary in these letters about business, all of them utilitarian, and they cannot be said to show that their writers used the English language easily and fluently. They managed to understand each other, nothing more.

[1] Ed. J. Gairdner, 6 vols., 1904; H. Bennett, *The P's and their England*, 1931.

English prose was still formless and indefinite, distributed among numerous local ways of speech, when in 1474 the first English printer began his work. William Caxton [1] (1421–91) has himself told how hampered he at first was by the anarchical state of his language. The unity constituted by the King's English in the fourteenth century had as yet been realized only in poetry. Evolution was, moreover, still in course, so that in his sixtieth year Caxton found the language very different from that spoken in his childhood. He asked himself how he could please every one. To make himself more certain of being understood he sometimes places the French beside the English word, as *chasse* and *hunt*. He wrote as he habitually spoke, avoiding too rustic terms, aiming at the comprehension of clerks and gentlemen, having his books revised by Master John Skelton, poet laureate of Oxford University. He thus succeeded in being intelligible, and he hardly went beyond this modest ideal. He is a mediocre translator, and the best of his prose occurs in his explanatory prefaces, in which he shows himself a good fellow and a man of cheerful disposition.

It is usual to number the discovery of printing among the causes of the Renascence. By helping the spread of knowledge it certainly favoured the great literary revolution which was at hand. But it is possible, at least in England, to ask whether its first effects were not to fortify and prolong the Middle Ages. To draw up a list of the books issued from the English printing-presses during almost fifty years is to cast up the balance-sheet of the past. It is barely possible to discern, here and there in such a list, a book which heralds the new age.

Caxton himself had nothing of the humanist. He was a Kentish man, a member of the Mercers' Company, who at twenty years old left England for the Low Countries. He settled in Bruges and there acted as a consul responsible for the trading interests of his fellow-countrymen. His stay in Flanders acquainted him with the most civilized court in Western Europe, that of the Dukes of Burgundy, to whose dominions Flanders belonged. In this court, although a great appetite for art and learning was manifest, letters were still confined in the medieval frames. It was with French

---

[1] His prologues and epilogues have been edited for the Early English Text Society by J. W. B. Crotch, 1927. See W. Blades, *The Life and Typography of William Caxton*, 2nd ed., 1882; E. Gordon Duff, *William Caxton* (Chicago, 1905); H. P. Plomer, *Caxton*, 1925; N. S. Aurner, *Caxton*, 1926.

literature that Caxton came to be impregnated, and to its propagation that he devoted his energies as translator and printer. Bruges was one of the first towns to take advantage of Gutenberg's invention, and Caxton, having been initiated by the printer Colard Mansion, finished an incomplete translation of the *Receuil des Histoires de Troye* by Raoul Lefèvre, chaplain to the Duke of Burgundy, and published it at Bruges in 1474. It was the first printed English book. The second was the translation of another French work, a moral and allegorical treatise on the game of chess.

When more than fifty years old Caxton returned to England, in 1476, and established the first English printing-press near Westminster Abbey. Amid much encouragement and protected by Earl Rivers and by the Duke of Gloucester, afterwards Richard III, he worked there until his death in 1491.

What is interesting is his choice of books for printing. He has right neither to the glory of having discovered printing, which belongs to Gutenberg and Schoeffer, nor to the glory of erudition won by the Aldi of Venice and the Étiennes of France, nor even to that of producing beautiful volumes. He was essentially a practical man, on the look-out for books likely to please, and also a man whose personal tastes were determined by his long sojourn on the Continent and by his age. But although his title to represent his nation has been questioned, it is impossible not to be struck by the fact that the library he formed is very like that of the Paston family. It contains the same mixture of poetry, chivalrous romances, moral allegories, and books of devotion.

He was a great admirer of Chaucer and printed *The Canterbury Tales* (1478) and *Troylus and Criseyde*, but he also found room for Lydgate and Gower.

He preferred prose, however, as a medium for the translations of French chivalrous romances which he made or had made—the *Recuyell of the Historyes of Troye*, *The Boke of Histories of Jason*, *The Lyf of Charles the Grete*, the *Morte d'Arthur*, *The Foure Sonnes of Aymon*. It was also into prose that he translated *The Historye of Reynart the Foxe* from the Dutch.

Among works of piety issued from his press were the Hours of the Church, a life of Christ, and a translation of *The Golden Legend* which had the largest circulation of all his publications.

Nothing shows the medieval character of his reading and his mind better than the *Aeneid* he published in 1490, which is translated not from Virgil but from a baroque romance of the Middle Ages.

If it be remembered that Caxton's immediate successors, Wynkyn de Worde, Richard Pynson, and the others, did not notably deviate from his lead in their choice of publications up to 1530, it becomes clear that the English Renascence began amid a considerable body of books which were penetrated by the medieval spirit. It might even be thought, so nearly complete is the absence of the books properly called classical, that the country remained outside the current along which Europe was being swept towards Greek and Roman antiquity. But in justice it should be said that the English found it more convenient to procure books of the newer kind from continental publishers, and to keep their own presses, still few in number, for popular books written in their own language.

What is most remarkable, from the literary point of view, is the development of English prose for which Caxton, a mediocre writer, was responsible. French prose, of which he definitely perceived the qualities, was his ideal. He admired 'the fair language of French, which was in prose so well and compendiously set and written, which methought I understood the sentence and substance of every matter' (*Recuyell of the Historyes of Troye*). He himself aimed at a like clarity and like ease.

In producing prose renderings of the medieval romances he followed the example of the French of the fifteenth century. He thus ensured a longer survival and wider popularity to these romances, which he made accessible to all men. In English, verse had hardly ever embellished them, and, had it not been for the minstrels, they would have fallen into neglect. Prose secured that the stories they enclosed became known. In more or less shortened form, these romances passed from hand to hand, chief among the wares the pedlar bore in his pack. In the chap-books of the Elizabethan period, they kept romance alive in the minds of simple people, awoke those dreams of extraordinary adventure to which many dramatists of the Renascence appealed and at which others of them mocked. By means of these compilations, the Middle Ages were kept from dying altogether, and sank, instead, to deeper and deeper strata of consciousness. Whatever may have been the value of the new works which sprang of the Renascence, the old stories still made the first and the favourite appeal to popular imagination. They shared the role with the ballads, which were multiplied in the same period as they, and which often epitomized in a few verses stories like theirs.

Among the prose versions of old romances published by Caxton there was, however, one which was to be not only food for the people but also a feast for the fastidious. Caxton was well inspired on the day he printed Sir Thomas Malory's *Morte d'Arthur*.[1] He tells us that when he had published the noble feats of Hector, Charlemagne, and Godfrey of Bouillon, he was 'instantly required' by 'many noble and divers gentlemen' also to imprint those of Arthur who belonged to the realm of England. In reply, he pleaded that 'divers men hold opinion that there was no such Arthur,' yet allowed himself to be persuaded. The translation he used was ready to hand, having been made by Thomas Malory, knight, member of Parliament and Lancastrian, who shared the misfortunes of his party and died in 1471. His translation was completed in 1469 and published in 1484.

Malory represents himself as translating a French book. In truth he seems to have had recourse to many books, so that his *Morte d'Arthur* is a compilation. He has brought together scattered romances and co-ordinated them, without eliminating the traces of disparity. In spite, however, of the immense parentheses which recount the separate adventures of Sir Balin, Sir Pelleas, Sir Palomides, Sir Bors, the history of Tristram and Isoud, we can distinguish in his work the lines of a dominant story, that of Arthur, which is logically followed by the tale of the Sangreal. Malory tells of Arthur's triumphant reign, the unfaithfulness of his wife Guenever who takes Launcelot for her lover, Launcelot's punishment by the failure of his quest of the Sangreal, the finding of which is reserved for the purer Galahad. He shows the knights disaffected to the king because of Guenever's sin, and relates Mordred's revolt and Arthur's death. The book ends religiously, for Guenever becomes a nun and Launcelot a hermit. Romantic though it be, we feel that it bears a relation to actualities. The painter of the evils of civil war in this legendary kingdom was a victim of the Wars of the Roses, and the fact sometimes brings a moving gravity and melancholy into his pages.

[1] Editions: H. Oskar Sommer, 3 vols., 1889–91; E. Strachey (Globe Edition, abridged and modernized, 1893); A. W. Pollard (Routledge). See Eugène Vinaver, *Sir Thomas Malory* (Oxford, 1929), and p. 198.

But both this application to the author's own time and the moral lesson which unites the adventures are uncertain, vague, and hesitating in Malory's work. Even the moral is inconsistent, for Launcelot and Guenever in their sin are cited as an example to true lovers. Hence the Puritan reproach, formulated by Roger Ascham: 'the whole pleasure of whiche booke standeth in two speciall poyntes, in open mans slaughter and bold bawdrye.' In fact, this over-loose compilation lacks unity both of thought and of plot.

It has, however, another unity, that of manner, tone, and atmosphere. Malory transports us to a strange country in a distant world, unreal, impossible, and yet imaginatively coherent—a country where all is tourneys and battles, where the only dwellings reared are castles; a country without agricultural life or trade, a region of mirage in which the marvellous is at home and fantastic personages are plausible.

It is the evocation of a vanished epoch, of a sort of golden age, a story of the Round Table written during atrocious civil conflict. It is a refuge, beneath hovering and all-diffused melancholy, from the hardships and crudities of the present.

The narrator of these fanciful tales found a style which fits them well—simple, even childish, monotonous, but harmonious and having poetic cadences. A clear, transparent, and smooth style with no fixed date, though it breathes a soft archaic odour. It betrays neither labour nor culture. The charm of this prose is that it is made up of poetic reminiscences inherited from a long line of earlier poems. The style is that of the fairy tales which are told to little children, and makes a Frenchman think of Perrault's stories; but it is the product of a period which was less wise than Perrault's and of a narrator less self-conscious than he. It is delicious prose of a particular kind, although unfit for other than its own purpose, as is apparent when the author attempts to reason. But when he relates he reaches excellence. An artist like Tennyson could do no better than translate almost literally Malory's story of Arthur's death and of the colloquy between him and Sir Bedivere. There are even good judges who prefer Malory's simple prose to the too elaborate verses of the Victorian poet.

The literary importance and influence of this collection cannot be exaggerated. It is England's first book in poetic prose, and also the storehouse of those legends of the past which have most haunted English imaginations. It is the work which kept the chivalrous spirit alive among the literate, the poets, and the gentry, while the people were fed by the chap-books. Whether such a book would have met with a like fortune in France is doubtful. The author does not sufficiently dominate his material for a French audience. He is incapable of making an explanation or giving a sign of self-consciousness. He repeats his tale like a marvelling child trying to tell faithfully what it has heard and not entirely understood. He gives a wide field to the imagination and does not trouble himself about the intelligence.

The first important prose work that appeared after Malory's was another translation from the French. It was Froissart's *Chronicles*, translated by John Bourchier, Lord Berners (1467–1533) [1] and published in 1523–5. Lord Berners's excellent prose, as animated, lively, and highly coloured as his original, yet represents a return to the fourteenth century, as does also his other book, *Huon of Bordeaux*,[2] which contains the story of the dwarf Auberon. These books appeared when the humanist movement had begun, and the first troubles of the Reformation were manifesting themselves. Without abandoning French, writers were about to add to it the direct study of Latin or even Greek, and on occasion to prefer to it the southern languages. The same Lord Berners was a pioneer of the new prose and a precursor of the Euphuists in his translation of *The Golden Book of Marcus Aurelius* from the Spanish of Antonio de Guevara. He is the connecting link between the two ages in prose, as Skelton and Douglas, on very different grounds, are in poetry.

[1] Reprinted by W. P. Ker in Tudor Translations, 6 vols., 1901–3, modernized and abridged by G. C. Macaulay (Globe Edition, 1895).

[2] Reprinted by the Early English Text Society, extra series, xl, xli, xliii, and l, 1882–7.

For recent work on Skelton, see I. Gordon, *John Skelton: Poet Laureate* (Melbourne, 1943); L. J. Lloyd, *John Skelton: Life and Writings*, 1938; W. Nelson, *John Skelton, Laureate* (New York, 1939); H. L. R. Edwards, *Skelton*, 1949; C. S. Lewis, *English Literature in the Sixteenth Century*, 1954; M. Evans, *English Poetry in the Sixteenth Century*, 1955; also *Complete Poems*, ed. P. Henderson, 1931 (2nd ed. 1948).

E. Vinaver's edition of Morte d'Arthur (3 vols., 1947), based on the recently discovered Winchester MS., for the first time gives what Malory wrote instead of Caxton's arrangement of it.

R. W. Zandvoort (in *Études Anglaises*, 1953) again claims priority for *Elkerlijck* over *Everyman*.

BOOK III—THE PREPARATION FOR THE RENASCENCE (1516–78)

CHAPTER I

THE PART OF THE HUMANISTS

1. *Special Characteristics of the English Renascence.*—The Renascence showed in England almost all the characteristics which it had throughout Europe: thought was liberated and broadened so that it broke its scholastic framework; destiny and morals ceased to be the matter only of dogma and became problematical; a rebellion against the spiritual authority was first incited by the Reformation, which was soon afterwards the enemy of this ally, the Renascence; men looked with a new wonder at the heavens and the earth as they were revealed by the discoveries of the navigators and astronomy; superior beauty was perceived in the literature of classical antiquity, particularly in the recently recovered works of ancient Greece.

At the same time, the Renascence had in England certain additional characteristics which were so special that they gave rise to a truly national literature. The difference was mainly in the time of flowering and in the quantitative mixture of elements, but it was also an outcome of the power each nation simultaneously acquired, when once it was enfranchised from the unifying Catholic discipline, of revealing its own character and of standing in opposition to other nations instead of blending with them. It was from the time of the Renascence that the various European nations began to follow the divergent paths which ended in the contrasts they now present.

The chief peculiarities of the English Renascence, as compared with the same movement in Italy and France, may be stated as follows:

The renewal affected literature later and more slowly in England than in those countries. Not because humanism was tardily introduced, for England's initiation into humanism was, if subsequent to that of Italy, yet quite as early as that of France. But humanism in England had for a long time no

decided effect on poetry and prose. The national language
was still immature. Prose lacked a strong tradition and
glorious precedents, and the best humanists still made use of
Latin. It is significant that the two books which appeared in
England in this period and attained to European fame—Sir
Thomas More's *Utopia* (1516) and Bacon's *Instauratio Magna*
(1620)—were both written in Latin. As for verse, it had,
since Chaucer, been irregularized, and it did not definitely
regain equilibrium and measure until Spenser's work began
in 1579: all the preceding years of the sixteenth century show
no more than a series of incomplete experiments, ground which
was won and then lost. In consequence, English literature
had its flowering season when the magnificent Italian literature
had already entered on its decadence, when France had produced Rabelais and Ronsard and his Pleiad, and Montaigne's
essays were appearing. Malherbe was nine years old when
Shakespeare was born. It was therefore in a generation
enriched by all the substance of France and Italy that England
realized for the first time her high literary ambitions.

Secondly, the Renascence held more aloof from the plastic
arts in England than in Italy or even in France. The English
Renascence occurred in a country which had no pictures or
statues except those bought abroad, and in which the most
determined reformers were zealously protesting against
images. It had therefore a more inward and moral effect than
the similar movements on the Continent. It reached its
triumph not before, but after, the Reformation, when the
Anglican religion had spread throughout the country and was
beginning, here and there, to be tinged with Calvinism. In
so far as the Renascence was an aspiration to every form of
beauty and the cult of every kind of energy, it was not quite
at ease in the already Puritan atmosphere breathed in this
country. There were doubtless free spirits in England, but
they were rebels and notorious. A morality which was
sincere and natural in the majority had, on pain of obloquy,
to be assumed by the others. The total result was increased
seriousness, increasing pangs of conscience, less serenity, and
intensified passion in the matter of faith and conduct.

On the other hand, although the spread of Protestantism all
over England caused her to break with the Middle Ages more
decidedly than France and Italy, her literature remained more
nearly medieval than that of either of those countries. The
fact is the more striking because literature in the preceding

centuries had been a less direct expression of national sentiments in England than elsewhere. English literature had
been almost all imported from France, had mainly consisted
of translations and adaptations. It had not assumed a truly
national shape. The greatest poet, Chaucer, had been
essentially French. None the less, the truth remains that,
although the Renascence and the Reformation beckoned to
new paths, England was faithful to the cult of the past longer
than the Continent. The fact is explained by the continu-
ance of popular influences. While in France the Renascence
was eminently aristocratic, in England it was always regardful
of the masses. It preserved and increased the vogue of the
ballads. The theatre, the home of the most magnificent
product of the period, was accessible to all men, appealed to
the humble as to the great. For the people follow in literature
fashions derived from former days, hold to them tenaciously
and do not abandon them.

A patriotism more and more intense and passionate, even
aggressive and disdainful, favoured this continuity by glorifying the annals of the nation, its history, legends, traditions, and
antiquities. While this patriotism gave rise to an ambition
to rival the masterpieces of Greece and Rome as well as those
of Italy and France, it inspired at the same time antagonism
to the foreign influences which seemed to threaten the national
genius. It was an obstacle to Italianism, that most potent
of the infatuations of the Renascence. It is impossible to
say whether in England, in this century, Italy were more the
object of wonder or of scandal, of admiration or of disapproval.
Increasingly England felt and wished herself to be different
from the rest of Christendom.

2. *The Beginnings of Humanism* (1490–1578).[1]—During
some thirty years, from 1490 until about 1520, when the
religious quarrels began, there was in England an efflorescence
of humanism which was accomplished only by a few elect
spirits, but was pure, serene, and full of hope. Some young
Englishmen were attracted to Italy by the desire to learn Greek,
knowledge of which had been carried thither by refugees after
the fall of Constantinople to the Turks in 1453. They were

---

[1] See *Cambridge History of English Literature*, vol. iii, Chap. I; Courthope,
History of English Poetry; Morley, *English Writers*, vol. vii; Jusserand, *Histoire
littéraire du peuple anglais*, livre iv, Chap. I. See also Green, *A Short History
of the English People*; G. Saintsbury, *A History of Elizabethan Literature*, 1899;
D. Bush, *The Renaissance and English Humanism* (Toronto, 1939), and C. S.
Lewis, *English Literature in the Sixteenth Century, excluding Drama*, 1954.

eager to see the manuscripts of the masterpieces these fugitive Greeks had saved and brought with them, and in quest of this revelation they journeyed to Florence, Bologna, Padua, Venice, and Rome. Thomas Linacre (1460–1524), grammarian, physician, and translator of Galen, should be named among them, and William Grocyn (1446–1519), both of whom returned to Oxford about 1490 and there established the teaching of Greek on sound principles. John Colet (1467–1519) found in Italy, perhaps while he listened to Savonarola, Ficino, and Pico della Mirandola, the inspiration of that enlightened and purified Christianity which he preached in London and Oxford, and founded on renewed study of the text of the New Testament and an historical examination of Saint Paul's mission. By the foundation of St. Paul's School in 1504, Colet also provided the first model for a reformed secondary school the teaching of which should be based on Latin and Greek. For this school he caused William Lily (1468–1522) to write and Erasmus to revise a Latin grammar which was to reign supreme in schools until our own day: it became in the eighteenth century, after some rearrangement, the *Eton Latin Grammar*.

Such prestige did the New Learning acquire from these three masters, that Erasmus, when he resolved upon a profound study of Greek, being dissatisfied with Paris and the college of Montégut, but too poor to go to Italy, made several visits to England, from 1499 onwards, as much to complete his own education as in search of an easier life. Under Colet's influence his studies took a more religious turn, and he devoted himself for a time to the reform of Christianity, which both he and Colet would have wished to see accomplished by persuasion, knowledge, and the purification of morals, without a break in unity.

(a) THOMAS MORE.—The other side of the nature of Erasmus, his admiration for antique thought and form shown in his *Adages* (1500), his wit, his mockery which had free play in his *Praise of Folly* (1509), was better echoed by another of his English friends, Thomas More (1478–1535).[1] It was under More's roof that he wrote the *Praise of Folly*, and of

---

[1] English works published in 1557. P. S. and H. M. Allen have edited a volume of selections (Oxford, 1924). Translations of the *Utopia* by R. Robynson (1551; with the original, ed. J. H. Lupton, Oxford, 1895) and G. C. Richards, 1923. Studies by R. W. Chambers, 1935; J. Delcourt (*Essai sur la langue de Sir Thomas More*, 1913); W. E. Campbell, *More's Utopia and his Social Teaching*, 1930, and *Erasmus, Tyndale and More*, 1948.

hair shirt. This apostle of toleration was, as chancellor, a persecutor of the first Protestants and ended by dying a martyr to his faith. The contrast between his Utopia and his own life betrays a principle of unreality. The ideas of his book were on a level with his intelligence rather than deeply rooted in his conscience.

Yet this book cannot be called the unstable product of a youthful imagination. More was thirty-eight years old when he wrote it, and more than one of its pages contains reflections suggested by his practical experience as a lawyer and a member of Parliament. When he sees in the existing society 'a conspiracy of the rich against the poor,' he is not guilty of mere rhetoric. He supports his assertion by facts which are contemporary and English, the enclosures of land which were depopulating the countryside, especially in the south-east, the eviction of small tenants because rich landlords found that grazing farms were more profitable than their holdings. The lessened demand for workers on the land was causing great misery, so that 'even a beast's life seems enviable' as compared with that of a labourer. When More attacks the barbarous penal laws he is aiming a blow at the executions with which, as a lawyer, he was too familiar in a country where twenty criminals could be seen hanging from a gallows in a row. He is the very antithesis of the judge Fortescue, who was proud of the bravery of English robbers. When he recommends houses of 'a gorgeous and gallant sort,' well lit by glazed windows, he is thinking of the healthy and pleasant dwellings he had seen in Holland and comparing them with the dark, inconvenient, and miserable homes of the London and England of his day.

This book is partly the work of a dreamer led by his fancy and a logician who systematizes his ideas. But it is also written by a satirist who attacks the errors and evils bequeathed by the Middle Ages. It is unlikely that More thought his conception could be realized in its entirety, but he very heartily wished to awaken the desire for certain necessary changes.

His *Utopia* stands alone as representing England's literary contribution to pure humanism. Ten years after he wrote it More himself was drawn into the religious controversy, and obliged, whether he would or no, to abandon the sphere of intellectual exercises for that of narrow ecclesiastical quarrels in which he is next found.

It is a great pity that he did not write a work of such general interest as *Utopia* in English. His humanist's culture is not evinced only by his Latin writings. He left behind him certain pages in English which show, no less than *Utopia*, the degree to which this admirer of Plato was impregnated with Socratic dialectics. The dialogue between the old prisoner Anthony and his nephew Vincent, which More wrote in his prison, to prove that he was neither more unfortunate nor more of a prisoner than the rest of mankind, is so admirable that Socrates might have approved it or envied him its author-ship. And if he be indeed the author of the historical fragment on Richard III attributed to him, he must be recognized as a rival of Tacitus, so vivid is the portrait he paints, so strong his colours, so intense his attack. It is to this fragment that the atrocious, implacable figure which has remained in men's memory is due, the character on which Shakespeare founded his famous tragedy. Whether the picture conforms to reality is doubtful, but artistically it is an astonishing success. It has unity of structure and effect far beyond anything hitherto achieved by an English chronicler.

The pages which prove More's solid classical culture repre-sent only a part of his rich and complex personality, curious of everything in life and nature, conscious of the variety in the souls of various men. His favourite pastime was to observe the habits and instincts of animals. He had a spontaneous and most lively dramatic talent, and although he never wrote for the stage, he dramatized, in the driest controversial treatises, living and comic characters, who speak their own language or even their native dialect. His English prose abounds with humorous passages such as his predecessors lacked. It contains also many turns of familiar talk, sayings and popular expressions which he seems to have been the first to coin or circulate. One wonders if he took them from current speech, or invented them entirely. His natural gaiety, 'the kind and friendly cheerfulness with a little air of raillery' which was, Erasmus tell us, expressed on his face, season his prose, as it showed itself in his speech throughout his life and on the very scaffold. We do not know whether to praise him most for his humour or his wit.

Nevertheless, we cannot follow those who have called him the earliest of the modern English prose-writers. This human-ist seems, if the doubtful case of *Richard III* be excepted, to have done all his artistic work in Latin. His English prose is all improvisation, and he lets loose in it, without rule or measure, his extraordinary lawyer's flow of language. His latest critic calculates that some of his sentences are as much as four yards long, measured line by line in the original edition. He never sought to mould English prose, which then, above all things, needed to be made light and more definite. He left this task entirely to men who were much his inferiors in genius, openmindedness, and liveliness of observation, men who recognized their duty of giving, on the model of the ancients, firmness and regularity to the structure of English sentences. Yet to More belongs the honour of having provoked one of the best prose works of his time, his biography by his son-in-law, William Roper, which was written about 1535 but did not appear until 1626, in Paris.[1] This is an admirable book from every point of view. Nothing could be simpler, clearer, or more pathetic than its story of More's last moments, and it makes an impressive advance in clarity and construction on More's own writings.

(b) THE EDUCATIONISTS: ELYOT, CHEKE, WILSON, ASCHAM.—The men who were inspired by classical antiquity after More were educationists rather than imaginative writers. They have more in common with More's masters than with More himself. But they have over him the advantage that they wrote their best work in English.

It is thus with Sir Thomas Elyot (1490–1546)[2] whose *Governour* appeared in 1531. This treatise on moral philosophy and education, written for those who would be called to govern their country, was founded on the Italian works of Pontano and Patrizzi and is full of the spirit of antiquity. It abounds with Greek and Latin reminiscences.

The influence of the civic morals of Rome is very evident in it, although Elyot was a convinced Christian. He adapts the manner of Plutarch to English history, for instance in the scene in which he shows the prince, afterwards Henry V, obeying the judge who sends him to prison, and the king congratulating himself on a fearless magistrate and a son submissive to justice. By this scene, of which the historical truth is most doubtful, Elyot inculcates the Roman respect for law. His prose is less of the people and less spontaneous than More's, but, on the other hand, more restrained and classical.

The humanism of a man brought up on antiquity is also the

[1] Ed. E. V. Hitchcock (E.E.T.S., 1935) and J. M. Clive (New York, 1950).
[2] Ed. H. H. S. Croft, 1880; S. E. Lehmberg (Everyman's Library), 1962.

most salient characteristic of a book written against the seditious, *The Hurt of Sedition, how grievous it is to a Common-wealth*,[1] by Sir John Cheke (1514–57), teacher of Greek at Cambridge.   This good Hellenist, noted for the love of Greek which he spread around him, gave in 1549 forcible expression to English conservatism in his *Hurt of Sedition*.   It is directed against the Norfolk rebels who were led by the tanner Kett. Already we have that hostile picture of popular risings which recurs half a century later in Shakespeare's *Henry VI* and *Coriolanus*.   Cheke shows himself vigorous in argument, eloquent, and occasionally homely and humorous.   He has both the tone and the arguments which are heard again from the Shakespearian Menenius Agrippa.

Form was almost as important to Cheke as matter, and he made attempts to reform the English language.   Sir Thomas Wilson (1525–81)[2] was concerned solely with style in his *Arte of Rhetorique*, published in 1553, in which this so-called English Quintilian recommends purity and simplicity of language.   He reviews and derides all the verbal affections of his time, and proscribes 'inkhorn terms,' 'outlandish English,' the barbarous legal language made up of deformed Anglo-Norman words, and the abuse of archaism by the 'fine courtier' who 'wil talke nothing but Chaucer.'

These men are good masters, sensible and sure, fashioning both mind and style by their precepts and example.   But their personalities are too restrained to have made a deep imprint on their prose.   Roger Ascham (1515–68)[3] had qualities which threw him more into relief.   He was the most popular of the educationists of his time, and the most pungent of the group of writers—Cheke, Wilson, Sir Thomas Smith, and Watson— who about the middle of this century transferred from Oxford to Cambridge the honour of guiding England along the paths of the Renascence.   Ascham was Cheke's friend, and in some degree his pupil, tutor to Elizabeth in her sixteenth year, a good Protestant, even tinged with Puritanism, yet prudent enough to be Mary Tudor's Latin secretary.   He left behind him two books of which one was devoted to the physical

---

[1] 1st edition 1549.   Reprinted by G. Langbaine (Oxford, 1641) and in Holinshed's *Chronicle*.   [2] Ed. by G. H. Mair (Oxford, 1909).
[3] Complete works, ed. Giles, 4 vols. (1864–5); English works, ed. Aldis Wright (Cambridge English Classics, 1904); Arber reprints of *Toxophilus* (1861) and *The Scholemaster* (1870); the latter also in Gregory Smith's *Elizabethan Critical Essays*, 2 vols. (Oxford, 1904).   See A. Katterfeld, *Roger Ascham, sein Leben und seine Werke* (Strasburg, 1879).

education of the young and the other to their intellectual instruction.

The first of them, *Toxophilus* (1545), is intended to revive the love of archery for which Ascham felt an almost romantic passion.   He even considers the bow to be a superior weapon to the cannon, and believes that the physical and moral health of his country is bound up with the practice of this obsolete sport.

His other book, *The Scholemaster*, was published in 1570, two years after his death, and contains his advice to masters on the teaching of Latin.

Ascham puts life into these treatises by his personal presentment of his ideas.   He brings forward his own practice and experience, his memories, and interesting anecdotes related first-hand.   His parentheses stimulate flagging attention.   His preoccupation with Latinity does not debar him from a moral point of view.   He admires the great writers of ancient Rome, but abominates, as papistical and corrupt, the Rome of his own time.   He vigorously attacks the Italianism of the English nobility, especially the dangerous sojourns in the country of licence which rich young men of wealth and fashion were wont to make.   He cares less for literary beauty and refinement than for solid and healthy education.

He also has the merit of having worked assiduously to advance the progress of the English language.   He is aware, he says in his preface to *Toxophilus*, that to write in Latin would have been 'more honest for my name,' but he decides to use English both to further 'the pleasure or commoditie of the gentlemen and yeomen of Englande,' and because everything has been written in English 'in a maner so meanly, bothe for the matter and handelynge, that no man can do worse.' Indisputably he helped to perfect the language by his use of it.   His style is much laboured, penetrated with Latin turns of phrase and Latin elegancies.   Numerous symmetrical, balanced, antithetical sentences, sometimes marked by alliteration, occur in his work, all that is best in the prose of the Euphuists without their eccentricity and false ornament.   It is true that Ascham in his Romanized dress is a little stiff and hampered.   But his faults are trifling as compared with the benefit prose derived from submitting to the discipline of the ancients, especially Cicero and Seneca, whose periodic style and nervous conciseness Ascham imitates by turns. The training which he imposed on himself and which he recommended for schoolboys had a salutary effect. He desired that a pupil should first translate a passage from Latin into English, and then, after a sufficient interval, be required to put his own English version back into Latin. By repeated use of this exercise Ascham himself acquired a relative facility of expression. The too heavy clothing of his thoughts finally became so pliable that the man, sincere, sensible and good-humoured, can be descried beneath it. He is one of the earliest writers of classical English prose.

These were the chief of the educationists, such of them as left a name behind them. The work which was being accomplished at this time cannot, however, be understood unless we add to their number all the nameless makers of the Renascence, all the unknown masters who were training their English pupils in the universities and the schools to admire and imitate the masterpieces of antiquity.

CHAPTER II

THE REFORMATION AND THE RELIGIOUS CONTROVERSIES FROM 1525 TO 1578

HUMANISM did not long remain without other admixture. Hardly had it affected literature when its influence was crossed and opposed by that of the religious Reformation. Most of the men of whom we have just spoken had to choose between the Pope and Luther or Calvin. The free development of their culture was interrupted and they were drawn into the religious struggle. In the year after that in which *Utopia* appeared Luther published his famous theses at Wittenberg. More's career was thereby transformed: the rest of his life was devoted to the defence of Catholic unity. Sir John Cheke died at forty-three years old of remorse for having abjured Protestantism under Mary Tudor. Ascham in his writings mingles Puritan ideas and pedagogic counsels. For others, controversy constituted all their life and the whole of their work.

Matter for controversy was from the outset mainly provided by the question of the translation of the Bible into English and of the dissolution of religious houses, both destined to influence language and literature importantly.

1. *Tindale. Translation of the Bible and the Book of Common Prayer.*—It was the question of translating the Bible which brought Sir Thomas More and William Tindale into conflict.

William Tindale (1484–1536) [1] was the first to be inspired by Luther's example, and as early as 1522 he began to translate the New Testament into English. As he was prevented from pursuing this work in England, where the king was still at this date a determined defender of orthodoxy, he took refuge on the Continent, and finally had his translation printed at Cologne in 1525. In spite of the measures taken by Henry VIII, it was introduced into England, where the ground had been prepared by Wyclif and where there were some local survivals of the spirit of the Lollards. Tindale's version of the New Testament, which was founded both on Luther's

[1] Complete works with preface by Foxe, 1572; modern edition in the Parker Society's Publications; *The Ordinance of a Christian Man*, ed. R. Lovett, 1886; selection by S. L. Greenslade, 1938. See J. F. Mosley, *William Tyndale*, 1937.

translation and on editions of the Greek and Latin texts elucidated by the commentaries of Erasmus, was a basis for the famous Authorized Version of 1611.

Tindale, who had been a pioneer during the dangerous years in which the Government of England was the champion of the papacy, maintained an active controversial defence of the Reformation. A good humanist, who had enjoyed a solid university education and knew the ancient and several modern languages, Tindale is a talented controversialist, especially in his treatise *The Obedience of a Christen man and how Christen rulers ought to governe*, which was printed in 1528. The advantage to the formation of vigorous, clear, and swift-moving English prose which arose out of the reformers' need to speak to the people is apparent in his work. In order to justify the translation of the Bible into the vulgar tongue, he not only uses the arguments based on good sense which appealed to the many, but also defends English against the orthodox allegation that it was incapable of rendering the original text adequately. He lays down that, on the contrary, 'the Greek tongue agreeth more with the English than with the Latin.' He discovers a deep-rooted affinity between English and Hebrew, thus first perceiving a truth of which the application had presently to be extended to the very spirit of the two peoples. Like the humanists, he makes mock of the scholastics who applied Aristotelian logic to the interpretation of Scripture, and he is again in agreement with them in condemning the medieval romances, the stories of Robin Hood and Bevis of Hampton, Hector and Troilus. But it is for reasons of morals that he rejects these tales, as licentious and ribald fables, not because he wishes another aesthetic ideal to be adopted. It is neither Homer nor Virgil which he would substitute for them, but only the Bible. From the first, he marks the agreement and the disagreement of humanism and the Reformation.

It was Thomas More, the most lettered and skilful of the Catholics, who replied to Tindale, particularly on the question of translating the Bible. In this controversy More does not appear to advantage. He himself had recommended the translation of Scripture and he was obliged to contradict his own proposition. He liked, moreover, to write in Latin, and it was incumbent on him in this dispute to use English. His position was the difficult one of a quiet scholar who is compelled to take part in a public meeting and to speak against liberty. He equivocated, hinted that the Church was not absolutely opposed to the translation of the Bible, but only to unfaithful versions falsified by heresy. But his acuteness showed him from the beginning how unfitting it would be to deliver up Holy Writ to the interpretation of the ignorant man in the street, 'suche blynd bayardis as wyll whan they rede the byble in englysch be more bysy than wyll bycum them.' He foresaw the swarming of the sects and the eccentricities of the Independents, and proposed a middle way. Let each bishop decide to whom in his diocese a copy of the translation might be entrusted and from whom it should be withheld or withdrawn.

But the public demand had already gone beyond such partial toleration. Tindale was persecuted and put to death in the Low Countries in 1536. Yet Henry VIII had broken with the papacy and had sent Thomas More to the scaffold in the previous year (1535). The Reformation was officially established in England, and Tindale's translation of the Bible, completed by Miles Coverdale in 1535,[1] was broadcast over the country. Four other translations were added to it during the next thirty years. The sacred texts of the Hebrews and the early Christians were in all men's hands, to be from this time a check or counterweight to the reading of Graeco-Roman classics, and to introduce into prose the biblical dialect which was to tinge so much of English literature. What is noticeable in these successive translations, and what was preserved by the Authorized Version of 1611, is the traditional prose which was adopted, one removed from pedantry and triviality, simple and yet a little quaint, to which the beauty of the original texts and a certain magic of style, especially perceptible in Coverdale, clings in varying degree. This prose, thus created, had incomparable influence. It appealed to all classes, penetrated by way of religious feeling to all minds, and gave a certain beauty to the speech even of the most ignorant and uncultivated, while it militated against the tendency to pedantry of the most learned. Its effects were especially conspicuous in the seventeenth century.

To the translation of the Bible, the Book of Common Prayer, drawn up under Edward VI in 1549,[2] was added. It is an anonymous compilation from the Latin missal, published under

[1] *Writings of Coverdale*, ed. Pearson (Cambridge, 1844).
[2] J. Dowden, *The Workmanship of the Prayer-Book*, 1899, and *Further Studies in the Prayer-Book*, 1908; E. Clapton, *Our Prayer Book Psalter*, 1934.

the direction of Archbishop Cranmer, and its cadences are such as to lift up the hearts of the faithful like poetry and to awaken the admiration of purely aesthetic critics. In this prayer-book Latin sonority has passed into a tongue which seemed hardly able to contain it. The mingling of the Saxon and French elements of the language is perfect. The disjointed and jarring character of pure Saxon has been eliminated. Everything connects, blends, harmonizes, for instance in the General Confession: 'Almighty and most merciful Father, We have erred, and strayed from thy ways like lost sheep. We have followed too much the devices and desires of our own hearts. . . .'

These chosen sounds must be imagined rolling from the lips of a clergyman who is a skilled reader and who gives the rhythm to the congregation. It must be remembered that these sonorous and melodious phrases were repeated every Sunday in every church in England. Only thus can the impulse be understood which such a model could give to a language as yet indefinite and in search of paths.

2. *The Dissolution of Religious Houses.*—The other great change in the reign of Henry VIII which reacted on letters was the suppression of the religious houses from 1535 to 1539.[1] To-day it is still difficult to say whether the measure was to the detriment or advantage of learning. There was an enormous destruction of books, deplored by the Protestants themselves, for instance by Bishop John Bale, one of the most determined enemies of the papacy. The Benedictine monasteries, which had been asylums for studious clerks, disappeared, and no like places of refuge arose in their stead. The numerous schools attached to many religious houses vanished also, and it was a long time before they were all replaced. Such of the Oxford and Cambridge colleges as were reserved for the religious became empty. The two great universities lost a considerable number of students. Higher education suffered: Greek, which had been brilliantly taught since the end of the fifteenth century, almost ceased, for a long period, to be studied. It was many years before the reformed foundations of schools and colleges compensated for the losses.

On the other hand, the end of the monasteries hastened the abandonment of scholastic philosophy which they had principally maintained, and this was favourable to a bolder spirit of intellectual enterprise. For the relations of the religious

---

[1] See *Cambridge History of English Literature*, vol. iii, Chap. III, and F. A. Gasquet, *Henry VIII and the English Monasteries*, 2 vols. (1888).

houses in England with sister houses on the Continent, relations established by the Reformers with their brothers in Germany, the Low Countries, and Geneva were substituted. Finally, the books which escaped the plunderers did not remain secreted and immobilized on the shelves of monastic libraries, but were henceforth read and studied. The great ardour of antiquaries dates from this time. The earliest of them was John Leland (1506?–1552), who was commissioned in 1533 to examine all the ancient monuments of the country, especially the archives of cathedrals, colleges, priories, and abbeys. He aspired to enrich the royal library with all the precious documents which had been delivered to the riflers, and was distressed to see young scholars sent from Germany to extract from them pages which went back with them to their own country, to rank there as national monuments. Leland spent six years travelling about England, exploring all the libraries, and he published a formidable list of the wealth he discovered. This was the limit of his capacity: his ambition to use his over-copious material was not realized. His *Itinerary* [1] served, however, to open a road, and at the end of the century it furnished Harrison [2] and Camden [3] and their like with material.

The same patriotic impulse is accountable for the many chronicles, Protestant in spirit, which appeared in the latter half of the sixteenth and the early seventeenth century. Edward Hall's *Chronicle*, published in 1548, traced the struggle of Lancaster and York and those of the first two Tudor reigns. Raphael Holinshed's *Chronicles*, which go back to remote origins, were written in collaboration with others, published in 1578 and continued to 1586, and were for long the great repertory of national history, used by Spenser and Shakespeare, among others. John Stow, between 1561 and 1604, issued eleven editions of his *Summarie of English Chronicles*. John Speed's *Historie of Great Britaine* was published in 1611; and William Camden's history of the reign of Elizabeth was written in Latin in 1615 and translated into French, and from French to English in 1625.

None of these authors is either a writer of great talent or

[1] *Itinerary*, first published by T. Hearne in 1710–12. Modern edition by L. T. Smith (1906–7).
[2] W. Harrison, *Description of England*, published in 1578 in Holinshed's *Chronicle*. Books II and III ed. by Furnivall, 1877–1908.
[3] W. Camden, *Britannia* (in Latin, 1586; English translation by P. Holland, *Britain*, 1610).

a veritable historian. Almost all of them collect evidence
uncritically and filch from their predecessors. They have a
mediocre talent for composition and cannot resist puerile
anecdotes. But they are all equally animated by the desire
to glorify the part played by England in the past as in the
present.

3. *Latimer and John Foxe.*—Besides these almost impersonal
productions, the Reformation provoked in the middle of the
sixteenth century the very living work of a preacher, Hugh
Latimer (1485–1555),[1] whose energy and good sense produced
some of the most pungent pages of English prose of the period.
At a time when religion wavered, when the country abruptly
passed from one form of observance to another at the will of
the governors, Latimer, in spite of one or two politic retrac-
tions, showed almost continuous zeal and courage in preaching
as he believed, against Catholicism during Wolsey's ministry,
against the bastard reform of Henry VIII, and against the
laxity of the Protestant clergy under Edward VI. He ended
at the stake, having refused, under Mary Tudor, to repudiate
his heresy. His last words to Bishop Ridley, the companion
of his martyrdom, are famous: 'Play the man, Master Ridley;
we shall this day light such a candle, by God's grace, in
England as I trust shall never be put out.'

These words have the accent of Thomas More, whom
Latimer resembles in his homely, almost jocular manner of
presenting his thought. He is like More, but has not his
underlying refinement or his frequent moments of detached
observation and reflection. Latimer's sermons are characterized by an absence of theology and dogmatic discussion.
Born of the people, a farmer's son, his mind had a popular
cast. His subject was morals, and he illustrated it by countless allusions to the most familiar things, proverbial turns
of speech, apologues and conceptions which were striking in
their simplicity.

He believed in the power of sermons and preached especially
against the clergy who did not preach. In his most celebrated sermon, that of 1594, 'Of the Plough,' he attacks the
laziness of the Protestant clergy. His wit is broad and he
scoffs at silent prelates with a comic use of alliteration: they
are 'pampering of their paunches,' 'mounching in their

---

[1] G. E. Corrie, *Latimer's Sermons* (Parker Society, 1844), and *Sermons and
Remains*, 1845; H. C. Beeching, *Sermons* (selected) in Everyman's Library,
1906. See R. W. and A. J. Carlyle, *H. L.*, 1900; H. S. Darby, 1953.

mangers.' He relates, with much go, how he went to carry
the gospel to a village grown unaccustomed to sermons, and
found the church empty, because it was Robin Hood's day:

It is no laughing matter, my friends, it is a weeping matter, a heavy
matter, a heavy matter, under the pretence for gathering for Robin
Hood, a traitor and a thief, to put out a preacher. . . . If the bishops
had been preachers, there should never have been any such thing.

A famous passage has its natural place in his argument:

I would ask you a strange question. Who is the most diligentest
bishop and prelate in all England, that passeth all the rest in doing his
office? . . . I will tell you. It is the devil. . . . He is never out of his
diocese. . . . He is ever at his plough.

And the devil will bring back popery:

Away with Bibles and up with beads! Away with the light of the
gospel and up with the light of candles, yea at noon-days.

There are two pages on this theme, and their energy and
redundancy are equally astonishing. The good Latimer's
phrases have the very same turn as those of the stump-
orators in London to-day. He keeps his audience breathless
by his mixture of mother-wit and feeling and his sudden
apostrophes. His great desire to be understood by the
most ignorant makes him a pioneer among prose-writers. He
simplifies and clarifies. By instinct and for his immediate
purposes he accomplishes a work analogous to that of a
pedagogue like Ascham. He often formulates his phrases
briefly and balances them symmetrically. Yet, preoccupied
as he is solely with religion, he is consistently careless of style.
Although literate himself, he never gives a thought to literature, which has given but little thought to him.

Beside Latimer, another and very different writer may be
ranged, the recorder of his last words on the stake and of the
deeds and sayings of all the English martyrs who suffered for
the Protestant faith and were the victims of Roman prelates
'from the yeare of oure Lord a thousande' onwards. It may
be claimed for John Foxe (1516–87) that he wrote the book of
this century which, after the Bible, made most noise. His
martyrology, *Actes and Monuments of these Latter and Perilous
Dayes* (1563), [1] is inevitably the work not of an historian but
of a partisan, but if the author be often credulous and partial,
he is also sincere. Each martyrdom is related with the
simplicity of an official report. There are no flowers of style,
but the wood-cuts in the original edition depict the tragic

[1] Ed. Cattley and Pratt, 8 vols., 1877. See J. F. Mozley, *John Foxe*, 1940.

scenes, the instruments of torture, the stake. Nothing did more than this work to spread hatred of the papacy in England and to maintain the spirit of heroism which was to appear again in the days of the Puritans. The book was known outside England, served the Huguenots as a breviary, and gave d'Aubigné material for 'Feux,' one of the books of his *Tragiques*. It was first written by Foxe in Latin, but was translated by him into an unadorned English, without literary form, minute and dramatic when it relates interrogatories and tortures. To-day it astonishes by the fury which animates it, and which can still hold a reader's attention, enormous though the volume be and terrible its monotony.

4. *Scotland. Lyndsay, Buchanan, and Knox.*—In Scotland the religious Reformation provoked a contemporary literary movement, evinced in the verses of Sir David Lyndsay, in the Latin works, both verse and prose, of George Buchanan, and in the treatises of John Knox.

Sir David Lyndsay (1490–1555)[1] is the last of the line of the Scottish poets of the fifteenth century. By the form of his poetry he connects with the Middle Ages, but his reforming zeal distinguishes him from his predecessors. His work consists of a series of virulent satires which herald d'Aubigné's *Tragiques*. Hence there is a certain contradiction between his matter and his manner. His denunciations of Rome are contained by the traditional frames. He is a Jean de Meun who writes a *Roman de la Rose* after Luther. There is the same discrepancy in his life as in his writings, for this fervent democrat, this associate of John Knox, was also the companion of James V from whom he received the high heraldic office of Lyon King of Arms.

Besides his *Satyre of the Thrie Estaitis*, of which we shall speak presently, he wrote *The Dreme* (1528), *The Complaynt* (1529), *The Testament of the Papyngo* (1530), *The Historie of ane nobill and vailyeand squyer, William Meldrum* (about 1550), and *The Monarchie, or Ane Dialog of the Miserable Estait of this World* (1552).

With prolix energy, without discrimination or beauty, but with a certain biting force, he denounces in these poems kings and prelates and their abuses and impostures. In his *Dreme* he descends into hell, where he sees popes, emperors, kings, cardinals, and archbishops chastized for the ambition which kept them from succouring and instructing the poor. His

[1] Works edited by D. Hamer, 4 vols. (Scottish Text Society, 1930–4). See W. Murison, *Sir David Lindsay* (1938).

vision brings him back to Scotland, and there he meets a poor lean man, in rags, 'with scrip on hip and pyikstaff in his hand,' who is preparing to leave the country. It is John the Common Weal, who will not return until Scotland has a good king.

Lyndsay's satires were at first predominantly social, but with years they became more and more Protestant. His last and most considerable poem, *The Monarchie*, is a history of the most famous kingdoms of the earth, beginning with Daniel's vision of the four beasts which became the empires of Babylon, Persia, Greece, and Rome. The author's basis is one of Knox's sermons. His octosyllabic lines are so virulent as to recall Skelton, whose verses they surpass in regularity, but also in an inexorably prosaic quality. Lyndsay has nothing of the poet except metre, but his brutal satire strikes hard and multiplies blows without flinching. Often coarse, he owed his immunity from persecution to his licentiousness. For Lyndsay as for Rabelais, ribaldry was a passport for daring.

The celebrated humanist George Buchanan (1506–82) [1] wrote almost wholly in Latin, and he therefore has here no place except as a witness to the classical culture of a Scot, and to the alliance between the Renascence and the Reformation which he represented. He had close relations with France, where he studied and taught, by turns in Paris and in Bordeaux where Montaigne was among his pupils. Reputed the first Latinist of his time, he was famous for his Latin verses and for his tragedies on the classic model, *Jephtha* and *Saint John the Baptist*. He had already distinguished himself by his satires against the Franciscans, the guardians of scholasticism, when, about 1560, he became one of the champions of Protestantism in his own country. It was at the moment when Scotland, impelled by Knox, was effecting her religious reformation. Buchanan, who until 1567 was Mary Stuart's tutor, became her determined enemy after the murder of Darnley, and wrote against her his *Detectio Mariae Reginae*. He ended as the stern schoolmaster of James VI, the pedant king, and wrote his *De Jure Regni apud Scotos* (1579) and his *Rerum Scoticarum Historia*. This was the last and most notable of a series of histories of Scotland which were written by Catholics and Protestants in the course of the sixteenth century and bear witness to the ardent Scottish patriotism. Buchanan has left behind him only two short

[1] Vernacular writings edited by P. Hume Brown (Scottish Text Society, 1892). Study by P. Hume Brown (Edinburgh, 1890).

treatises in Scots, but they are remarkable. His career shows what disturbance humanism suffered by the Reformation; party spirit is violently manifested by this man whose tastes first led him to pursue intellectual culture and learning for its own sake.

Buchanan left the glory of being the first great Scottish prose-writer to John Knox.[1] Knox (1505–72) was the reformer, the Calvin of Scotland. However fervently Lyndsay and Buchanan may have espoused the cause of reform, he was the Reformation itself. It was when he had taken refuge in Geneva with Calvin that he wrote, in 1558, his pamphlet against the two queens who were barring the spread of Protestantism in Scotland and England, *The First Blast of the Trumpet against the Monstrous Regiment of Women*. In 1559, back in Scotland and all-powerful there, he tormented and terrified Mary Stuart by his bold preaching, and until his death he pursued his ardent Calvinistic apostolate.

Knox, who wished for immediate effect, wrote in the language of his country. His *History of the Reformation of Religioun within the Realme of Scotland* is not the work of a professional writer, but of a man of action who relates history in which he played a great role. His composition is not good, but his book is full of matter, of vigorous and picturesque passages in which humour and satire mingle. His stories of the murder by the men of the reformed religion of their persecutor, Cardinal Beaton, and of his own interviews with Queen Mary, have been found worthy to be compared with the most expressive pages of Saint-Simon. Knox, who wishes to appeal to England as to Scotland, avoids the dialectal peculiarities of his mother tongue, and writes so as to be understood on both sides of the Tweed.

In all these men, and especially the Scots, there is something which presages a new era, social as well as religious, an age of democracy as well as of Protestantism. There are signs of a progress towards the triumph of the Presbyterians and the Puritans. In the meanwhile, the reformers' need to speak to the people frequently led them to use the vulgar tongue rather than Latin, and it is undeniable that they largely contributed to the advance of English prose, that medium which the humanists had too often disdained.

---

[1] Complete works ed. D. Laing, 6 vols. (Edinburgh, 1846–64). Life by P. Hume Brown, 2 vols., 1895. See also Andrew Lang, *John Knox and the Reformation*, 1905; Edwin Muir, *John Knox*, 1929; Lord E. Percy, *John Knox*, 1937.

CHAPTER III

POETRY—ITALIANISM, WYATT AND SURREY—SACKVILLE AND
THE 'MIRROR FOR MAGISTRATES'—GASCOIGNE

POETRY [1] owes less to the reformers. They kept aloof from it as secular and frivolous. It was humanism which provoked the renewal of poetry, and especially the influence of the Italian Renascence. The task involved was considerable, for verse had to be saved both from the languor which had overtaken it with such as Stephen Hawes and from the artistic disarray which such as Skelton had brought upon it. Everything had to be done over again. Under Henry VIII two poets of the court undertook the task, and it was in Italy that they found both models and stimulus. These pioneers, whose labours were ended by premature death, were Wyatt and Surrey.

1. *Wyatt.*—Sir Thomas Wyatt (1503–42),[2] who made sojourns in France and Italy, brought back from the latter country, in 1527, the admiration for lyrical poetry which he found there, and a desire to fashion English verse on the model of the Italians, or of the ancients seen through an Italian medium.

His first object was to restore to English verse the nobility, grace, and harmony it had lost. But as he groped after this ideal he showed how difficult was his enterprise. He seems at first to have perceived only the law of syllabism, and it is possible to find, doubtless in his earliest work, verses in which there is no discoverable regularity in the use of accents. So uncertain is his prosody, that we are driven to ask whether he were unaware of the iambic rhythm, or whether he pronounced such words as *bannèr, suffèr, [dis]pleasùre, fearèth,* as iambuses, throwing the accent on to the last syllable. His rhymes manifestly fall on unaccented syllables.

Gradually, however, he attained to comparative regularity. He went further than this. He borrowed from the Italians

---

[1] J. M. Berdan, *Early Tudor Poetry* (New York, 1920).
[2] A. K. Foxwell, *The Poems of Sir Thomas Wiat,* 2 vols. (1913, also in 1 vol.); E. M. W. Tillyard, *The Poems of Sir Thomas Wiat, a Selection and a Study,* 1929; K. Muir, *The Collected Poems of Sir Thomas Wyatt* (Muses Library), 1949. See E. Bapst, *Deux gentilshommes et poètes à la cour de Henri VIII,* 1891; E. K. Chambers, *Sir Thomas Wyatt and Other Studies,* 1933.

poetic forms which were unknown to his fellow-countrymen.
Sometimes he uses Dante's *terza rima*, sometimes Serafino's
strambotti, octaves rhyming as *abababcc*, and sometimes he
imitates the Petrarchian sonnet. It was this last importation,
effected in France at much the same time by Marot and Mellin
de Saint-Gelais, which had by far the largest consequences.
This was due not only to the beauty of the form, but also to the
fact that the sonnet was then the principal vehicle for the
direct expression of personal feeling, without recourse to fiction
or allegory.

It was by the sonnet that lyricism again entered English
poetry. Whether it were translated or imitated mattered
little. It rendered the music of feeling or passion. It called
forth the rare word, the metaphor, subtlety and condensation.
Its very brevity necessitated artistic labour.

Wyatt wrote no memorable sonnets, but he blazed the
track. His imitations of Petrarch brought bold and new
images into English. He speaks of love who

> Into my face presseth with bold pretence,
> And there campeth displaying his banner,

and tells that, upon rejection,

> . . . to heart's forest he fleeth,
> Leaving his enterprise with pain and cry.

This impassioned language was current and normal fifty years
later, but before Wyatt it was entirely unknown.

Wyatt's sighs and supplications are Petrarchian. He is
himself in other sonnets in which he pulls himself together and
tells his mistress hard truths. His nature was frank and
manly, like the proud portrait which Holbein made of him.
The groans of humility suited him ill:

> My heart I gave thee, not to do it pain,

he says; and again:

> For he that doth believe bearing in hand,
> Plougheth in the water and soweth in the sand.

He bids farewell not to his mistress only, but to love also:

> Farewell, Love, and all thy laws for ever;
> Thy baited hooks shall tangle me no more:
> Senec and Plato call me from thy lore
> To perfect wealth, my wit for to endeavour.

And he bids love:

> With idle youth go use thy property.

He does indeed renounce love poems for satire. And his satires, imitated from Horace and Alamanni, are among his happiest innovations, reflecting his energetic and bold character. The courtier, withdrawn from the court, relates the vice and wretchedness he has seen. He mocks the gallants who advance their fortunes by marrying old rich widows. He tells, after Horace and Henryson, the fable of the town mouse and the country mouse, perhaps less happily than those predecessors, but with a proud accent to point his moral reflections.

The cavalier tone of his personal sonnets and his satires recurs in a few poems which are true songs, for instance, that beginning, 'Madam, withouten many words,' in which he calls upon his mistress to answer him yea or nay, and that last summons to his lute which has kept its place in most anthologies:

> My lute, awake! perform the last
> Labour that thou and I shall waste;
>   And end that I have now begun:
> And when this song is sung and past,
> My lute, be still, for I have done.

2. *Surrey*.—Although he speaks of his vanished youth, Wyatt died young, at thirty-nine years old, so that he gave no full measure of his powers. Still less did Surrey do so, for he was sent to the scaffold by Henry VIII when only thirty.

The names of these poets are permanently linked in literary history. Born fourteen years after Wyatt, Surrey seems to have been the disciple of the older man, whose name he celebrates in fine verses. The Earl of Surrey (1517–47) [1] was thus not obliged, like Wyatt, painfully to discover the rhythm of verse. Almost all the verses he left behind him are regular and harmonious. His nature was less energetic than Wyatt's, but he was a better artist. The accomplishment of his short life is remarkable. His personality, that of a great gentleman and a poet, is like a first sketch for Sidney's.

Much more dominated than Wyatt by the Petrarchian convention, Surrey sang in sonnets his entirely imaginative love for Geraldine, or Lady Elizabeth Fitzgerald. The elegiac tone is natural to him. His special note is that of love for nature, and with happy effect he mingles descriptions of nature with his love plaints.

But it is perhaps in some impersonal sonnets that his merit as an artist shows itself best. There may be a satirical allusion

[1] Poems edited by F. M. Padelford (Seattle, 1920; revised 1928). See E. Bapst, op. cit., on p. 221, n. 2.

to a contemporary personage in his sonnet on Sardanapalus, but it should be read for its absolute value, its dignified swing, its structural force, and its effort to condense thought:

> Thassyrian king in peace, with foule desire,
> And filthy lustes, that staynd his regall hart,
> In war that should set princely hartes on fire:
> Did yeld, vanquished for want of marciall art.
> The dint of swordes from kisses seemed strange:
> And harder, than his ladies syde, his targe:
> From glutton feastes to souldiars fare, a change:
> His helmet, farre above a garlands charge.
> Who scarce the name of manhode did retayn,
> Drenched in slouth and womanish delight,
> Feble of spirte, impacient of pain:
> When he had lost his honor, and his right:
>   Proud, time of wealth, in stormes appalled with drede,
>   Murthered himself to shewe some manful dede.

A like grandeur distinguishes the sonnet which praises Wyatt for his translation of some of the Psalms of David. The humanist is betrayed in an allusion to Alexander preserving Homer's poems in an ark of gold, and is revealed elsewhere also, even in the love effusions, for instance in that curious lyrical piece, 'When raging love,' in which the poet consoles himself for his heartaches by thinking of the countless ills endured by the Greeks before they became masters of Ilion.

Nature and the poets of antiquity alternately console Surrey for his lover's griefs and his sadness when he is in prison. His most intimate poem is that in which, 'prisoned in Windsor he recounteth his pleasure there passed':

> Where I in lust and joy,
> With a king's son, my childish years did pass,

the allusion being to his close friendship with the Duke of Richmond, natural son to Henry VIII. The elegy depicts his early joys—games, hunting, the 'secret groves' and the 'wild forest,' above all the pleasures of friendship:

> The secret thoughts, imparted with such trust,
> The wanton talk.

No other poem gives in so short a compass a richer description of the luxurious and chivalrous life of a young nobleman:

> The palme-play [1] where, despoiled for the game,
> With dazed eyes oft we by gleams of love
> Have missed the ball, and got sight of our dame,
> To bait her eyes, which kept the leads above.

---

[1] Tennis

Remembering that nearly all Surrey's verses have a just and sure harmony, one cannot exaggerate the loss which English poetry suffered by his premature death. Less directly influenced by the Italians than Wyatt, he had a perfectly just sense of what befitted the poetry of his nation. For the sonnet on the Italian model cultivated by his friend—two quatrains followed by two tercets—he substituted the less elaborate and easier English form which Shakespeare afterwards adopted, three quatrains with different rhymes followed by a couplet. But his chief title to glory is that he introduced blank verse into English when, probably in the prison which he left only to go to his death, he translated the second and fourth books of the *Aeneid*. He may have been induced to make this translation by the example of Cardinal Ippolito de' Medici (1541). The innovation is in the pure spirit of the Renascence. It was to be attempted in all modern languages, with unequal results. How indeed was it possible not to blush for rhyme which none of the ancients authorized by their example, and not to try to dispense with it when translating their hexameters? Surrey's blank verse is simply the decasyllabic or heroic metre shorn of its rhymes. Of classical origin, it is learned verse, in no way popular. That Surrey was able immediately to give it almost all its distinctive characteristics is remarkable. It had to be saved from too close resemblance to rhymed decasyllabic verse; it was necessary that the sense of the words should not be complete at the end of each line, for this would have caused the lack of rhyme to be felt and produced wearisome monotony. To avoid this defect, Surrey decided to imitate Virgil in dividing lines, letting the sense run on from one line to another. But he did this too little, and without the sure touch and facility which his imitators acquired long after him. His line is stiff and lacks ductility. But it catches the epic tone, and shows itself much more apt to render Virgil's poetry than a rhymed line. This partial translation, which was little removed in date from that of the Scottish Douglas, proves that a revolution had been accomplished between 1520 and 1540. If Surrey's verses are far from attaining to the smooth Virgilian beauty, he has dignity and often strength. Thanks to him, English poetry acquired a magnificent instrument, which, once perfected, became the metre of the drama and of the epic.

Wyatt and Surrey published nothing in their lifetimes. It was not until ten years after Surrey had been legally murdered that Richard Tottel, the printer, brought their verses out, together with those of some inferior authors, in the famous collection of songs and sonnets commonly known as *Tottel's Miscellany*.[1] The influence of the two poets could not therefore be felt immediately, nor did it take effect as soon as the *Miscellany* appeared, numerous though the readers of this collection were. A whole generation passed before the lead of Wyatt and Surrey was followed. The very form of the sonnet was almost forgotten, and the name was used to designate short poems of very varying structure, often mere songs. These two poets must be admitted to have been much in advance of their time, English poetry to have been unripe for their ingenious essays. Yet they were in no way in revolt against the national tradition. Wyatt was a great admirer of Chaucer, had read the old poet assiduously. Nor did he reject the French models traditional in his country, for he made translations of Mellin de Saint-Gelais. But his Italianism did not take root in English poetry or bear fruit there until forty years after his death. Almost all the work of the French Pleiad was produced before England had made a step in advance. She did not even keep the position which these two young courtly writers had won for her.

3. *Sackville*.—Thomas Sackville (1536–1608),[2] the only poet after Wyatt and Surrey and before Spenser who left memorable verses behind him, reverted to the medieval tradition. He was, none the less, a humanist who gave England her first classical tragedy. But chance willed that his only contribution to poetry, other than drama, was the *Induction*, which was followed by *The Complaint of the Duke of Buckingham*, written in 1563 for the *Mirror for Magistrates*. This *Mirror* was a series of stories concerning the misfortunes of the great figures in English history, and was written by several poets. Sackville conceived the idea of the collection, and his verses constitute its only merit.

The conception is in itself evidence of the patriotism which was impelling Englishmen to explore their annals. This enormous poem is founded on Lydgate's *Falls of Princes*, which was an adaption of Boccaccio's *De Casibus Virorum Illustrium*, previously imitated by Chaucer in his 'Monk's Tale.' The authors of the *Mirror for Magistrates* cull their examples not

[1] First published in 1557. Reprinted by Arber; scholarly edition by H. E. Rollins, 2 vols. (Harvard, 1928–9).

[2] *The Mirror for Magistrates*, ed. L. B. Campbell (1938). Sackville's contributions ed. by M. Hearsey from MS., 1936. See p. 229.

from universal but solely from English history, but this effect of
recrudescent patriotism cannot be called a literary innovation.

Sackville's *Induction*, written in the seven-line stanzas
(*ababbcc*) beloved of Chaucer, takes us back to the vision and
allegories of the *Roman de la Rose*. As a dark winter night
is coming on, and the poet is mournfully reflecting on the
miserable end of the great ones of the kingdom, and wishing
he could describe them in order 'to warn the rest whom fortune
left alive,' he sees approaching the sad shape of Sorrow, who
offers to guide him in to the realms of the dead, where he will
hear their complaints. Led by her, he sees at the gate
Remorse, Dread, Revenge, Misery, Care, Sleep, Old Age,
Malady, Famine, and War. He crosses the Acheron, passes
near Cerberus, and enters the kingdom of Pluto, where, first
of the fallen princes, the Duke of Buckingham comes to
relate to him his woes.

It is difficult to imagine a gloomier series of stanzas. The
darkness is uninterrupted, and it is this very excess of misery
which constitutes the novelty of the poem. Never, since
Dante's *Inferno*, had the Middle Ages conceived a vision
so tensely and implacably sinister. A stronger brush was
needed, a palette richer in sombre hues, a more solemn tone,
than any which belonged to the trouvères. The best of those
old verses, even Chaucer's, had a certain frailty. The language
was too slight, the rhythm not sufficiently marked. But
Sackville used an English which had contracted its grammar
and dropped its terminations, and he re-established alternating accents more regularly than even Wyatt and Surrey.
Just because he wrote at a time when the accentual rhythm
of verse was in process of being reconstituted, he exaggerated
his scansion with a powerfully monotonous effect, which he
further emphasized by repeated alliterations.

The men of the Renascence who re-established rhythm were
preoccupied by ancient metres. It was they who first used
the words iambus, trochee, and spondee to denote the combinations of accentuated and unaccentuated syllables in their
lines. Chaucer gave no thought to anything of the sort, but
was guided by ear alone, and escaped the more rigid laws
observed by the earlier poets of the sixteenth century, or
rather such few of them as wished to restore metre. Versification wavered for some time between anarchy and excessive
regularity before it reached equilibrium. Sackville belongs
to the small number faithful to scansion, and he hammers

out his syllables with striking emphasis but monotonous persistence. He has, however, undeniable artistic sense, and he uses this very ding-dong to reinforce the energy of his gloomy pictures. Spenser was inspired by him when he painted the most lugubrious scenes of *The Faerie Queene*, for instance the Cave of Despair, and even more when he wrote the melancholy stanzas of his *Complaints*, especially *The Ruins of Time* and *The Tears of the Muses*. Sackville really deserves to be called the connecting link between Chaucer and Spenser. He lacked the variety of both these great poets perhaps because he soon left poetry for politics, ending as Lord Buckhurst and Lord High Treasurer. We have to judge his lyrical powers from a single lyric. His verses were isolated in a generation of which the poetic faculty was mediocre, hardly existent. He deserves the glory of having helped to renew English poetry.

4. *Various Poets. Gascoigne.*—Nothing could be emptier than this period. A bare mention suffices for the 'tragedy' of *Jane Shore*, which was inserted by Thomas Churchyard in the *Mirror for Magistrates*, and was correctly versified but no more; for the *Eclogues* of Barnaby Googe (1563), poor in rhythm, Protestant rather than poetical; for the epitaphs, epigrams, songs, and sonnets in which George Turberville modestly imitated Wyatt and Surrey; and for Thomas Tusser's advice to farmers and their wives, swelling in bulk from 1557 to 1573, *Hundreth Good Pointes of Husbandrie, A Hundreth Good Poynts of Huswifery, Five Hundreth Pointes of Good Husbandry*. Tusser's collection of practical counsels are completely prosaic, yet have some go and wit, and they are written in popular four-accented lines which seem to move at a gallop.

Verse continued for the most part to appear in collections or miscellanies, issued by a bookseller and induced by the success of *Tottel's Miscellany*. They were of diminishing interest. They included *The Paradyse of Daynty Devises* (1576), by Richard Edwards, choirmaster of the Chapel Royal, and the *Gorgious Gallery of Gallant Inventions* (1578), collected by Thomas Proctor.

Only one writer deserves less cursory notice, George Gascoigne (1525?–77),[1] who essayed to grope his way along all

[1] Complete works ed. by W. C. Hazlitt, 2 vols. (1869–70), by J. W. Cunliffe 1907, and for the C.U.P. 1910. See also the study of Gascoigne by F. E. Schelling (Boston, 1893) and C. T. Prouty's *George Gascoigne* (O.U.P., 1942).

the new paths opened by the Renascence, although he made
no great advance on any of them. A soldier and a poet, he
was an amateur of poetry. Besides drama, he wrote in his
youth love poems and slightly scandalous confessions, his
Hundreth Sundrie Flowers, 'bounde up in one small Poesie:
Gathered partely by Translation in the fyne outlandish Gar-
dins of Euripides, Ovid, Petrarke, Ariosto, and others, and
partly by invention out of our owne fruitfull orchardes in
England.' These *Flowers* only appeared in 1573. Meanwhile the aging author had become pious and moral. It was
then that he wrote *The Glass of Government,* in 1575, his satire
in blank verse, *The Steel Glass,* in 1576, and *The Droome of
Doomesday.* To these should be added the short metrical
treatise called *Certayne Notes of Instruction concerning the
making of verse or ryme in English.* Whatever form he chose,
Gascoigne was almost always first in the field, and he is re-
nowned for having written the first prose story taken from
real life, the first prose comedy, the first tragedy translated
from Italian, the first masque, the first regular satire, and the
first treatise on English prosody. But this versatility proves
him prolific rather than artistic. He writes easily, without
brilliancy or distinction. His blank verse is correct, but
flat and dull; it reminds us of a hammer striking on a wooden
anvil. He has, however, a curious mind, he is discreet, and
there is go in his verses. His few innovations were so soon
exceeded that hardly a trace is left of them. At one time a
disciple of Italianism, he afterwards repudiated this fashion.
His *Steel Glass,* which is his best-known work, compares the
truthful metal mirror of olden days with the too flattering
glass, doubtless of Venetian crystal, used by the gallants and
ladies of the poet's time. Here Gascoigne denounces the
profanity and luxury of modern manners. He would revert
to ancestral customs, and in his *Notes* he analogously advo-
cates the reduction of the vocabulary to monosyllables, to
the only words which were, in his opinion, of truly English
origin. It is curious to notice how nationalism awoke in all
these men, who at one time were humanists or Italianate, and
with nationalism the desire to bar out foreign importations.

[1] Ed. by C. T. Prouty (New York, 1942).

Note. For further study on subjects of this chapter, see L. B. Campbell,
Tudor conceptions of history and tragedy in A Mirror for Magistrates (Berkeley,
California, 1936); J. Swart, *Thomas Sackville. A Study in Sixteenth Century
Poetry* (Groningen, 1949), and C. T. Prouty, *George Gascoigne,* 1942.

CHAPTER IV

THE THEATRE FROM 1520 TO 1578 [1]

1. *Humanism in the Theatre.*—English dramatic writing produced no masterpiece in this period, yet felt its way along the most various paths, and acquired an experience without which the Elizabethan drama would have been impossible. It partook both of the past which had survived, and of the future for which it was preparing.

The miracle plays were performed almost till the end, although, since the Protestants looked askance at them, they gradually lost ground, and the cycles of the different towns disappeared, one after another, as the Reformation advanced. In any case, these plays did no more than prolong their existence. They no longer changed: they merely persisted in the form which they had assumed in the fifteenth century. The interesting point is that they still had a large public, and that dramatic innovations did not supplant them, but were introduced side by side with them.

Moralities, on the other hand, did not only continue to be much appreciated, but were also modified and renewed in accordance with circumstances. Those produced until about 1520 were Christian and no more. They may be said to have had neither place nor date. But the moralities came to be impregnated with the spirit of the Renascence or the Reformation. Two distinct groups of them appeared, which voiced respectively humanist and Protestant tendencies.

Tedious though was the morality *Magnificence*,[2] written by John Skelton about 1516, it yet showed a new standpoint. It did not merely, like its predecessors, represent the struggle between Heaven and Hell. Skelton, who seems to have aimed at warning Henry VIII against mad extravagance, does not deal with the great problem of Christianity, but enforces a particular moral lesson. His hero, Magnificence, is brought to ruin by a succession of bad counsellors, and would kill himself were he not saved by the intervention of Good Hope,

---

[1] A. W. Reed, *Early Tudor Drama* (London, 1926).
[2] Edited by A. Dyce, *Skelton's Works* (1843), and by R. L. Ramsay (1906).

Circumspection, Perseverance, and others. This is the first specimen of a laicized morality.

In its two successors the spirit of the Renascence is much more clearly marked. They are inspired neither by the usual moral lesson nor by religious faith, but by the love of knowledge. Manifestly they were born in academic circles in which knowledge is the ideal goal and in which the devil is named Ignorance.

The morality of *The Four Elements*,[1] which was printed in 1519, and of which fragments are extant, is very curious. It is contemporary with More's *Utopia*. Like More, the author is under the influence of the tales of Amerigo Vespucci. He teaches geography, cosmography, almost all the sciences known to his time. The Messenger, who speaks the prologue, discourses gravely on science and deplores the lack of learned books in England and English. Only frivolous books, he says, are written in English, and only the rich man is esteemed wise in England. Yet true wisdom is in knowledge, in knowledge of God who can be known only by His works, and therefore in the study of nature. The play leaves theology on one side. The subject is the instruction of the child Humanity, son of 'Natura Naturata.' He is entrusted to Studious Desire, but his progress is interrupted by the temptations of Sensual Appetite, who takes him to the tavern. The child has interpreted ill the words of Nature, who bade him use his senses. Only at the end of the play does he again show a taste for knowledge.

Sensual Appetite here plays the part of clown, as does his friend Ignorance, who detests philosophers and astronomers and boasts of his own power, saying that he is mightier than the king of England or France, that he is the greatest lord alive, and has more than five hundred thousand servants in England. He addresses the audience directly:

> For all that they be now in this hall,
> They be the most part my servants all,
>   And love principally
> Disports, as dancing, singing,
> Toys, trifling, laughing, jesting;
>   For cunning they set not by.

A geography lesson produces a burst of patriotism. Studious Desire instructs Humanity that the earth is round; Experience displays a globe, enumerates the countries she has visited,

[1] Edited by W. C. Hazlitt in Dodsley's *Old English Plays*, vol. i (1874), and by J. S. Farmer (*Six Anonymous Plays*, 1905).

dwelling on America, and deplores that Spaniards, Portuguese, and Frenchmen have gone farther than Englishmen:

> O, what a thing had be then,
> If that they that be Englishmen
> Might have been the first of all
> That there should have taken possession.

She would have wished all these countries to have been civilized and converted to religion by the English.

A like ardour to instruct fills John Redford's pedagogic morality, *The Play of Wyt and Science*,[1] which dates from the end of the reign of Henry VIII.   Reason, after the manner of a highborn father, wishes to marry his daughter Science to Human Wit, the son of Nature.   It matters not that Wit is neither well born nor rich:

> Wherefore, syns they both be so meet matches
> To love each other, strawe for the patches
> Of worldly muckel syence hath inowghe
> For them both to lyve.

But Wit for long lacks wisdom.   In his youthful eagerness to know he imprudently attacks Tediousness and is saved only just in time by Honest Recreation.   She, unfortunately, does not satisfy him, and he leaves her and falls asleep in the lap of Idleness.   Without knowing it he has become a fool, when, at last, he reaches the presence of Science, who repels him for an ignorant suitor.   But in a mirror he sees himself as he is and is disgusted.   After a term of chastisement and hard labour, he again attacks Tediousness, this time with a good sword, and slays him.   Science, who has watched the encounter from the summit of Mount Parnassus, now accepts her destined spouse, first warning him:

> But if ye use me not well, then dowt me,
> For, sure, ye were better then wythout me!

This is an ingenious and well-arranged morality, which is pervaded by strong rationalist conviction.   It resumes the spirit of the Renascence well, and bears witness to the appetite for knowledge which caused schools and colleges to be born in the land.   The comic element is supplied by an episode in which Ignorance is heard blundering through a lesson in the alphabet given him by his mother, Idleness.   The mistress, who represents the old somnolent methods of teaching, is no less ridiculous than her idiot pupil.

[1] In *Specimens of the Pre-Shakespearian Drama*, ed. J. M. Manly, vol. i (1897).

2. *The Reformation on the Stage.   Lyndsay.   John Bale.*—
Very early, the Reformation attempted to take possession of
the morality and use it for its own ends.   Passion, inevitably
unjust and sometimes brutal, gave life to more than one
Protestant morality play.   They appeared in the north and
in the south.   The first in date was written by the Scot Sir
David Lyndsay, whose reforming zeal we have already seen.

His *Satire of the Thrie Estaitis* [1] was played in 1540 at Lin-
lithgow before the King of Scotland, the bishops, and the people.
It is as political as it is religious.   The three estates are the
nobles, the clergy, and the merchants, and all three are pilloried
together, censured for giving too much ear to Sensuality,
Wantonness, and Deceit.   The grievances which John the
Common Weal, the man of the people, has against them are
just enough, and it is pleasant to see him obtain the needed
reforms with the help of Good Counsel and Correction.

Lyndsay's special attack is against the Church.   Dame
Veritie, who desires access to the king, finds her way barred
by the lords spiritual, scared at her advent.   An abbot wishes
to cast her into prison, and a parson recommends that she be
put to death, under cover of the king's momentary subjection
to Dame Sensuality.   The same priest summons Veritie to
declare by what right she is addicted to preaching.   He
threatens her with the stake, and when she refuses to retract,
Flattery, a monk, exclaims:

> Quat buik is that, harlot, into thy hand?
> Out, walloway! this is the New Test'ment,
> In Englisch toung and printit in England:
> Herisie, herisie! fire, fire! incontinent.

In a comic interlude the social satire is dominant.   Pauper
recounts his misadventures.   He used to keep his old father
and mother by his labour and owned a mare and three cows.
When his parents died the landlord took the mare as a heriot;
the vicar seized the best cow at his father's, and the second
best at his mother's, death.   The third cow went the same way
when his wife died of grief, when also the vicar's clerk bore off
the uppermost clothes of the family.   There is nothing left
for Pauper to do but to beg.   The parish priest has refused
him Easter communion because he no longer pays tithes.
He has only one farthing in his pocket with which to plead for
justice.   A Pardoner arrives, boasting of his relics and insulting the New Testament, which sells to the injury of his

[1] In Hamer's edition, see *supra*, p. 218, n.

trade. With his last farthing Pauper buys a thousand years' indulgence, but when he asks to see his purchase a fight ensues and the relics fall into the gutter.

These passages give an idea of the violence of the attack and of the life it imparted to the morality.

The Protestants of England were no less ferocious. Their most famous dramatic champion was Bishop John Bale (1495–1563), who even attempted to turn the fixed and traditional miracle plays to Protestant uses. Under the name of tragedies, comedies, and interludes, he wrote scenes in harmony with the reformed faith, taking them from sacred history and principally from the life of Christ. But he gave the chief of his efforts to morality plays, combined with history which was sometimes contemporary, as in his *Proditiones Papistarum* and *Super utroque Regis Coniugio.* The most interesting of his dramatic essays is, however, his allegory *King Jehan,* [1] in which he recasts history to his liking. He makes of the deplorable John a great king, hated and calumniated by the clergy. For John had been bold enough to rebel against Rome, and all his faults, crimes, and cowardice are therefore wiped out. He is represented as a man misunderstood, a noble victim, the first Protestant. This play merits a particular place in the history of the theatre. It is the half-open chrysalis, the morality play whence the historical drama is about to emerge. Real and allegorical characters are mingled in it. John is betrayed by Dissimulation and threatened by Sedition. Moreover, abstractions are changed in the course of the play into living beings. Sedition, for instance, becomes Cardinal Stephen Langton, Usurped Power the pope. This is a travesty of history and yet history, and, through the medium of another and Elizabethan work on the same reign, it was to leave its mark on Shakespeare's *King John.*

3. *Heywood's Interludes.* '*Calisto and Meliboea.*' — John Heywood's (1497?–1580) [2] interludes or farces, written under Henry VIII, cannot be called Catholic answers to Protestant attacks since they preceded the offensive of the Reformers. Two of them were printed as early as 1533. Heywood, a good Catholic and the friend of Thomas More, wrote in the medieval tradition, in the spirit of the fabliaux which certainly did not

[1] Edited by J. M. Manly in *Specimens of the pre-Shakespearian Drama,* vol. i.

[2] *Dramatic Writings,* ed. by J. S. Farmer, 1905. See *The Play of the Weather* and *Johan Johan* in Gayley's *Representative English Comedies,* vol. i., 1903, and R. de la Bere, *John Heywood, Entertainer,* 1937.

spare churchmen. He was original in avoiding morality
plays and in having no purpose but to amuse. He has no
notion of ecclesiastical or theological controversy. His
interludes are mere comic dialogues, scenes from fabliaux
sometimes modelled on the French. But he is of his own
nation almost the only representative of this school of dramatic
writing. The four interludes which he certainly wrote are
controversies in burlesque. In *Witty and Witless*, James and
John discuss whether it is better to be a fool or a wise man:
they are echoing the *Dyalogue du fol et du sage* performed at the
court of Louis XII. In *Love*, an unloved lover and his un-
loving mistress seek, each of them, to prove himself the more
miserable, while another couple, a lover beloved and a man
who is neither loved nor a lover, dispute the right to be called
the happier. In *The Play of the Weather*, ten characters demand
of Jupiter that he send them weather suited to their needs or
desires, and the god finally decides that each of them shall be
satisfied in turn. In *The Four P's*, four characters, a Palmer,
a Pardoner, a Potycary, and a Pedlar, discuss which of them
shall tell the biggest lie. The pilgrim declares that in all his
travels he has never seen a woman lose patience, and the others
themselves allow that he has won the prize.

These plays are, it is seen, without plot, but Heywood puts
life into his characters and expresses himself with a drollery
which recalls Chaucer. There is a grotesque description of
hell equal to the Sompnour's in the prologue to his Tale.
Good humour reigns everywhere. Yet these writings are
hardly dramas. If, as is probable, Heywood also wrote *The
Pardoner and the Friar* and *Johan Johan*, the story of a husband deceived by his wife, Tyb, and Sir Johan, the parish
priest, he came much nearer to farce in them. Their characters
and incidents conform excellently to the old comic tradition,
and their dramatization could not be more vigorous. In these
two pieces Heywood was inspired by French originals, *Farce
nouvelle d'un pardonneur, d'un triacleur et d'une tavernière* and
Farce de Pernet qui va au vin. Although he wrote under
Henry VIII he never even suggests the Renascence.

Not, that is, unless the comic monologue *Thersites*, played
about 1537, may be ascribed to him on the evidence of style.
Its subject and its allusions are loaded with classical reminiscences. The play is a free adaptation from the Latin of
Ravisius Textor, or Jean Tixier de Ravisé, professor of rhetoric
in Navarre College in Paris. Antiquity supplied the material

for this farce, which had many analogies with the *Franc Archer de Bagnolet*, and which brought the braggart on to the English stage for the first time.

Another novelty isolated in the reign of Henry VIII was the adaptation of the famous Spanish play *Celestina* which was printed in 1530 as *Calisto and Meliboea*.[1]   The English play-wright has kept only the first four of the sixteen acts of his original.   He has changed the long crowded drama with its tragic conclusion to a romantic comedy having a moral and cheerful ending.   The character of the procuress Celestina, the descendant of Dame Siriz and the prototype of Macette, is indeed the same in the English as in the original version, but before she throws Meliboea into the arms of Calisto, the girl's father intervenes to save her on the brink of the abyss.   Thus the didactic instinct cuts short a romantic drama.

4. *Progress of the Theatre after 1550.*—There was no further change in the first half of the century, but from 1550 onwards innovations came thick and fast.

It is about the middle of the century that the formation of troops of professional players, in addition to the amateurs who performed in the miracle plays, can be clearly traced. In more than one school and more than one college of the the universities there were performances especially of classical pieces, but usually they were written by the masters and acted by the pupils.   But the people of the provinces as well as those of the capital wished to be amused, and they were no longer satisfied with the miracle plays and moralities.   Inter-ludes, otherwise farces, were in great demand and were provided by professional actors.   These were at first poor wretches, always under suspicion, who were harried by the authorities as rogues and vagabonds.   Before they could be left in peace they had to obtain the patronage of a magnate, a baron at the least.   There was no lack of such willing pro-tectors who appreciated their services.   The first company to obtain letters patent was Leicester's, in 1574, but it was not the first to stroll about the country.   In London the players were at the mercy of the civic authorities, who made their life hard, less perhaps from Puritan prejudice, than be-cause the highly popular dramatic performances constantly gave occasion for disorder, and by attracting a great concourse

[1] Hazlitt's *Dodsley*, vol. i. *Six Anonymous Plays* (series i, ed. Farmer, 1905).

of spectators might spread the plague, during these years in which it was endemic.

Against the persecuting lord mayor the actors invoked the help of the queen and the magnates. Their chief plea was that they contributed to the queen's pleasure and had need of practice in order to be worthy to play before her. The Privy Council supported them against the City. They first played in London in the courtyards of certain inns. Then, to escape constant annoyance and prohibitions, some of them built, in 1576, their first theatre, outside the city but on its confines, on waste land in Shoreditch.

London meanwhile enjoyed more select performances. The Inns of Court were a home for the drama of classical tendencies, and a connecting link between the stage of the universities and that of the popular theatres.

That the queen might be ensured a supply of worthy actors, the choristers or children of the Chapel Royal were trained to perform plays, both those specially written for them by the master of the Chapel Royal, and others. These boys, both singers and actors, performed for the public as well as for the court, and were for some fifty years the dreaded competitors of adult and professional actors. Their example was followed by other London schools—St. Paul's, Westminster, and Merchant Taylors'—where the most gifted pupils were trained to act and were proud to contribute to the royal diversions. Nothing, not Puritan disapproval nor civic alarms, could stem the growing passion for the theatre which was felt by the whole nation—nobles, burghers, and people.

(a) THE CLASSICAL INFLUENCE. COMEDY.—The first English comedy of the classical school was *Ralph Roister Doister*,[1] written about 1533 by Nicholas Udall (1506–56), head master successively of Eton and Westminster. Instead of making the Westminster boys act Plautus, Udall wrote for them, according to the laws of the classical drama, a comedy in five acts, inspired by Latin comic plays. He borrowed some characters from the ancients, but took others straight from English life. The hero Ralph recalls the Pyrgopolinices and Therapontigone of Plautus, is swaggering, stupid, and fatuous as they. Since the play is intended for schoolboys, Udall does not make him a libertine as in the Latin original, but a man really in love, even sentimentally and tearfully amorous. As he endows him also with avarice, so that he keeps an eye on his

---

[1] Reprinted by Arber and Manly; also in Everyman's Library No. 492.

lady's dowry, the character is confused and lacks verisimilitude. Side by side with Ralph appears Merrygreek, a parasite from ancient comedy, but one who plays his part for fun rather than self-interest. It is the parasite about to be changed into Mascarille or Scapin.

Besides these imitated characters, there is the heroine, Dame Constance, who is courted by Ralph, a worthy and chaste matron annoyed by an impudent fool. When she knows that she has been slandered to the merchant Goodrich, whom she loves honourably, she sends up to heaven a fine prayer for protection. About her are her maids, one young and the other old, real English servants painted with merry realism. In fact, Udall accepts aid from Plautus, but has no superstitious veneration for him. His aim, like that of his contemporary Rabelais, is to amuse, 'for mirth,' he says, 'prolongeth life and causes health.' The principal scenes are that in which Merrygreek reads to Constance a love-letter from Ralph and makes it insulting by revising the punctuation, and that in which the roisterer besieges his mistress's house and in spite of a warlike disguise—Merrygreek has put a hencoop on his head for a helmet—is routed by the dame and her maids.

Udall may have had a moral purpose—he may have desired to satirize vainglory—but his chief aim was to cause innocent laughter. He has not only produced a farce on the classical model, but has also constructed a plot without expelling gaiety. His verse is stiff and stilted, but his language has savour.

There is even more go in a farce performed about the same time in Christ's College, Cambridge. This takes nothing from antiquity except its distribution in acts and its regular construction. Subject and characters are completely English and completely rustic. *Gammer Gurton's Needle,*[1] which was printed in 1575, was written by a Master of Arts of the university, reputedly by a certain William Stevenson. Gammer Gurton loses the needle with which she sews breeches for her servant Hodge. The good-for-nothing Diccon persuades her that it has been stolen by her neighbour, Mother Chatte, and quarrels and recriminations follow. The whole village is turned upside down. The parson intervenes, and Diccon takes advantage of the confusion to steal a ham. Finally Hodge utters a scream and the needle is found sticking in his breeches, and all is thereupon discovered. This story is not refined, but the dialogue has go; the rhymed verse, nimbler than Udall's,

[1] In Manly, vol. ii, and *Five pre-Shakespearian Comedies* (World's Classics, 1934).

lends itself to comic effects; the realism is not adulterated by borrowings from antiquity, and there is an unsurpassable drinking-song, 'Back and side go bare.'

(b) THE CLASSICAL INFLUENCE. TRAGEDY.—But farces, even when they were divided into acts in the ancient manner, could not lead to dramatic progress. They had had a place in the miracle plays. The novelty was all in the isolation of the comic element. It was in tragedy that the national theatre and the theatre of antiquity came together most significantly.

Like the Italians and the French, the English were far more inspired by Seneca than by the Greek theatre.[1] He was a somewhat dangerous model, for his were oratorical tragedies, and it is a moot point whether they were written to be staged or to be declaimed. He used again the mythological themes of the Greeks, but used them, like a romantic, neither for their national sentiment nor because he believed in their legends, but for their brilliancy. He knew nothing of dramatic movement, and there is no action in his tragedies. His characters rarely voice real sentiments: their speeches abound with maxims; their language is emphatic and lyrical, full of choice metaphors which show great force of oratory and real subtlety in analysis. Long monologues alternate with passages made up of short questions and answers, each crowded into a single line. Seneca's political allusions are frequent and he often attacks tyrants. Most of these characteristics recur in the work of his imitators, but what they have taken from him by preference is certain of his expedients, sometimes his choruses and more often the phantom who has the duty of explanation. Above all, they have been impressed by the atrocity of his subjects, and have learnt from him to associate the idea of tragedy with that of crime, nearly always monstrous crime. *Agamemnon* and the horrors of the Atrides, *Oedipus, Medea, Phaedra,* and; above all, *Thyestes* and the horrible banquet of Atreus, led to tragedies of atrocious vengeance like *Titus Andronicus* and *The Duchess of Malfi.*

Five of Seneca's plays were separately translated and perhaps performed between 1559 and 1566, before the translation, published in 1581, of his *Ten Tragedies.* As early as 1562

---

[1] *Cambridge History of English Literature,* vol. v, Chap. IV; J. W. Cunliffe, *The Influence of Seneca on Elizabethan Tragedy,* 1893; F. L. Lucas, *Seneca and the Elizabethan Tragedy,* 1922; H. B. Charlton, introduction to *The Poetical Works of Sir William Alexander* (Manchester, 1921), ed. by Kastner and Charlton (2 vols., 1921–9); T. S. Eliot, introduction to *Seneca his Tenne Tragedies* (Tudor Translations, 1927); T. H. McGrail, *Sir William Alexander,* 1940.

Thomas Sackville and Thomas Norton produced the tragedy of *Gorboduc, or Ferrex and Porrex*,[1] which was imitated from him although it had an independence. Sackville was the author of the *Induction* to the *Mirror for Magistrates* and the best poet of his day, and both playwrights were lawyers and politicians. Their tragedy was given in one of the Inns of Court.

Seneca's influence is apparent in the uninterrupted seriousness of the play; in the sustained nobility of the style; in the almost abstract character of the scenes, where all the action falls to messengers and to confidants, male and female; in the abundant speechifying, and also in the sanguinary plot. King Gorboduc abdicates in favour of his two sons, Ferrex and Porrex, who, like another Eteocles and Polynices, at once take up arms against each other. Ferrex is slain, and their mother, whose favourite son he is, kills her other son, Porrex, the slayer. The people are angered, rise in rebellion, and put father and mother to death. Anarchy, usurpation, and the death of the usurper ensue.

In spite of these piled-up crimes, the play is cold and lacks movement and drama. Its authors were better fitted to express ideas than to put life in characters. They had a didactic aim, for they wished to depict the misfortunes of a kingdom to which the succession is uncertain—a constant preoccupation of Elizabethan politicians—and the horrors which accompany civil war and result from anarchy. Their tragedy would assuredly have interested Corneille had he known it. It is Seneca after the style of lawyers and members of Parliament. The authors have a certain originality because of the didactic sense which, in spite of everything, connects *Gorboduc* with the moralities, and because of the patriotic feeling which made these young humanists choose their subject from the annals of Great Britain, as the subject of *King Lear*, with which it has analogies, was thence taken. They stand less apart from the national tradition than at first appears from their superficial resemblance to Seneca, that is, from their use of choruses, and their cult of gloomy effects combined with their rejection of the spectacular. But the symmetrical plan of their scenes—Ferrex and Porrex consulting their good and their bad adviser in turn, advisers who are almost as much abstractions as vice and virtue—betrays an artless simplification inspired by morality plays rather than by Seneca.

[1] In Manly's *Specimens*, vol. ii.

That the moral of the play may be the more distinct, and perhaps also that spectators unused to such heights of seriousness may be diverted, each act opens with a pantomime in which the lesson it conveys is illustrated.

This is therefore no mere academic tragedy. It is a work which stands first in a line of succession, the first unrelieved English tragedy and therefore the play which led to Kyd's *Spanish Tragedie*. It brought the idea of fatality on to the English stage. In spite of its great defects it established a high artistic level. Finally, it was the first play in which the blank verse formed under the influence of antiquity was used. The metre which Surrey had invented for his translation of Virgil served Sackville and Norton when they emulated Seneca. They handled it forcibly and with dignity, but were incapable of giving it the ductility necessary to the stage. Twenty-five years were to pass before their initiative was followed triumphantly. Their merit is that, though they did not reach success, they made the attempt.

(c) VARIOUS INFLUENCES.—*Gorboduc* was significant, but appeared in isolation. Round about this play there were many tentative efforts and importations from abroad, all of them pointing English drama along different paths. It has been possible to group several plays under the title 'Prodigal Son Series.' [1] This time the prototype was a work by a Neo-Latinist, the Dutchman Gnaphaeus whose *Acolastus* had been translated by John Palsgrave in 1540. He was imitated with great talent and with original additions in *Misogonus*, performed about 1560. The author, uncertainly identified as Thomas Richardes, wrote a strongly constructed and well-arranged play, enlivened by frankly comic scenes. The morality *Nice Wanton*, which appeared about 1560, connects with the same series and is a commentary on the adage 'Spare the rod and spoil the child.' In 1575 George Gascoigne produced his *Glass of Government*, imitated both from *Acolastus* and from the *Rebels* of Macropedius.

George Gascoigne, ever in quest of novelty, is the best witness to the diversity of the influences operative at this time and of the sources whence plays derived. Besides *The Glass of Government* he wrote *The Supposes*, a prose translation of a comedy by Ariosto, and *Jocasta*, a tragedy which purports to be a translation from the *Phoenissae* of Euripides, but is in truth a rearrangement of the Greek tragedy by the Italian Lodovico Dolce.

[1] See for this group *Cambridge History of English Literature*, vol. v, Chap. V.

Italian influence is yet more apparent in a free adaptation by an unknown author of the Florentine Grazzini's *La Spiritata*, under the title *The Bugbears* (1561), in which a son obtains three thousand crowns from a miserly father by frightening him at night with noises attributed to ghosts, and is thus enabled to marry his mistress. Other plays inspired by Italian comedies also appeared, but only their names have been preserved.

(*d*) FORMATION OF THE NATIONAL DRAMA.—Each of these classical, neo-classical, and Italian influences had its part in blazing the trail to the English national drama, which absorbed the most diverse elements. But there is a group of plays then acted which were not adaptations but truly English, and although they have weaknesses and an element of the ridiculous, they reveal the national drama as already almost a reality. They conform to that broad type which was finally adopted for drama and was followed by Shakespeare and his contemporaries.

Dramas of this type still partook of the morality plays, at least in right of certain characters, but they tended more and more to stage the scenes of an episode of history or a romance, and they were wont to relieve tragedy or romance by scenes of broad comedy, more or less skilfully related to the principal plot, thus observing the great tradition of the miracle plays.

The most striking of these plays are *Appius and Virginia* (1551?), *Damon and Pythias* (1564), *Horestes* (1567), *Gismond of Salerno* (1567), *Cambyses* (1569), and *Promos and Cassandra* (1578).[1]

Three are obviously connected with the moralities. Like Bale's *King John*, they mingle abstractions and real characters. *Horestes* is entitled ' A Newe Enterlude of Vice Conteyninge the Historye of Horestes' (Orestes). *Appius and Virginia*, of which the ridiculously emphatic language remained dear to Shakespeare's Pistol — 'The furies fell of Limbo lake' — dramatizes the well-known story of Virginius, who slew his daughter to save her from the wicked judge Appius. Appius is impelled by the vice called Haphazard, and Conscience and Justice appear to him. Homely and comic scenes alternate with tragedy. There is a curious mingling of all the earlier dramatic elements with a classic theme.

[1] *Appius and Virginia* and *Damon and Pythias* are printed in Hazlitt's *Dodsley*, vol. iv; *Promos and Cassandra* in Hazlitt, *Shakespeare's Library* (1875), vol. vi; *Cambyses* in Manly's *Specimens*, vol. ii; *Gismond of Salerne* in J. W. Cunliffe's *Early English Classical Tragedies* (Oxford, 1912).

Cambyses is yet more significant. The author is usually identified as Thomas Preston, Master of Arts of King's College, Cambridge, a learned man who became master of Trinity Hall. The marked and yet artless bad taste of the style has thrown doubt on this authorship, yet the play shows signs of having been written by a humanist, for Herodotus is followed step by step, and there are many mythological reminiscences. The full title, as printed, is very characteristic, *A Lamentable Tragedie mixed full of plesant mirth containing the Life of Cambises, King of Persia, from the beginning of his kingdome unto his Death, his one good deede of execution, after that, many wicked deedes and tyrannous murders committed by and through him, and last of all, his odious death by Gods Justice appointed.*

Preston's method is that of the authors of the miracle plays. He cuts up the story from Herodotus into scenes as they did the Scriptures. Not the whole of the story is in his play, but nearly all of it. He makes no attempt to weave a plot or by simplification to give unity to characters. Cambyses is represented in all the diversity and chronological incoherence of his actions. He begins well by ordering the execution of a prevaricating delegate, then, impulsive under the influence of wine, commits a series of atrocious crimes, almost all of them instantaneously, and passes immediately from the exaltation of love at first sight to passionate and murderous fury against his new-made bride. The playwright, by refusing to make any selection among the deeds of his hero, has rendered him lifelike and complex enough, has shown his double physical and moral nature and given him a temperament. There is here a character which ought already to be called Shakespearian.

Cambyses is not always on the stage, but gives place to buffoons. We can discern, in the raw, the expedients of a playwright who, chiefly by varying his scenes, appeals to a heterogeneous public, caters for coarse as for other tastes in order to reach all his audience.

Allegorical mingle with historical characters, the better to bring out the moral, the most important abstraction being the vice called Ambidexter, whose part it is both to impel to evil and to ensure the punishment of the guilty. Ambidexter is a cynic who takes pleasure in discovering and encouraging human perversity, and revels in the sight of foolishness. In his chuckle we seem already to hear Iago, even more Gloucester (Richard III) winning Queen Anne's heart by false protestations of love. This is the sardonic, diabolical, and sharp-sighted sinner, bad all through, without a trace of conscience, snapping his fingers at prejudices, his philosophy a fundamental atheism.

The connection of the buffoonery with the tragedy is weak, yet exists and is already a little Shakespearian. Thus, Cambyses has just decided to make war on Egypt when three soldiers enter, rejoicing in the prospective expedition, counting on slaughter and plunder. The truth, as undoubted in the days of Cambyses as in the sixteenth century, is illustrated that war is not the exclusive concern of princes and generals, but is as much the common soldier's business as the king's. Similarly Shakespeare, when he deals with Falstaff's enrolments, shows the seamy side of the glorious profession of arms, adopting the point of view he keeps in all his popular scenes, whether English or Roman. It is the tradition of the miracle plays combined with that of the morality plays.

In *Cambyses* the development of the plot is spectacular. The murders are not recounted, as in *Gorboduc*, but the playwright carefully stages them in full. He reproduces the execution of Sisamnes, who is beheaded and scalped—the artless stage directions stipulate for a false skin—his scalp being afterwards pulled down over his ears. On the stage, Cambyses, to prove that he is not drunk, pierces the son of Praxaspe full in the heart with an arrow.

At the same time, this author carries pathos to the highest point. He puts into the mouth of the dying child of Praxaspe touching complaints which bring tears perforce. The scene recalls little Isaac ready to go to the stake in the mystery of *Abraham*, and anticipates the child Arthur in Shakespeare's *King John* seeking to move Hubert who has been ordered to burn out his eyes. But Preston reaches a yet higher degree of pathos. He sends a mother to mourn over the body of her son, and causes Cambyses to have the child's heart cut out that the father may know it was wounded in the very centre. After this, how could an audience be satisfied with only hearsay of butchery, messengers' tales?

To compensate for these episodes, Preston gives his public an open-air scene, a garden in which a fair lady and a lord stroll along the paths while the lord supplies the absence of scenery by describing the landscape and the flowers. Thus a breath of fresh air blows through the horrors of the melodrama.

This play reveals on examination all the characteristics of

English drama of the great period. It lacks only two things, genius and style, or rather, perhaps, only one, genius made manifest in style.

The awkwardness of Preston's writing was so complete and his bombast so ridiculous that his play, after a long term of popularity, became the laughing-stock of succeeding dramatists. Shakespeare amused himself by parodying it in Falstaff, who says, when he wishes to use fine language, 'I will do it in King Cambyses' vein.' Preston's rhetoric is in the highest degree both frantic and artless. Some of his metaphorical epithets have the most ludicrous effect, as when a character speaks of her 'christall eyes,' or the mother of little Praxaspe of her 'velvet paps.' Moreover, the playwright is so little at his ease with the fourteen-syllabled rhymed lines which he uses for tragic passages, that he mutilates grammar by the suppression of articles or by most astonishing inversions in the very places in which he aims at simple statements of fact.

Undoubtedly the great lack was of a metre fitted to drama, a ductile line which would leave freedom of movement to the playwright. Failing this, verse might have been relinquished for prose. In verse, the attempt made in Gorboduc had not yet been pursued, and prose had been tried only by Gascoigne in his Supposes. English drama made decided progress when a flexible metre had been adopted, more or less generally, and when prose was used with increasing frequency. As for the remaining and too prominent traces of the morality play, it was not difficult to get rid of them. Even in Cambyses they appeared only in the name of characters. To eliminate them from that play it would have been necessary only to rebaptize a few supernumeraries, including Ambidexter, who were still called after abstractions. Richard Edwards, the author of Damon and Pythias, a far better if a possibly less significant play than Cambyses, contrived to do without abstractions altogether. He produced a tragi-comedy which, save for its versification, would not have seemed out of place had it appeared among a number of others of the great period. The same praise could be given to Whetstone,[1] who in 1578 wrote Promos and Cassandra, from which Shakespeare derived Measure for Measure, that gloomy comedy. Hitherto all had been experiment, but the advent of the undeniably great works was very near.

[1] See T. Izard, George Whetstone; Mid-Elizabethan Gentleman of Letters (New York, 1942).

BOOK IV—THE FLOWERING OF THE RENASCENCE (1578–1625)

CHAPTER I

GENERAL CHARACTERISTICS OF THE GREAT PERIOD

I. *The Translations. Their Number and their Influence.*[1]— Although the great Renascence period, often somewhat inexactly called the Elizabethan age, came to be markedly original, its literature had its rise among a multitude of ancient and foreign influences. The rich soil was fertilized by a deep layer of translations. By 1579 many of the great works of ancient and modern times had been translated into English, almost all of them by 1603, the end of Elizabeth's reign. Some of these translations formed current reading and some became as popular as the best writings of English authors. There were certain of them which had an influence equal to that of the masterpieces of the age.

It is easier to notice the rare exceptions constituted by the few important works which were omitted than to enumerate the Greek and Latin authors done into English during the century. It is surprising that, at a time when Platonism awakened so much enthusiasm and inspired so many poets, Plato was, save for some fragments, neglected by the translators, and that, while the English theatre was enjoying an unmatched flowering season, the Greek tragedians were forgotten. Aeschylus and Sophocles were not touched. Nor was Euripides, save for his *Phoenissae*, of which Gascoigne, in 1559, produced a version entitled *Jocasta*, but one which he borrowed from the Italian. Of the Latins, Plautus was overlooked except for *Menaechmi*, which was translated by Warner in 1595, although English comedy more than once followed in the footsteps of Plautus.

[1] Many were reprinted in the Tudor Translations (two series, 1892–1909 and 1924–7). See *Cambridge History of English Literature*, vol. iv, Chap. I, Franck Schoell, *Études sur l'humanisme continental en Angleterre à la fin de la Renaissance* (Paris, 1926), and F. O. Matthiessen, *Translation: an Elizabethan Art*, 1931.

Among the moderns, no translation was printed of Machiavelli's *Il Principe*, although this book was a veritable guide to many statesmen, and was commented on and, above all, attacked by many writers. Nor was there any translation of Rabelais—the first appeared in 1653—although he was known to several authors and imitated by them.

Of famous books, few besides these escaped. Practically all the others, of the past and of the present, were brought under contribution. It is true that all the translators were not able to use their originals directly, as was Philemon Holland, that good humanist and 'translator-general of his age,' who gave his country Livy (1600), Pliny the Elder (1601), and Suetonius (1609), not to mention Plutarch's moral writings (1603). But most used Italian and, in particular, French versions as intermediaries. Thomas North retranslated Plutarch's *Lives*, basing himself on Amyot's text (1579).[1] Thomas Nicolls, citizen of London, borrowed his Thucydides (1550) from the French of Claude de Seyssel, whose own translation of the Greek historian had been based on the Latin of Laurentius Valla. Adlington's version (1566) of the *Golden Ass* of Apuleius was taken from Guillaume Michel's translation, his *Ethics* of Aristotle (1547) from the Italian, and his *Politics* (1597) from Leroy's translation. Sometimes French was an intermediary even between Italian and English, as for Bandello, who reached England by way of Belleforest's version.

These indirect translations were often not the least remarkable for their literary merit and their influence. The instance of Thomas North is typical. He improved on Amyot's homely style, and by the quality of his idiomatic English produced a really national book. So lucid are his narratives, with such ease and precision does he tell his stories, that he does not suggest a translation. With a less sure and a more fanciful touch, but with a style which is full of go, John Florio, in 1603, gave Montaigne's *Essays*[2] to England. Like Plutarch's *Lives*, they became the everyday reading of many. Next to the Bible, they were the most widely known of foreign productions.

The translations in verse are more unequal. Some are deplorable, like Stanyhurst's *Aeneid* (1582), in which the

---

[1] In Tudor Translations, 1895 and Nonesuch Press, 1929–30.
[2] In Tudor Translations, 1892–3, Everyman's Library, etc. See Mme Longworth-Chambrun, *G. Florio* (Paris, 1921); F. A. Yates, *John Florio*, 1934.

impossible hexameter is used, together with a most baroque vocabulary, interspersed with contemporary slang and vulgarisms. This is an involuntary caricature of the most harmonious of poets. Phaer's *Aeneid* (1562), while without such absurdities, lacks any positive merit, as do the translations by Golding[1] of the *Metamorphoses* of Ovid (1565–7), by Sir John Harington of *Orlando Furioso* (1591), and by Carew (1594) and Fairfax (1604) of *Gerusalemme Liberata*.

Du Bartas, who was admired as a Huguenot no less than as a poet, who was called the 'treasure of humanism and jewel of theology,' was happier than Ariosto or Tasso, for Sylvester, between 1592 and 1606, produced a vigorous translation of his *Semaines*, as bombastic and fantastic in style as the original, abounding in the composite epithets which the French soon rejected, but which found a home in English poetry, the English language being more adapted and propitious to their use than the French. This translation met with a considerable and prolonged success.

But the masterpiece of verse translation was incontestably Chapman's Homer. Thanks to Chapman, the *Iliad* (1598–1609) [2] became a great Elizabethan poem, vehement, rich in verbal audacities. It was doubtless far removed from the serene Greek simplicity, but its energy and brilliancy were such as to impassion, two centuries later, the young Keats, who had no access to the original sources of Hellenism.

These translations from du Bartas and Homer really became part of the treasure of Elizabethan verse, as the versions of Plutarch and Montaigne belong to the great prose. The same might be said of the passages from Ovid and Lucan, reproduced by a poet like Marlowe, or of du Bellay's *Visions* and *Ruines de Rome*, as rendered by a master of rhythm like Spenser. Side by side with these patent and frankly avowed translations, dissimulated borrowing and plagiarizing were frequent in this period in which literary copyright was disregarded. It will be seen that the sonneteers were the most considerable of the borrowers. English style and prosody were formed by these countless translations. They profited the great, the writers who were not robbers, but who found their language waxing rich and pliable by the schoolboy exercises to which it was subjected.

2. *Italianism*.—Among the foreign influences one was incon-

1 See p. 257.   2 Temple Classics, 1897–8; Shakespeare Head, 1930–1.

testably dominant, that of Italy.[1] Elizabethan literature, which came to be the expression of the national genius, had its birth in Italianism. The word may seem too narrow when the large number of French works then circulating in England are considered, and also the influence exercised by Spain, especially through the medium of the chivalrous romances— *Palmerin*, *Amadis*, and Montemayor's famous *Diana* were all done into English by Anthony Munday before the end of the century—and through the picaresque romance *Lazarillo de Tormes*, which was translated in 1576. Since, however, France and Spain were themselves impregnated with Italian culture, the English were apt to find Italy even in what these other countries produced. And in these years Italian books, like the journey to Italy, were the great matter in England. As well as the works already cited, Castiglione's *Cortegiano*, translated by Thomas Hoby in 1561, should be mentioned, the book whence the Elizabethan gallants derived the principles of courtliness. Of more consequence to the development of drama and the novel in English were the tales of the *novellieri*, the short stories told so dramatically, vivaciously, and skilfully by Boccaccio, Cinthio, Bandello, Straparola, and their like. It is not easy to imagine how English drama would have been nourished without these comic or tragic and often licentious stories, these tales of pleasure, love, violence, blood, and tears. No complete translation of them was made at this time, but many of them appeared scattered among successive collections, such as those of Fenton and Painter in 1567, Whetstone in 1582, Turberville in 1587.

The meeting between the English and the Italian spirit which had already enriched Chaucer's poetry brought a wealth of splendour to sixteenth-century England. The English character was, however, already at this time too definite and too insular merely to reflect a foreign country. The Reformation had not yet penetrated the nation deeply, nor absorbed it wholly, but it had made so distinct an impression that there was necessarily a reaction against the prestige of the country which was the seat of Catholicism, and in which the Renascence had flowered with a sensual ardour reminiscent of paganism. By the second half of the century there were two opinions about Italianism; the new dangers to which Italy exposed her admirers were cited in opposition to her

[1] Einstein, *The Italian Renaissance in England* (1892); M. A. Scott, *Elizabethan Translations from the Italian* (1916); Mario Praz, *Machiavelli and the Elizabethans* (Oxford, 1928).

artistic attractions.   We have seen that Roger Ascham, good humanist and good Protestant, gave up to this dispute half his *Scholemaster*, a book professedly about a method of translating Latin.   It is true that the very violence of his attack throws into relief the fascination by which his contemporaries were held.   He complained of the translations through which the products of Italian licence were steadily flowing into England, and his invective did not stem this stream.   But Ascham's disapproval and that of the Puritans forced even the 'devils incarnate,' as they named those who returned from the peninsula, to depreciate the country which had at once dazzled and corrupted them.   Usually the Italianate Englishmen criticized the books they themselves had imported, the morals which had corrupted theirs, the decadent civilization which had given them a taste for forbidden pleasures.   Though depraved, they felt that they still were not as the Italians.   Italy, which excited the licentious imagination of the English, came little by little to be for them a land of unspeakable debauchery, the country of Machiavellism, crime, and poison.   It was their Utopia of irregularity.   Thus both action and reaction must be discerned in the undeniable Italianism of the period.   From being the stimulus and the model of England, Italy came to stand for the antithesis to the national character, which it defined by force of contrast.   The literature of England was enriched by an immense looting of Italian treasures, and the spoils carried back to the island were there exhibited, not only as marvellous works of art, but also as objects of reprobation.

3. *Patriotic Exaltation*.[1]—More than three-quarters of the sixteenth century passed before English literature did more than grope its way.   Elizabeth, who was to name the great period, had been twenty years on the throne before a definitive step had been taken.   By two successive advances, the one made in 1578, while Drake was sailing round the world, the other in 1589, on the morrow of the Armada, England caught up with her continental rivals, if indeed she did not outpace them.

About the year 1578 appeared John Lyly's *Euphues* and Spenser's *Shepheard's Calendar*, and all Sidney's work, in verse and prose, was written at about the same time, although it was not published until after his death.   The impulse for this

[1] See Jusserand, *Histoire littéraire du peuple anglais*, Vol. ii, Book v, Chaps. I and II.

production was derived from patriotism. It sprang from England's growing consciousness of strength, her pride of prosperity, the spirit of adventure which animated her sons and caused them always to aspire to the first place, and her faith in her own destiny.

Everything, even religion, combined to stimulate and reinforce this patriotism. For very many, Protestantism, now triumphant, was no more than deliverance from foreign supremacy. It was summed up in the rejection of the papacy. It broke the bonds which had for centuries connected England with the Continent by subjecting her to Rome. If the English still conceived of union with Europe, they dreamt, with Sidney, of a confederation of all the Protestant states with England at their head, an association of the powers of good which should be ready to affront the powers of evil personified in Philip II, the Catholic monarch. The majority favoured an entirely insular Christianity, monopolizing divinity for national ends. The Hebraic spirit was beginning to be substituted for the properly Christian spirit. The extreme formula of this over-weening religious egoism was expressed by Lyly, who, in 1580, declared of God that He always had a tender care 'of England, as of a new Israel, his chosen and peculier people,' and who ended by announcing that 'the living God is only the English God.'

For most men, the exactions of God did not go beyond those of patriotism. Except for the still limited group to whom their faith was all in all, the Puritans who made it their first business to seek salvation, the people turned from such austere cares and gave themselves up to enjoying life. These were still the days of Merrie England. The ardour of the first reformers, their vehement preaching and the heroism of the martyrs under Mary Tudor, might give another impression, but in truth the country was still indifferent, if not sceptical, eager not for religion but for games and pleasure, ambitious of the free development which is the very spirit of the Renascence. The intellectual paganism of humanism rested on the broad basis of an instinctive paganism scattered wide among the people.

The manner of the official Reformation in England excluded edification. Several times over, the English in the sixteenth century passed from one form of religion to another, as a herd might change masters, without enthusiasm or revolt. Kept in the beginning of the Reformation within bounds of ortho-doxy by Henry VIII, the champion of the papacy, they allowed him, on the occasion of his divorce, to implicate them in the schism, and then accepted a sort of Anglican Catholicism, with a new pope in a king who was the slayer of women and the most hypocritical and bigoted of bloodthirsty princes. Under Edward VI they became real Protestants, and followed the services of their church in a Lutheranized prayer-book. Mary Tudor easily re-established Roman Catholicism among them, and might perhaps have reunited England to the papacy permanently, had not the prevalent indifferent and conciliatory spirit been alarmed by the burning of the Protestant martyrs, and had not the queen's marriage to Philip II irritated and disquieted patriotism. When Elizabeth restored Protestantism she did it amid general rejoicing, but as pope she was political, not devout, well fitted to govern men who desired independence of Rome, but were in no wise inclined to profound conviction or to proselytism. Public opinion supported the queen when she restrained the Puritans as when she opposed the Catholics.

4. *The High Conception of Poetry*.[1]—It was this tepid religious feeling which allowed literature to spring to vigorous life and the Renascence to flower. To the tardiness of the Reformation in closing its grip on the country England owes the glory of her drama, her most magnificent literary achievement, and also a large part of the glory of her other poetry under Elizabeth and James I.

This love of letters had its beginning in the patriotic pride which was impelling England to claim a pre-eminent place in every field of activity. She was nearly a whole century behindhand in maritime discovery and seafaring. With one bound she caught up with her rivals, Spain, Portugal, and France, striving to outdistance and oust them. For the first time she was actuated by the spirit of imperialism. It gave birth to a swarm of tales of distant exploration and ensured their success, stories which do not exactly belong to literature, but were an element of literary animation and fertility. While Englishmen like Richard Eden, about the middle of the century, were translating and reproducing foreign stories of adventure, they were also becoming adventurers themselves and celebrating their own discoveries. In 1589 Richard Hakluyt published his great work *The Prin-*

---

[1] *Elizabethan Critical Essays*, ed. Gregory Smith, 2 vols., 1904; G. Saintsbury, *History of Criticism*, Vol. ii, Book iv, Chap. V, 1902; J. E. Spingarn, *A History of Literary Criticism in the Renaissance*, 1899. See also p. 257.

*cipall Navigations, Voiages and Discoveries of the English
Nation made by sea or over land . . . at any time within the
compass of these 1500 yeares*, and in 1598 he issued a much
augmented edition thereof. His task was continued by
Samuel Purchas, who, in 1625, brought the chronicle up to
date in *Hakluytus Posthumus*.

Literature was swept onwards by this spirit of conquest and
self-glorification. England balanced her literary accounts and
was ashamed to realize her poverty as compared to France, her
indigence by the side of Italy, and her virtual destitution in
comparison with antiquity. The latest in the field, she
decided, arrogantly, to become the first. She had faith in
her own genius and language, and also in her prosody if she
could but reduce it to order. Hitherto she had been paralysed
by timidity or by a certain languor, but she was now ready to
be bold. She was prepared to venture on the various *genres* in
which the ancients and the moderns had won distinction—
pastorals, epics, comedies and tragedies, lyrics of every
form, every kind of prose, romance, criticism, history, and
philosophy.

A magnet to draw her into each of these paths was the faith
in the greatness of letters, and particularly of poetry, with
which the Renascence had gradually inspired her. This
faith made the poet the first of men. It was in 1579 that the
Puritan Stephen Gosson, who had stigmatized poetry as a
school of immorality, provoked Sidney's eloquent retort, his
Apologie for Poetrie, written at the same time and in the same
spirit as Spenser's lost treatise—*The English Poet*. Sidney
recalls that to the Romans the poet was the *vates*, the diviner
or prophet, and establishes his superiority over the historian
and the philosopher. 'Of all Sciences,' he says, '. . . is our
Poet the Monarch.' This gallant champion of jousts and
battlefields considered that the poet deserved the laurel-wreath
as much as the soldiers.

Spenser proclaims that heroes and famous poets are born
together. He shows that civilization and poetry advance side
by side. In particular, he insists that poetry is 'a divine gift
and heavenly instinct not to be gotten by labour and learning,
but adorned with both; and poured into the witte by a certain
enthousiasmos and celestiall inspiration.' It is true that this
Platonic doctrine was common to the men of the Renascence,
but it seems especially to have penetrated English poetry,
which had almost its sole theoretical basis in a belief in the

necessity of poetic enthusiasm.   The Greek word recurs in
English poetry in various vernacular forms, all of them proof
of the assimilation of this article of faith.   It is this enthusiasm
which Shakespeare calls a 'fine frenzy,' which Drayton calls
a 'fine madness' when he is praising Marlowe or a 'clear rage'
when he is praising Shakespeare.   None are poets who are
not possessed of this demon.   Drayton expects the poet to see
'brave translunary things.'   The classical Daniel, a writer of
pure and noble verse, is criticized by Spenser because

> Yet doth his trembling Muse but lowly flie,
> As daring not too rashly mount on high.

And Drayton disdainfully considers Daniel's 'manner better
fitted to prose.'

There was insistence that the candidate for poetic glory
should have exaltation, and this quality therefore became a
current one, genuine in the great, simulated in others.   The
object of their transports was beauty, to which Spenser
addressed a magnificent hymn, and which Marlowe, in a
famous passage and with poignant melancholy, declared to
be beyond complete expression:

> If all the pens that ever poets held
> Had fed the feeling of their masters' thoughts,
> And every sweetness that inspired their hearts,
> Their minds, and muses on admirèd themes;
> If all the heavenly quintessence they still
> From their immortal flowers of poesy,
> Wherein, as in a mirror, we perceive
> The highest reaches of a human wit;
> If these had made one poem's period,
> And all combined in beauty's worthiness,
> Yet should there hover in their restless heads
> One thought, one grace, one wonder, at the least,
> Which into words no virtue can digest.

The generation lived in this fever.   Poetry was then neither
the privilege of a caste nor the apanage of a few.   It was
widely disseminated, heated men's brains, and sometimes
turned their heads, gave a lyrical turn to the whole of literature, beflowered and falsified the prose which was all poetic.
To the poets whose names are known those many anonymous
writers must be added whom a set of verses, or a song, sometimes exquisite, proves to have had at least their hour of
illumination.   Every one felt the breath that was passing—
the passion for artifices of language, the perception that words
hold something beyond their meaning, the pleasure in savour-

ing words, the pleasure in the beautiful or at least in the fantastic. The courtier was surprised to find the man of the people as ingenious as himself. 'The age is grown so picked that the toe of the peasant comes so near the heel of the courtier, he galls his kibe,' says Hamlet, as he listens to the grave-digger's punning. The awakening of mind and imagination was sudden, lively, and general. It occurred first at court, but soon spread throughout the nation.

5. *The Spirit of Independence. The Rejection of Strict Rules.*—For all the extensive borrowing from abroad and avowed respect for ancient precedents and traditional rules of conduct, and in spite of the passing fashions which temporarily made a law of the strange or the eccentric, the general impression conveyed is one of frank and free boldness. A wide initiative was left to individuals. This is apparent if the language and versification, the common instruments of poets, be studied. There was no established grammar to fix and stereotype syntax. The first English grammar, Ben Jonson's, was written under James I, but it perished when the author's house was burnt, and appeared in fragments only after his death. There was more than one *Art of Poetry* compiled, but none of them had acknowledged authority.

In the matter of grammar, the critics of to-day are surprised to discover that the separation of the parts of speech was not yet recognized. A dictum on Shakespearian grammar may be extended to the whole language:

Any irregularities whatever, whether in the formation of words or in the combination of words into sentences, are allowable . . . almost any part of speech can be used as any other part of speech. An adverb can be used as a verb, . . . as a noun, . . . or as an adjective. . . . Any noun, adjective, or neuter verb can be used as an active verb.[1]

The restriction was to the intelligible, and must be acknowledged not always to have been respected. On the other hand, writers were incessant creators, perpetual innovators. Words were not labelled and immobilized. There was something improvised and energetic in the mode of their use which became impossible in periods of fully constituted grammar.

Prosody also retained a mobility and pliability which had the happiest effect on true artists, although it misled the others to such licence that in the end verse relapsed to prose. It cannot be said that a fixed prosody existed at this time, that the value

[1] E. A. Abbott, *A Shakespearian Grammar*, p. 5. See also W. Franz, *Shakespeare-Grammatik*, 3rd ed. (Heidelberg, 1939).

of each word had been established once for all and independently of its use. While in lyrics and solemn poetry words had their full and constant phonetic value, in dramatic verse they were increasingly governed by circumstances, and suffered contractions and extensions entailed by the need of speed or emphasis. One word might be taken to contain a varying number of syllables. Words were elastic, could shrink or expand. The astonishing blank verse of the theatre, especially of Shakespeare's plays, provides inexhaustible material for the study of these varying inflections which almost always are found to conform to one law, to follow nature, that is true passion or feeling.

Versification was not reduced to a single principle, but sometimes acknowledged the syllabic and sometimes the accentual law. Some verses are governed by no rule except that of the recurring *ictus*, or beats. They disregard both number of syllables and number of regular feet.

The great mass of the verse is at once syllabic and accentual. The heroic or decasyllabic line, either blank or rhymed, has precedence, and is found on analysis to contain, as a rule, five iambic feet. But it remains syllabic only in virtue of the elastic prosody. And it allows of very great diversity in the placing of accents and the character of feet. It is a much varied, sometimes a very subtle, subject of study. The line differs, moreover, with different poets. Spenser's rhymed line is very different from Donne's; Marlowe's, Dekker's, Fletcher's, and Massinger's blank verse are of widely diverse types; and such metrical evolution can be discovered in the course of the poetical career of Shakespeare, considered by himself, that it has been possible to found on it the chronology of his dramatic works.

Analogous remarks apply to the combinations of rhymes and stanzas. The couplet or rhymed distich, which was to be adopted almost exclusively by the classical school, was already used frequently, but in its structure there was a freedom which subsequently disappeared. Its rhythm is varied because the place of the pause is shifted and because the sense is often continued from one line to another. The line is rarely self-contained, as it came to be later, and it keeps, if it does not enlarge, the freedom of movement which Chaucer had given it.

English poets were curious of every happening in continental literature, and were aware of the rules for the use of masculine and feminine rhymes introduced by the Pleiad. In France, the principle of the alternation of the two kinds of rhyme was established when Sidney and Spenser began to write. Sidney was enough awake to the law to observe it, with very happy effects, in some of his songs. But no one in England seems to have had the idea of making it absolute. Its establishment in France may be regretted. When alternation became the rule, the artistic, that is the free use of the two kinds of rhyme, had to be suppressed, and alternation gradually became a mnemotechnic device. It did not leave to the poet the decision of whether he would write a particular poem in masculine or in feminine rhymes, or a duly proportioned mixture of both, nor did it allow him to fortify ideas or feeling by suitable rhyme. Where choice should have been, or remained, free, a police regulation was introduced, and was accepted with surprising unanimity, not only for songs, but also for the longest narratives. At one blow, some harmonious combinations were ruled out, for instance the tercets of the sonnet, which was debarred from the *abc abc* disposition of lines. English poetry did without such rules. In the classical period it almost reached the point of abandoning the feminine rhyme altogether, or relegating it to the domain of humorous verse. But Elizabethan poetry proscribed nothing, and used feminine rhymes abundantly, never, however, in obedience to a mechanical external law, but always to produce an effect of sweetness and melody. This small point shows the divergence of form between the poetry of France and of England at the Renascence. In consequence, it was more possible in England than in France to refine on the varieties of the stanzas for which France had supplied the model and to multiply their types.

Note. For further study of matters treated in this chapter, see L. T. Golding, *An Elizabethan Puritan: Arthur Golding* (New York, 1937); W. Ringler, *Stephen Gosson: A Biographical and Critical Study* (Princeton, 1942); and J. W. H. Atkins, *English Literary Criticism.* Vol. ii, *The Renascence* (Cambridge, 1947).

CHAPTER II

THE PIONEERS: LYLY, SIDNEY, AND SPENSER

THE habitual distinction between prose and verse must be momentarily suspended in order to present together the three men who, about 1578, simultaneously, although with very unequal resources, were initiators of the literature dedicated to beauty. It is a distinction which loses importance at this time, because poetry penetrated everywhere. The prose of such romances as *Euphues* and *Arcadia* is entirely poetic. Only the drama really needs separate study. Lyly, except for his dramatic work, Sidney, and Spenser are rightly presented side by side.

1. *John Lyly*.[1]—John Lyly (1554–1606) is the first in date of the writers who consciously and persistently used an artistic style and whose chief aspiration it manifestly was to say a thing well. It is even possible to ask if Lyly had any other clearly determined aim. But that his art was mainly artifice is a matter of little importance. He fulfilled the expectations of his fellow-countrymen so opportunely that his studied and strange way of writing set the fashion for a long period. For a good dozen years the 'euphuistic' manner which he inaugurated reigned at court and spread thence through almost all literature.

The father of euphuism was born of a family of grammarians. He was the grandson of the William Lily who was the friend of Erasmus and More. After studying at Oxford, 'where I tyred at a drie breast three yeares,' he went to London, and there, with the help and patronage of Lord Burleigh, was able to live by his wits, at first in the guise of a moralist. In 1578, at the age of twenty-four, he published his famous *Euphues, or the Anatomy of Wit*, a book filled with wise lessons and bristling with attacks on irreligion and immorality. The hero, Euphues, or the Well-endowed, is a young Athenian— a disguise for an Oxford man—noble, handsome, quick-witted, and with a passion for travelling, but also presumptuous, apt

---

[1] Complete works, ed. by Bond, 3 vols. (Oxford, 1902); *Euphues*, ed. M. W. Croll and H. Clemens, 1916. See A. Feuillerat, *John Lyly* (Cambridge, 1910); V. M. Jeffery, *John Lyly and the Italian Renaissance*, 1928.